AF322879

HISTORICAL RECORDS AND STUDIES

THE MONOGRAPH SERIES

The Voyages of Christopher Columbus, as told by the Discoverer

Unpublished Letters of Charles Carroll of Carrolton and of his
Father, Charles Carroll of Doughoregan

Forty Years in the United States of America (1839-1885)
By the Late *Rev. Augustus J. Thébaud, S.J.*

Historical Sketch of St. Joseph's Provincial Seminary, Troy, N. Y.
By the *Right Rev. Henry Gabriels, D.D.*

The Cosmographiae Introduction of Martin Waldseemüller
In Facsimile

Three Quarters of a Century (1807 to 1882)
By the Late *Rev. Augustus J. Thébaud, S.J.* Two Vols.

Diary of a Visit to the United States of America in the Year 1883
By *Charles Lord Russell of Killowen,* late Lord Chief Justice of England

St. Joseph's Seminary, Dunwoodie, New York, 1896-1921
By the *Rev. Arthur J. Scanlan, S.T.D.*

The Catholic Church in Virginia (1815-1822)
By the *Rev. Peter Guilday*

The Life of the Right Rev. John Baptist Mary David (1761-1841)
By *Sister Columba Fox, M.A.*

The Doctrina Breve In Facsimile

UNITED STATES CATHOLIC HISTORICAL SOCIETY
MONOGRAPH SERIES XI

PIONEER CATHOLIC JOURNALISM

By

PAUL J. FOIK, C.S.C., Ph.D.

GREENWOOD PRESS, PUBLISHERS
NEW YORK

CONTENTS

PREFACE

In this study on early Catholic periodical literature in the United States the purpose has been to trace the origin, scope, progress, and design of newspapers and magazines from the earliest times down to the year 1840 inclusive. The importance of such an inquiry can best be estimated by those who have, at some time or other, had occasion to pore over the files of some of these pioneer journals in quest of some precious morsel of information dealing with a particular phase of history. It must be obvious to all that in the period which witnessed the rapid growth of the Catholic Church in America to full vigor, there will also be found important occurrences which display the influence exercised by the press in that great development.

The forerunner of the real Catholic newspaper was what may be called the Irish national journal, which, while it was not distinctively Catholic in purpose was, nevertheless, so sympathetic in tone towards those of the ancient Faith that it deserves a place in any treatment of Catholic journalism. Certain other periodicals, national in their tendencies, for similar reasons are included in this work. Spanish periodical literature, while it produced no notable results on Catholicism in America, has been discussed on account of the important part played by one of its editors in the early Catholic newspaper activities of New York City. The *Michigan Essay* is considered the pioneer of all Catholic journals, since it owes its beginning to the Rev. Gabriel Richard, one of the early missionary priests of the Northwest.

The whole disposition of Catholic journalism during these first decades seems to have been to promote harmony by removing from the pathway of Protestants the groundless prejudices and prepossessions which had grown into social barriers, due chiefly to the circulation of misrepresentations and calumnies by the enemies of Catholicism in Europe and America, and to the supineness of the Catholic body in the face of such gross fabrications.

The history of the Irish nation has been inseparably bound up with the history of the Catholic Church in the Emerald Isle. This traditional fidelity to the belief of their fathers more than aught else has made Irishmen the object of persecution the world over. The strong living faith and intrepid zeal of the early Irish immigrants caused them to defend with vigor their civil and religious liberties through the power of the press.

In tracing the history of the pioneer efforts in Catholic journalism we shall also have occasion to touch upon the deleterious influence exercised by journals hostile to the Faith, and of certain other papers relying in a great measure on Catholic patronage, but whose editors made religion the cloak by which immeasurable harm was produced to the Catholic cause in America.

The two journals of this early epoch which have survived the trials and the vicissitudes of time shall be treated with great fullness from their establishment down to the present time.

Until the year 1840 the general policy of Catholic journalism was a defense of Catholicism by vigorous appeals to reason and dogmatic principles. The period was above all one of spirited controversy. The Church and her tenets during this epoch were very imperfectly understood. There was a predisposition on the part of all sectarian and secular journals to misrepresent her doctrine in every conceivable way. After the year 1840, there began among the Protestant bodies a canvassing of opinions brought about by the successful conflicts waged against the sectarians by Catholics. The newspapers of this period give a contemporary view of the rise and spread of Catholicism in America.

In this inquiry the author owes much to the encouragement which he received from professors while attending the Catholic University of America. He acknowledges with feelings of gratitude, the many suggestions and criticisms offered by Dr. Charles Hallam McCarthy, Professor of American History. He also is indebted to Dr. Frank O'Hara, Professor of Economics, and the Very Rev. Dr. Patrick Joseph Healy, Professor of Church History, for the interest they have displayed during the progress of the work.

PIONEER CATHOLIC JOURNALISM

CHAPTER I

The Michigan Essay

The earliest effort in Catholic pioneer journalism began in the first decade of the nineteenth century when, in August 1809, the Rev. Gabriel Richard of Detroit made possible the publication of the *Michigan Essay, or Impartial Observer.* If we examine the conditions in the Northwest at this time, the absolute need of a newspaper in the vast and sparsely settled territory of Michigan is evident. Its people were, for the most part, French, unacquainted with the English tongue, and many of them rude and uninstructed even in their own language.[1]

Those who know the history of this territory in those early days will remember also the activities of Father Richard as an educator.[2] The establishment of this periodical was part of his comprehensive scheme for the enlightenment of the people of his own flock and of the territory at large. As an initial step in such a plan for the uplifting of his fellow-citizens, the newspaper was perhaps the best means that he could have employed.

We may regard this scheme of Father Richard as one of the determining causes which gave to this country its first Catholic periodical. Another consideration which hastened its establishment was the loss occasioned by a disastrous fire that swept Detroit in 1805. Hardly a building was saved from the fury of this great conflagration. Father Richard and his flock were compelled to seek temporary quarters until he could devise some means towards the rebuilding of St. Anne's Church. With this object in view, he journeyed to Baltimore in 1806, and it was on this occasion that he purchased a printing press and a font of type. These he brought

[1] "Contributions to American Educational History," edited by Herbert B. Adams. "History of Higher Education in Michigan." Serial No. 11 by Andrew C. McLaughlin. Government Publication, Bureau of Education, whole No. 174, Circular of Information No. 4, Washington, Government Printing Office, 1891, p. 11.

[2] See article by Rev. J. J. O'Brien in "Historical Records and Studies," the United States Catholic Historical Society, New York. Vol. V, part I, Nov., 1907, pp. 77-94.

See also *Metropolitan Catholic Almanac,* 1855, pp. 43-57. *Annals of the Propagation of the Faith,* 1800 to 1830.

overland to Detroit and set up at Spring Wells in the house of Jacques Lascelle.[3]

Many persons have claimed for this press the honor of being the first one to be set up throughout the Northwest, but it is even questionable whether it was the first in operation in Detroit itself; for there were proclamations issued to the people of this vicinity by Lieutenant Governor Hamilton as early as the year 1777. These were dated from Detroit showing, presumably, that they were printed there. Strange to say, these were the only printed documents that were, over a long stretch of years, credited to Detroit as the place of issue. We may reasonably conclude from this that the Lieutenant Governor's proclamation was dated from Detroit but printed elsewhere. Another press was owned by Alexander and William Macomb, who received it from England in 1785; but there is no evidence that it was ever put in operation.[4] It has been further asserted that the *Michigan Essay* was the first paper printed in the Northwest. Various newspapers were already printed in the Territory before 1800. Cincinnati and Chillicothe early boasted of this means of enlightenment.

It is known that Freeman and Son started a newspaper in Cincinnati in 1795. Chillicothe established two papers about the same period. Before the close of the century at least thirteen were being printed in the Northwest.[5] That the *Essay* was the first periodical edited in that part known as Michigan is a well established fact.[6]

Many misstatements have also been made regarding its real publisher and editor.[7] The regular collection and dispatch of news in those days presupposed a widespread interest in public affairs. This qualification Father Richard possessed to a remarkable degree, as is well attested by every local historian of eminence;[8] but his religious duties and the extent of his missionary labors did not enable him to give his time to the publishing and editing of this paper. He therefore placed the publication of the

---

[3]"Historical Records and Studies," Vol. V, Part I, pp. 85-86.

[4]*Catholic News*, New York, Sept. 17, 1891, p. 5. Report of Don C. Henderson's Speech before the West Michigan Press Association held at Kalamazoo. Also "Michigan Historical and Pioneer Collection," Vol. 13, p. 394 and p. 489. Also the Detroit *Free Press*, May 30, 1888.

[5]"Circular of Information No. 4," Bureau of Education, Serial No. 11, p. 11 *et seq.*, full reference cited above. Also the "History of Printing in America," by Isaiah Thomas, Worcester, 1810.

[6]"Michigan Historical and Pioneer Collection," Vol. 13, p. 394.

[7]The most reliable account is Silas Farmer's "History of Detroit and Michigan," Vol. I, pp. 670-671. He went to Worcester, sought out this periodical in the library of Isaiah Thomas, and had a photograph made of each sheet of its first and only issue.

[8]See Cooley's "Michigan," pp. 307-311; also O'Brien in "Historical Records and Studies," cited above.

Essay in the hands of a capable layman, who could devote his time exclusively to the work, while the priest himself acted merely as supervisor.[9]   That Father Richard was neither the publisher nor the editor of the *Michigan Essay* is found by an examination of the first issue of that periodical.   Probably he contributed to the French portion, but it is distinctly stated on the first page that the paper was printed and published by James M. Miller.

A brief retrospect of the period preceding the establishment of the *Michigan Essay* will disclose many facts of interest, touching the history of journalism.   Various methods have from time to time been used for the circulation of news, but we can claim for Detroit and its vicinity the most primitive stage of development,—the "spoken newspaper."   Such, indeed, was the means that Father Richard first used to arouse interest among the people, which was afterwards to ripen into a more active and intelligent participation in the affairs of government.   He appointed a town-crier, whose duty it was to publish, every Sunday, from the doors of St. Anne's, news items and matters of general concern to the waiting congregation and to the public at large.   We are told, that not infrequently, the crier announced even auction sales, horse races, and the date of the next fox-hunt.   Sometimes notices were written and posted in some convenient place near the church. For a while the duties of the crier were fulfilled by Theophilus Mettez,[10] the sacristan of St. Anne's.   Regularly, after Mass on Sundays, he stationed himself on the steps of the Church, within view of all and there made such announcements as the eager people were anxious to hear.[11]

Though the town-crier performed his duties to the satisfaction of all, his labors, nevertheless, were confined within narrow limits. In the first place, matters of local interest were his chief concern. When, perchance, he did have news from afar, it rarely circulated beyond the vicinity of Detroit. Consequently the arrival of Father Richard's press in the territory was hailed with great enthusiasm.

As regards the paper about which we are chiefly concerned the expectations of its promoters soon came to naught.   The *Michigan Essay, or Impartial Observer* began its career on August 31,

---

[9]"History of Detroit and Michigan," by Silas Farmer. "Catholic Periodicals Published in U. S." Supplement to a list printed in *Records* of Cath. Hist. Soc. of Philadelphia, by Rev. T. C. Middleton, p. 6, Vol. IV.   Campbell, "History of Michigan." Textbook, "American State Universities," "Michigan Pioneer and Historical Collection," Vol. XIII, p. 394.

[10]Theophilus Mettez afterwards became printer and publisher.   See "Records and Studies," cited above; and pp. 74, 94.

[11]"History of Higher Education in Michigan," by Andrew C. McLaughlin, cited above, p. 11.

1809. It was the intention of the publisher that the paper should appear every Thursday.[12] Exactly how many issues did appear we do not know. Five copies of the first publication are all that have been discovered up to the present time. Some have concluded from this that the periodical immediately ceased to appear.[13]

This initial number of the *Essay* has a history peculiarly its own. Of the copies still known to exist, one was possessed for a short time by a friend of the publisher, whose home was in Utica, New York. Perhaps it had been sent by Mr. Miller himself to his home town; for we know that prior to 1809 he had resided there. From Utica, it was sent to Isaiah Thomas, of Worcester, who was writing a history of printing in America. The following note, written in the margin of the first page of the periodical, suggests at least that there might have been more than one issue:

Utica, N. Y., Aug. 31, 1810.

Sir:

I send you this paper published by a friend of mine to insert in your "History of Printing." If he sees your advertisement he will send you more, perhaps, of later date.

We have no conclusive evidence that more than one number was issued.[14] Brown's "Campaign of the Western Army" incidentally mentions that "only three numbers were issued," but this must not be regarded as an authentic statement, since the author seems merely to indicate that the paper had a very brief existence.

After the discovery of the copy already described three others were found in the City of Detroit. One of these numbers, held for over fifty years by Thomas Lee, of Leeville, recently came into the possession of H. E. Baker of the Detroit *Tribune*. Another copy was saved from oblivion by William Michell, who discovered it among some old papers. A third copy of Vol. 1, No. 1 is at present in the Detroit Public Library. There was still another number of this issue in the old Detroit Museum. We may suppose that this remaining copy is still in existence although we have no accurate information concerning it.

When the *Michigan Essay, or Impartial Observer* was introduced to the people it was a four page paper, nine and one-quarter inches by sixteen inches in size. The statement, so frequently repeated that the paper was printed mostly in French is unreliable.

---

[12]"List of Catholic Periodicals," *Cath. News*, and "Speech of Henderson," cited above.

[13]Farmer, "History of Detroit and Michigan," Vol. I, pp. 670-671. See also "Records and Studies," cited above.

[14]The "Michigan Pioneer and Historical Collection" says that eight or nine copies appeared but no other testimony is furnished to support this claim. It is accompanied with some misstatements of facts.

That the periodical was called the *Essai du Michigan* is also without foundation. An examination of the first issue reveals the fact that there were only one and a half columns in French, and that the remainder of the paper as well as the title were in English.[15]

There is nothing in the first issue to indicate that the *Essay* was to be the mouthpiece of the Catholics of Michigan. Its columns were open to any gentlemen of talent, provided such persons abstained from controversy. We can reasonably suppose, however, that it was the intention of the founder to reflect, in some measure at least, the opinion of the Catholic people in the territory. The most we can claim for the *Essay,* then, is that it was a semi-Catholic periodical. This conclusion is based principally upon the circumstances attending its establishment. Its chief purpose was to inform, to entertain and to educate. Articles from various newspapers, foreign and domestic, furnished the bulk of the news section. The items of foreign interest were taken mainly from the London *Morning Chronicle* and the Liverpool *Aurora;* and such information appeared four or five months after the events occurred. Incidents printed four or five weeks before in the New York *Spectator,* the Pittsburg *Commonwealth,* and the Boston *Mirror* were news for the *Essay.* Strange to say there was not one item of local interest in the first issue of sixteen columns; and but one short notice that bears somewhat of the nature of an editorial, in which the publisher makes clear that he intends to assume an impartial attitude in political affairs, and invites contributions for his newspaper from all gentlemen of talent.

It must have been the intention of the publisher to print from time to time original verse or selections from the English poets, with the view, no doubt, of entertaining readers, and at the same time creating in them a taste for good literature. At any rate, we see in this first issue excerpts from Young's "Night Thoughts" entitled "Futurity"; also two other poems on "Evening" and "Happiness." There were also prose articles on "Politeness," "Early Rising," and "Husbandry."

A very peculiar arrangement was made about subscription rates. One would naturally expect that city subscribers on account of their proximity to the office, would receive the paper cheaper than outsiders. On the contrary, the people of Detroit were asked to pay five dollars a year; residents of Upper Canada and Michigan four and a half dollars; while the more distant subscribers could receive it for four dollars. Advertising space did not exceed fifty cents a square for three insertions and twenty-five cents a square

---

[15]Farmer, "History of Detroit and Michigan"; "Records and Studies," cited above.

for each subsequent one.[17]   Only one advertisement appeared in
the first issue, that of St. Anne's school.   The publisher also gives
notice that he is about to print several works; among others he
mentions "Nine Days' Devotion to the Sacred Heart of Jesus."[16]

This periodical, like a frail and delicate morning-glory, lifted
its ambitious head to the rising light of progress but withered away
in the noon-day sun of one hot August day.   Why did this venture into the field of journalism fail so prematurely?   It has been
said that the *Essay* perished on account of insufficient patronage.[19]
Perhaps if Father Richard could have given to this work his personal attention, this project would have had a measure of success.
Perhaps also if the subscription price was more reasonable the
paper, small as it was, would have found many patrons.   We
know that journals of later and better times and of more ad-
vantageous circumstances barely subsisted, and some even suspended publication for a while, because they were not making expenses.

Though the *Essay* was so early doomed to failure, its press continued in service for a number of years.   Several publications of
a religious and of an educational character were printed.   Many
books of devotion, tracts, prayer-books and catechisms in the
Indian dialect and in the French, but set up in English type, were
published for Father Richard's missions throughout the territory.[20]   Even the laws and the official documents of the Territory
were run off on this small hand-press, and a biographer of good
Father Richard states that "he always made sure that this work
was properly executed."[21]   For a while the type-setting was done
by A. Coxshaw, who came West in 1808.[22]   General Brock's
proclamation during the War of 1812 was printed by this press.
After the war many newspapers sprang into existence in Michigan, but the one that still remains the proud boast of the people is
that pioneer of them all, the *Michigan Essay, or Impartial Observer*.

---

[17]Farmer, "History of Detroit and Michigan"; "Records and Studies" cited
above.

[18]*American Catholic Quarterly,* Phila., 1893, Vol. XVIII, p. 98. "Records
and Studies," cited above.

[19]"Michigan Historical and Pioneer Collection," Vol. VI.

[20]*Ibid.,* Vol. XIII; Records and Studies," Vol. V, Part I, p. 87.

[21]"Cyclopedia of Michigan. Historical and Biographical." Article on Rev.
Gabriel Richard, p. 321.

[22]*American Catholic Quarterly,* Philadelphia, 1893, Vol. XVIII, p. 95,
et seq.

CHAPTER II

The period that ushered in the French Revolution wrought many changes in the condition of Europe, but nowhere, except in France itself, were institutions so modified, and modes of thought so affected, as in the British dominions. England had just passed through one of the severest conflicts of her history, the Seven Years' War. Hardly had her guns ceased their thunders in this contest, when her American Colonies revolted and carried their struggle for liberty to a successful issue. The mother country was still bewailing the misfortune which the egregious folly of her misrule had brought about, when the tumultuous chaos of the great Napoleonic Wars, like another deluge, spread destruction and desolation upon a world already sickened with a thousand woes. The waves of enmity and discontent rose high and swept across the whole of Europe. No country on the Continent stood unshaken by the blows of that bitter conflict. Far and wide, swift as the cannon's shot, proceeded the cry of liberty, prophetic sound, that made kings tremble on their thrones, and awoke within the hearts of men a new and strange enthusiasm. This flood had not yet abated its fury, when Ireland, still burdened with the chains of English oppression, attempted to tear off the trammels of a wicked system based upon royal prerogative.

The soul of this movement was the Society of United Irishmen, founded in 1791. Its primitive idea was to unite Catholics and Protestants, to bring about a much needed parliamentary reform for Ireland, and to improve its system of government.[1]

As early as 1792 the Society warned the Government of England against a continuance of its abuses, and threatened that unless reforms were forthcoming, the people would soon be driven to embrace Republicanism. The great minds of Ireland, at last thoroughly aroused, sought objects on which to employ their energies. Their thoughts were directed towards every means that would speedily alleviate the hardships and sufferings of their fellow-countrymen. Then was born that intellectual activity and moral earnestness which was to stir the souls of all true Irishmen, not only in their native land, but also in that of their adoption—the United States of America.

This movement made itself forcibly felt through the medium

---

[1]"History of Irish Periodical Literature," by Robert R. Madden, London, 1867, Vol. II, p. 235.

of the press. The chief organs of the United Irishmen were the Belfast *Northern Star* [2] and the Dublin *Press* [3], both established in the nineties. The chief editor of the *Northern Star* was Samuel Neilson.[4] With him were associated eleven others of whom a number, and also of the contributors of the *Press* later were counted among New York's foremost citizens. Dr. Madden states that "the grand object of these papers seems to have been to keep the example and events of the French Revolution constantly before the eyes of the people."[5] The Dublin *Press,* during its brief existence, had many able contributors, among them the poet Thomas Moore who, however, did not contribute matter of any particular moment.

The "Montanus" letters of Thomas Addis Emmet, written in the *Press,* excited the most attention. William Sampson, another of New York's exiles, wrote over the pen name, "Fortesque." Dr. William James Macneven, their companion, was also a man of considerable culture.[6]

While these Irish patriots were still in the midst of their struggles for liberty in the Emerald Isle, branches of the Society were being formed in America. We see traces of these activities as early as 1794. Mathew Carey, William Duane, and others assisted the efforts of the parent society by their fearless advocacy of its doctrines, and that in the face of a Federalist opposition, which was at that time beginning to manifest itself.[7] Reprints of the principal articles in the *Press* were published from the Philadelphia office of the *Aurora,* the mouthpiece of the Jeffersonian party.[8] Philadelphia, the headquarters of the American branch of the United Irishmen gave aid and impulse to their friends across the sea, supplying them with funds; and arms were even promised should necessity demand such assistance.[9]

The English Government looked with some apprehension on the strength and influence wielded by this sympathetic organiza-

---

[2] Madden, "History of Irish Periodical Literature," Vol. II, pp. 225-235.

[3] "The United Irishmen, their Lives and Times," by R. R. Madden, Vol. II, Series 2, pp. 294-304.

[4] Samuel Neilson, an Irish exile, settled at Poughkeepsie, New York. See "History of Irish Periodical Literature," cited above.

[5] *Ibid.,* Vol. II, p. 233.

[6] *Ibid.,* Vol. II. Also "The United Irishmen, their Lives and Times," Vol. II, Series 2, under their respective names. See also biography of Arthur O'Connor for details regarding the *Press* in Vol. II, Series 2; "Ninety-eight and Forty-eight," by John Savage, New York, 1856, pp. 203-4.

[7] "Journal of the American Irish Historical Society," Vol. IV, p. 89, 1904. Article by Edward O'Meagher Condon on "Irish Immigration to the United States since 1790."

[8] *Ibid.,* p. 89, "Ninety-eight and Forty-eight," footnote p. 205.

[9] "Journal of the Amer. Irish Hist. Soc., cited above.

tion in America, and Sir Robert Lister, then Minister to the United States, set to work systematically to check, if possible, this concerted movement made by the members and friends of the Society in America.[10]

Sir Robert's efforts were, unfortunately, only too successful. He was on terms of closest intimacy with some of the highest officials of the American government, and persuaded them that the presence of these Irish enthusiasts was a menace to American institutions and liberty.[11] The psychological moment arrived when the rebellion broke out in Ireland in 1798. Under pretence of danger from the Society of United Irishmen, and their sympathizers in this country, President Adams took occasion to address a message to Congress, impressing members with the necessity of passing some suitable legislation relative to the admission of foreigners to the country and their residence here.[12] By the passage of this Alien Law a dangerous autocracy was established. Foreigners remained in the country at the mercy of the President. If they earned his displeasure, or if they were regarded as "dangerous," they might be compelled to undergo a term of imprisonment, to suffer perpetual disqualification from the rights of citizenship or be obliged in the end to quit the country. At best they were merely tolerated since fourteen years must have elapsed before they received the full rights of citizenship.[13]

As might naturally be expected, the opposition press, controlled principally by Irishmen,[14] challenged the President's action and criticised the Alien Law with a just severity. But Mr. Adams was not to be daunted. He succeeded in influencing Congress to pass a law which would make it a seditious libel to reflect on the conduct of the Chief Executive or to question the motives of Congress.

When the English Minister heard of the passage of the law his joy knew no bounds. In a letter written in 1799 to the Governor-General of Canada he related that some of the Federalists had "taken the law in their own hands and flogged one or two

---

[10]*Ibid.*

[11]*Ibid.*, p. 89.

[12]"The Irish in America," by Edward O'Meagher Condon, p. 259.

[13]*Ibid.*, p. 259. Also "Journal of the Amer. Irish Hist. Soc." cited above, p. 89.

[14]"Journal of the Amer. Irish Hist. Soc., Vol. III, p. 64, article on "Men of Irish Blood Who have Attained Distinction in American Journalism," by Michael Edmund Hennessy of the Boston Daily *Globe*.

Matthew Lyon of Vermont was the first Irishman to suffer under the Sedition Law. John Daly Burke was another. President Adams intended to hand Burke over to the British authorities. Aaron Burr, knowing of this intention, informed Burke and facilitated his escape. For fuller details see "Journal," cited above, Vol. III, p. 62 *et seq*.

printers of the newspapers whose comments had offended them"; he told how this conduct "had given rise to much animosity, to threats, and to a commencing of armed associations among those opposed to the laws, particularly among the United Irishmen." "Some apprehended," he added, "that the affair may lead to civil war."[15]

This unjust attack on the liberty of Irish immigrants was also carried on with even greater malevolence at the seat of government in England. In this persecution Rufus King, the American Minister at the Court of St. James, was to play a conspicuous part. The failure of the Irish Rebellion in 1798 led to the imprisonment of many of the leaders of the Society of the United Irishmen. In the latter part of that year, however, Thomas Addis Emmet, acting as spokesman for his compatriots, obtained from the British Government a promise of perfect freedom[16] for them, on condition that they would immediately quit English territory, never to return. They applied to the American Minister for passports to the United States; but Mr. King, in accordance with the wishes and sympathies of President Adams, refused to grant their request. Mr. Marsden, the Under Secretary of State, informed the prisoners, then confined in Fort George, Scotland, that Mr. King had remonstrated with the British authorities, and bitterly opposed the emigration of these unsuccessful patriots to America. When asked by them why Mr. King hindered their departure to the United States, the Under Secretary evasively replied: "Perhaps Mr. King does not desire to have republicans in America." This refusal on the part of Mr. King to assist the Irish State prisoners gave a pretext to the government of Great Britain to detain them four years longer in confinement.[17]

At last the day of their deliverance came. About 1804 or thereabouts, the released patriots landed in America. Shortly after their arrival these exiles learned with feelings of pain, the monstrous misrepresentation to which the majority of Irishmen were subjected. The influence exercised against them by a hostile press was enormous; added to this were the bitter prejudices of Puritanical Federalists who scorned these foreigners as "bog-

---

[15]*Ibid.*, Vol. IV, pp. 89-90.

[16]The text of this treaty and its history, written by Dr. Macneven, may be found in "Pieces of Irish History, Illustrative of the Conditions of the Catholics of Ireland, of the Origin and Progress of the Political System of the United Irishmen and of their Transaction with the Anglo-Irish Government," by W. J. Macneven, New York: Bernard Dornin, 1807, p. 169 *et seq.*

[17]Condon, "The Irish in America," pp. 260-261. See also Letter of Rufus King to Henry Jackson, Esq.; also Letters of Thomas Addis Emmet to Rufus King in "Pieces of Irish History, etc.," cited above, pp. 281 *et seq.*, and in the files of the *Shamrock* for 1816.

trotters" and "wild Irishmen."[18]   Dr. Macneven, writing shortly
after his arrival in New York City, does not exaggerate the condition of affairs existing in this country, when he states that "the
same virulence and invective, the same violation of truth, the
same distortion of fact, that marked the conduct of the English
faction towards the United Irishmen in Europe, have been revived
against them here by the retainers and hirelings of the same
enemy."[19]

Self-protection, the bond that united the Irish in Ireland in '98,
now united these exiles and their sympathizers in America. The
latter union was, however, a peaceful one, and consisted in the
formation of such associations as the Juvenile Sons of Erin,
Friends of Ireland, St. Patrick Benevolent Society, and the like.
The principal and very often the only local news items of the
early Irish periodicals were the addresses and proceedings of such
organizations. The purpose of these associations was, in some
measure, the promoting of the external interests of Irishmen,
especially the neutralization of existing prejudices sown broadcast
by an unfriendly press, not only in America but also in Europe.
Hence it became necessary to encourage the formation of Irish
periodicals in which the affairs of that nation might be truthfully
stated. That need was to be met by Irish weeklies published
principally in the two great centers of population, New York
and Philadelphia.

---

[18]"The Irish Scots and the Scotch Irish," by Hon. John Linehan, p. 72.
[19]Macneven, "Pieces of Irish History," cited above.

CHAPTER III

The Shamrock, or Hibernian Chronicle

The establishment of the first Irish National periodical in this country was a project of no slight magnitude, when we consider that a strong racial and religious prejudice existed against Irishmen in most of our large American cities.[1] This journalistic effort received its first impulse in the City of New York, which was a favorite port of entry for Irish immigrants, many of whom were content to make the metropolis their future home.

The distinction of publishing and editing this weekly newspaper, begun in 1810, belongs to Edward Gillespy, of whom very little is known aside from the fact, that he was a strong sympathizer in the movement, which had for its object the emancipation of the Catholics in Ireland. The prospectus of the *Shamrock, or Hibernian Chronicle,* as the paper was called, explains the motives which led the publisher to present it to the people. He pointed out the advantages to be derived from a journal in which the momentous events occurring in Ireland would be correctly presented without taint of fiction or prejudice. At a period when the whole of Europe was engrossed in the devastating wars of the great Napoleon, it is not at all surprising that many incidents of peculiar interest to Irish Americans passed unnoticed by the daily press. To keep people in touch with the important affairs affecting the state of Ireland, and to supply the deficiency of intelligence from their native land, were objects that engaged the zeal of this pioneer in National journalism. For the accomplishment of this design, the publisher communicated his plans to the leading editors of Ireland and requested them to send regularly the files of their papers.

From the beginning this weekly journal gave a definite scope to its labors, which it followed without much deviation during the entire period of its existence. Besides the news section there was also a literary department in which general topics on religion and morality were treated, and in which patriotism and a firm adherence to republican principles of government were earnestly advocated. In addition to this matter there was a poets' corner where could be found selections from Irish bards or original verse from American contributors. Dr. Macneven was an occasional writer for this column. The *Shamrock* has much valuable

---

[1] The principal source for the facts regarding this paper are the files of the periodical itself and in places where the dates are indicated in the narrative, references will not be given.

information regarding the arrival of Irish immigrants at New York. The names of thousands of passengers and the ships on which they arrived are recorded from week to week, so that we can place an almost correct estimate on the amount of immigration at all ports during that decade preceding 1820, when no statistical records of Irish settlers were kept.

The sources from which the *Shamrock* largely drew its news were the Dublin, Cork, and Belfast papers. On account of the slow progress of packet ships, Irish news was delayed sometimes for months. How unsatisfactory and obsolete such means seem now contrasted with the news-gatherings of the twentieth century! It was not an uncommon thing, especially during the war of 1812, to stop the press for fresh material that had come by stage coach.

A synopsis of the first numbers will indicate the variety of matter that filled the columns of subsequent issues. The *Shamrock* was printed at first on a folio sheet, fifteen by eighteen inches in size. There were four pages of five columns each to the paper. In the initial number of December 15, 1810, the chief intelligence from Ireland consisted of a lengthy report of an Aggregate Meeting, taken from the Dublin *Freeman's Journal*. The question under consideration at this meeting was the Repeal of the Union. O'Connell addressed this assembly with a vigorous appeal for the Catholic cause in Ireland. The third page contained some space-fillers and a list of new Irish publications. One especially worthy of note as, perhaps, furnishing historical data about settlements in New York, is entitled, "A Guide in the Wilderness, or History of the First Settlement in the Western Counties of New York, with Useful Instructions to the Settlers, by Judge Cooper of Cooperstown to William Sampson, Barrister."

A valuable piece of information on the same page may be found useful for the student of Irish history. It is a report of a mandate from Napoleon Bonaparte summoning to Paris the entire body of the members of the Irish Ecclesiastical College at Rome. He ordered a report of their revenues to be made previous to confiscation. The archives of this learned and interesting body of men contained some of the most rare and valuable documents of Irish history extant. This collection went to swell the vast literary stores accumulated from all nations in the Bibliothèque Nationale.

Very little domestic news is found in the first issue. With the exception of the Poets' Corner, the last page is taken up with advertisements, which highly displeased one of the subscribers. After a notice concerning the sale of some excellent pointers and fox-terriers, the publisher printed the following information concerning the sale of human beings:

For sale: A likely healthy, black woman, about twenty-three years of age. She is accustomed to house-work and is strictly honest. Any person wanting the like may be supplied by applying to Michael Landy's New Intelligence Office, 23 Maiden Lane.

Also the following notice:

For sale: A healthy black man, about fifty years of age. He understands farming and house-work and is strictly honest.

A third advertisement is about "a fine, healthy, colored boy" bearing the same qualities for usefulness as those already mentioned. The vigorous protest of the indignant subscriber to the *Shamrock* taught the editor a lesson, and he never again inserted such advertisements.

Twelve days elapsed between the first and second issue of the paper. The chief foreign news item was Grattan's speech in support of the Catholic claims. Another question of vital importance to the Catholic Bishops of Ireland was the report of the English Parliamentary leaders on the Royal Veto of Episcopal nominations.

The two questions of greatest importance to the Catholics of Ireland, and they were of special interest to their friends and kindred in the United States, were the agitations for the Repeal of the Union, and for Catholic Emancipation. In examining the files of the *Shamrock,* we are able to trace the history of the progress of this movement to guarantee larger liberties to Irish Catholics. Frequently, there were pithy editorials on these absorbing problems, which were engaging the best efforts and energies of Daniel O'Connell, that great statesman and champion of Catholic rights. His actions were followed most intently by the friends of civil and religious liberty on this side of the Atlantic, and societies to help along that cause were formed in the principal cities and towns. Thus American sympathy and public opinion were aroused, which must have encouraged the great Irish Liberator during those years when the struggle was fiercest and when victory was yet far off.

A contemporary view of the War of 1812 may be obtained by referring to current numbers of the journal. In fact, by taking up the discussion of the war in its editorial columns and by giving a report of the campaigns, the paper failed to give to Irish news that time and attention which its prospectus so definitely outlined.

We may depend upon it that the *Shamrock* was heartily in sympathy with America during the course of the war. For did not the American Eagle, symbolic of liberty, stand ever at the top of its first page, bearing an Irish shield and clutching in its talons a sprig of shamrock. Under this picture were the words: "Fostered under thy wing, we die for thy defence."[2]   The number of Irish in the City and State of New York who fought in the War of 1812 was considerable.   One organization in particular, made up exclusively of Irishmen known as the "Irish Republican Greens,"[3] was already well drilled in anticipation of hostilities. The *Shamrock* of April 20, 1811, gives a splendid account of their maneuvers.   It may be a matter of interest to state that these soldiers did excellent service under General Smyth, and were present at the capture of Fort George and Fort York. When the war commenced, there were frequent notices in the *Shamrock* appealing to Irishmen to enlist in the service of the United States.   The responses to such patriotic invitations were immediate and generous.   A striking instance of this promptitude is recorded in the *Shamrock* of August 20, 1814.   We learn there that Irishmen, fifteen hundred strong, enlisted and proceeded to Fort Greene, Brooklyn, where the chief engineer assigned them their posts.

Much space was devoted each year to detailed accounts of the celebration of St. Patrick's Day.   Usually, the last issue before the seventeenth of March was given over to the narration of some event or anecdote in the life of Ireland's Patron Saint. Then, for a month or six weeks following the festival, the speeches and banquet toasts, given by such associations as the Juvenile Sons of Erin, the Friendly Sons of St. Patrick, or St. Patrick Benevolent Society found a place in this newspaper.   The toast lists generally were of an amusing variety and show the spirit which ruled these assemblies.

Apropos of St. Patrick's Day celebrations, it may be interesting to note that in the issue of April 27, 1811, there appeared the report of a sermon delivered at Bardstown, Kentucky, by the proto-priest ordained in the United States, the Rev. Stephen Theodore Badin.   On the morning of March 17, he made a short but solemn address, showing the meaning and purpose of the devotions of the day.   This so impressed the citizens of Bardstown and the surrounding country, that some non-Catholics present at the morning service solicited Father Badin to give another address in the afternoon.   He did so beginning with a summary view of what he had said in the morning, and then entered into a discussion of certain doctrines of the Catholic Church.   Not-

---

[2] When the *Shamrock* became quarto size the following quotation is found under the title.   "What a people can do, the people of America have done. What a people ought to do, the people of Ireland are considering."

[3] For a more detailed account of the "Irish Republican Greens" consult R. S. Guernsey in "New York and Vicinity During the War of 1812 15." John D. Crimmins also mentions them in "Irish American Historical Miscellany."

withstanding his foreign accent, he was listened to with fixed attention by a very large audience, "which retired at a late hour both instructed and pleased."

That the editor had much sympathy with the Society of United Irishmen, is shown by the interest he displayed when occasion demanded some expression of opinion. During the course of the year 1811 Peter Finnerty, the editor of the *Press,* a United Irishman and a Catholic, was before the English bar of justice to answer a charge of libel on Lord Castlereagh. After a bold defence of the liberty of the press, he was finally sent to Lincoln jail. The *Shamrock* followed the case with greatest attention, and, when the sentence was passed, a meeting of friends of the liberty of the press was called at the Union Hotel, Williams Street, New York. At this gathering Dr. George Cuming occupied the chair, and Edward Gillespy, editor and publisher of the *Shamrock,* acted as secretary. A resolution of thanks was tendered to Peter Finnerty for his able defence of the liberty of the press. This expression of opinion was an example for similar demonstrations in other American cities. Their sympathetic utterances were recorded in full in the *Shamrock.* Hardly a week passed that the editorial column did not teem with spicy paragraphs, condemning the tyrannical action of the British authorities in their censorious treatment of the Irish press.

The enthusiasm displayed on such occasions by the editor generally pleased the native Irish in America. At the close of the first year's publication the journalist had reason to feel that his efforts had been appreciated, and the results for which he so earnestly labored realized.

During the course of the year 1812, Gillespy's health began to fail. He was unable to attend to all the departments of his business with the care an ever growing concern demanded. Consequently, in the issue of September 5, he states that he had come to the resolution of forming a partnership. By this assistance he hoped to augment the circulation of the *Shamrock,* which despite its brief existence could already boast of the largest patronage of any weekly paper in the city. He expected to devote himself to the business and circulation department, leaving to his associate the task of editing the paper.

These plans were not immediately realized and Gillespy struggled on as sole editor until June 5, 1813, when the paper suspended publication. From the character of some of the editorials in the beginning of the year 1813, signs of this impending crisis were evident. The paper was becoming a losing investment. On May 15, the editor, with feelings of regret and disappointment, announced to his subscribers that he had found it utterly impossible to continue the publication. The cause which he assigned for his forced withdrawal from the editorial labors was the failure of many of his subscribers to pay. He estimated the sum of these unpaid subscriptions to be in excess of four thousand dollars. The editor expressed the hope, however, that the suspension would be only temporary. He expected to be able to start anew after the restoration of peace. Thus lack of patronage was, perhaps, not the only reason for suspending publication. The circumstances of the war had operated materially against the purpose for which the journal was established. The dearth of intelligence from Ireland, occasioned by the frequent encounters between English and American vessels must have been another motive for the suspension of the paper.

When it resumed publication on June 18, 1814, it dropped the latter part of its title, *Hibernian Chronicle*. Mr. Gillespy had induced Thomas O'Conor, a devout Catholic and patriot,[4] to become his partner in the task of editing the paper. The new editor was a man of some literary ability. He was well fitted to take up the work of publishing this weekly journal, since he had warm sympathies for anything that would help the cause of Catholics in Ireland, In fact, he had taken an active part in the Irish Rebellion of '98, and was on terms of closest friendship with the other exiled United Irishmen, particularly Dr. Macneven.

Thomas O'Conor came to America in 1801, and soon after his arrival became associated with William Kernan in founding a settlement in Steuben County, New York, but as this venture did not prove a success, he returned to New York City, where, at the opening of the War of 1812, he began editing a paper, called the *War*, of which Samuel Woodworth was the proprietor and publisher. The latter afterwards became well known as a poet, novelist, and Swedenborgian preacher. O'Conor did not continue long as editor of the *War*, although it had been established at his suggestion. After the tenth issue his connection with that newspaper ceased, and in partnership with Stephen Wall, an Irishman, he started another paper. As both were men well versed in military affairs, under their joint labors the *Military Monitor and American Register* soon showed signs of success, but after the issue of April 12, 1813, O'Conor severed his relations with the paper.[5]

Between this date and June 18, 1814, when he entered on his new labors as editor of the *Shamrock*, he was engaged in writing a "History of the Revolutionary War in America." This was a duodecimo volume of about three hundred pages. Another of

---

[4] Thomas O'Conor was the father of Charles O'Conor, a lawyer of national fame.

[5] "Bibliographia Catholica Americana," by Rev. Joseph M. Finotti, New York, 1872, pp. 209-11.

Thomas O'Conor's literary and historical efforts was written at odd moments while he was editor of the *Shamrock*. This book bore the elaborate title "An Impartial and Correct History of the War between the United States and Great Britain." It was published by John Law, 62 Vesey Street, New York, during the course of the year 1817. The narrator spares no pains to give an authentic and satisfactory account of the events that occurred during the war just closed. In this history he does not forget the part performed by Irish Americans in the momentous struggle. Besides the information, he supplies many interesting documents of great value to historians of later time.[6]

The *Shamrock* continued under the joint editorship of Gillespy and O'Conor until January 28, 1815, when Gillespy severed his connection with the enterprise. At the time of its reappearance the paper becomes quarto size with eight pages instead of four as formerly. It teems with war news and expressions of patriotic feeling. To humble the arrogance of Great Britain in the eyes of the world was the cherished object of every Irish heart. Frequent and enthusiastic communications seem to indicate that Irishmen of every rank and station were anxious to display their valor and to defend the honor of the American Republic. Much matter for the student of American military history is to be found in the *Shamrock,* but hardly a thing that would interest the ecclesiastical historian.

The *Shamrock* under the sole editorship of O'Conor dragged out a precarious existence. Another suspension occurs during the month of September. From the frequent appeals to his subscribers, it is evident that the editor was barely making ends meet. He struggled on until August 17, 1816, when forced to it by lack of funds, the newspaper again ceased publication. Five months elapsed before another issue was attempted. In the meantime, some of the editor's friends came to his assistance with capital sufficient to place the journal once more on a paying basis.

During the earlier part of this year, the *Shamrock* was led by circumstances to depart from its original restricted field of action, and plunge violently into a campaign against the election of Rufus King for Governor of New York. Thomas Addis Emmet came out openly in the press and attacked him with the overwhelming force of his rare and brilliant mind. In March a systematic op-

---

[6]The following documents may be found: (1) President's Message to Congress of June 1st, 1812; (2) Report of the Committee of Foreign Relation of June 3, 1812; (3) The Act declaring War between the United States and Great Britain; (4) The Treaty of Peace; (5) Niles's "List of Prizes captured during the War"; (6) Treaty of Peace of 1783. See Finotti, *op. cit.*, p. 212.

position headed by Emmet raged in New York.[7]   As these exiles of Erin smote this Caesar with their trenchant quills, well might they, like other Cinnas and Cascas, triumphantly raise the shout:

> "Liberty! Freedom! Tyranny is dead!
> Run hence, proclaim, cry it about the streets."

The power of Rufus King was broken. It is true that he continued in public life until 1826 but he was no longer "the first man in the country." His whole behavior against the Irish while at the Court of St. James was exposed by speeches, by letters, by editorials. Even his own correspondence was used against him with telling effect. He was defeated for the Governorship of New York, and in 1816 gave up the cherished ambition of his life, the hope of becoming chief ruler of the nation.

After this exciting campaign the history of the *Shamrock* becomes uneventful. The paper when it resumed publication in December, 1816, promised to grow without interruption, but within the short space of nine months it again fell a victim of its delinquent subscribers. The periodical was revived in 1819 as a monthly magazine, called the *Globe,* but lasted only one year. It is a fact not generally known, that the *Shamrock* rose again like a ghost from its tomb about the middle of the year 1822. The first issue appeared on June 10, with M. Toohey as publisher and Thomas O'Conor again as the editor.[8] We know that it was still in existence in 1824, for in the issue of September 7, there is a local item about the consecration of the Cemetery adjoining St. Patrick's Cathedral.[9] It is doubtful whether files of these last years are extant. All our information regarding the journal's existence is obtained by references in contemporary periodicals. At that time the paper was published twice a week, on Wednesday and Saturday, whereas the original *Shamrock* appeared only on Saturdays.

When the *Shamrock* was started in 1810 its printers were Largin and Thompson, 181 Water Street, between Bleekman and Burling Slip. In 1811, a business and circulation department for the paper was established at 24 William Street. Towards the end of the year 1812, Pelse and Gould printed a few issues. Soon afterwards, in 1813, the proprietors of the *Shamrock* seem to have purchased a press and a font of type. We see in the paper at that time an advertisement stating that "plain and ornamental printing will be done at the *Shamrock* Office, 24 William Street."

---

[7]Some of Thomas Addis Emmet's letters to Rufus King of earlier date were used at this time. Published in "Pieces of Irish History," cited above, p. 281, *et seq.*

[8]*United States Catholic Miscellany,* Vol. I, No. 3, June 12, 1822.

[9]*Ibid.,* Vol. III, No. 9, September 11, 1824.

When the paper passed entirely under the control of O'Conor, a new business office was opened at 30 Nassau Street, and the printing of the years 1816 and 1817 was done for a while by Clayton and Fanshaw, 62 Pine Street, and lastly by Van Pelt and Riley, 9 Wall Street, near the corner of Broad Street.

In forming a correct idea of these early journals we ought to bear in mind that the telegraph, that mighty cooperator in our modern system of journalism, was not in practical use until 1835. The universal network of railways that so facilitate communication at the present day was then but the dream of visionary minds. Considering then the times and the difficulties of news gathering, the subscription rate of three dollars a year for New York, and fifty cents extra outside the State was not by any means unreasonable. Had all the subscribers conscientiously paid their dues how much anxiety, trouble, even failure would have been spared the editor. In fact when the paper passed into O'Conor's hands, he had to make allowance for the remissness of some of his subscribers. He was compelled to raise the price of the paper to four dollars a year, so that he might have sufficient money wherewith to support his family. The only other revenue that the paper brought was obtained from a few advertisements, for which the rates were one dollar a square for the first insertion, and fifty cents a square for each subsequent one. We may account in part for the advance in the subscription price of the paper in its later years by the fact, that no advertisements were published.

We have now to enquire whether or not the *Shamrock* fulfilled the purpose for which it was begun. The editor, in describing the effects produced in three years, gives ample testimony to the influence it had already exercised. When we remember the prejudices that dominated the upper classes of society, that to be a Catholic and Irishman meant ostracism, we should really feel gratified to see the least signs of an amelioration of their condition. These efforts, which the *Shamrock* in some measure helped to bring about, had better be told in the characteristic style of the Irish editors:

"When the United States was declared free, sovereign, and independent, persecuted Irishmen contemplated with joy, and embraced with avidity, the advantages held out by the enlightened legislature of this country, and thousands crowded to its shores forsaking friends, relatives and country, for the enjoyment of political liberty. In this drain on the population of Ireland, Britain foresaw consequences which would ultimately lower her from the pre-eminence which she had among the nations and that her wicked policy, which she seemed not able to control, was rapidly increasing the physical strength of a country designated by Heaven to humble her arrogance and to annihilate her tyranny. Here then were powerful inducements to perpetuate in the United States malignant prejudices against Irishmen; and when we reflect that her power of corruption and misrepresentation was so great, as even to instill a large portion of hatred into the breasts of one class of native Americans against another, we cannot wonder that she succeeded in her favorite object of injuring the character of Irishmen. Nothing but a total ignorance of the political state of Ireland and the true national character of the Irish people could have induced men, naturally fond of liberty, to be deceived by the wiles of the British serpent. To obviate this, more than any other consideration, induced us to establish a paper in the columns of which a picture of Ireland, writhing under the scourge of British tyranny, would be exhibited to the American people, or to such of them as were dupes of British artifice. Several well written essays on that subject were from time to time published in the *Shamrock,* and proofs drawn from Irish records, at once conclusive and convincing, to corroborate which there have been several letters from native Americans, acknowledging the effects which the reading the *Shamrock* produced in their minds, by changing their opinion respecting Irish character generally."[10]

The editors felt great satisfaction that so much had been accomplished in so short a time. We have every reason to believe from the consistent spirit of this journal that these good results were extended and increased by later issues of the paper. If the *Shamrock* did nothing more than to soften the prejudices against Ireland, its purpose was fulfilled.

---

[10]The *Shamrock,* June 5, 1813.

CHAPTER IV

The Globe and Emerald

As the struggle for Catholic Emancipation waxed strong in
the British Isles, a keener interest was awakened in America, in
foe as well as in friend. The garbled accounts of Irish affairs
in the English press were clipped with great eagerness by hostile
newspapers in this country. Chiefly to counteract this vicious
influence that was poisoning the minds of our citizens, recourse
was had to the antidote of Irish journalism.[1]

The purpose of the *Globe and Emerald* may be summed up in
the words of the English orator and statesman, Fox, which were
adopted as the motto of the paper and inserted below the title:
"Man has a right to equal and impartial government."[2] Boldly
and fearlessly did this journal assert the rights of Irishmen to
American citizenship. The paper did not devote much of its
attention to religious affairs, although the political rights of
Catholics were always ably defended. When the *Truth Teller*
was established in 1825, the *Globe and Emerald* stated: "We believe there is no journal in this city devoted to a defence of the
Roman Catholic religion, and even we, who have so often claimed
for the members of that Church a full participation in all political
rights, have never attempted to enter the arena of theological
controversy."[3]

This periodical was published every Saturday, and was essen-
tially a journal of politics, literature and the arts. Its first page
was entirely devoted to literary subjects. The remaining seven
pages gave attention to the following matters of special interest
to its patrons: The political news of England and the Continent,
items of domestic concern in America, a column or two which wit
and humor strove to make diverting, news on Irish affairs, clipped
from London and Dublin papers, editorial comments treating
frequently of the progress of the Emancipation struggle and
finally a column devoted to the muse. During the course of the
year 1825 we find letters of Bishop England taken from the
United States Catholic Miscellany. One of these epistles, addressed to the Irish Roman Catholics of the United States, occupied
five columns of the journal.

The first issue of the *Globe and Emerald* appeared in January,
1824. The paper was published simultaneously in New York and

[1] *Globe and Emerald,* Prospectus, Vol. I, 1824.
[2] *Ibid.,* Vol. I, 1824.
[3] Vol. II, No. 12, March 19, 1825.

Philadelphia. Its proprietors were Clerke and Mortimer. The latter conducted the Philadelphia office while Byrne and Milford were publishers of the New York paper.[4] A number of advertisements in the newspaper seems to indicate that it was receiving Catholic patronage. Bishop Fenwick's Bible is advertised in several issues. We also find there a notice of "An Abridgement of the Old Testament" by Rev. Dr. John Power of St. Peter's, New York, and Doyle's Book Store offers for sale a long list of the latest Catholic publications.

At the present time the subscription price of four dollars for a weekly paper would be considered high. But we must not judge the rates of 1824 according to our standard of today. The expense of conducting the *Globe and Emerald* in two cities and without any press of its own must have been considerable. There are many facts in this regard that must not be overlooked. When we deduct what the printer and editors received for their labor we find there was not much left to line the pockets of the proprietors. Moreover, we ought not to lose sight of the fact that the paper contained eight large quarto pages of finely printed matter gathered at no slight inconvenience and cost from all parts of Europe and America. Under the circumstances the wonder is that this journal had a continuous existence of over three and a half years; especially when it is considered that in 1825 another paper of a much wider scope became its competitor in New York City.[5]

At the close of the year 1825 the editors of the *Globe and Emerald* were sued for libel[6] but fortunately their fine did not exceed twenty dollars.[7] In the beginning of the year 1825 fire broke out in Fanshaw's printing office. This occasioned a delay of one issue of the newspaper. For a few numbers the printing was done by J. C. Johnston, 181 Pearl Street.[8] The growing patronage of its chief competitor, the *Truth Teller,* caused the proprietors in 1826 to surrender the field entirely to the new paper.[9] The *Globe and Emerald,* however, lived on under the new management of Pardow and Denman until September 29, 1827, when it discontinued publication.[10]

---

[4] *Globe and Emerald,* Vol. I, 1824.

[5] The *Truth Teller* was established in 1825 under the joint ownership of Pardow and Denman.

[6] *Globe and Emerald,* Vol. II, Dec. 17, 1825.

[7] *Ibid.,* Vol. III, Jan. 1826.

[8] *Ibid.,* Vol. III, Aug. 1826.

[9] *Ibid.,* Vol. III, May, 1826.

[10] *Ibid.,* Vol. IV, Sept. 1827.

CHAPTER V

The Truth Teller

New York already possessed two papers the purpose of which was to defend the cause of Ireland and its people in America. It was soon to have another journal, in which Ireland and Catholicism were the chief topics of discussion. Until the birth of the *Truth Teller*,[1] on April 2, 1825, the attitude of New York Irish journals seems to have been to treat religion incidentally only in so far as it affected the vital issues of Irishmen in their native land. In fact, Protestants could read these papers without fear of having their religious convictions disturbed or altered by such perusal.

In this respect the *Truth Teller* adopted a different position from that of its predecessors. We can not mistake its purpose if we read the editorial address in the initial number of the paper. It is exceedingly difficult to discover the reason which prompted the editor to write about a matter so irrelevant to the cause of Irish Catholics in America, especially at a time when his pen should have been directed against the malignant prejudices reviving in almost every American city. The spirit of this editorial, aimed principally at the subservient press in England and incidentally at the Evangelical movement then in full swing in Ireland, shows that the article may have previously appeared in the London *Truth Teller*, whose editor was William Eusebius Andrews.[2]

That this staunch and energetic Catholic should have lent his assistance towards the establishment of a Catholic newspaper in America ought to occasion no surprise, since he was known to the people in this country as an apologist, who had written many able works on controversial subjects. In 1816 he published "The Historical Narrative of the Horrid Plot of Conspiracy of Titus Oates." In 1822 he contributed eighteen pamphlets on the "Ashton Controversy," and at the time the New York *Truth Teller* was established, he was completing a masterly refutation of the calumnies contained against Catholics in Foxe's "Book of Martyrs."

Andrews was born at Norwich, England, in 1773 of humble parents, who were converts to Catholicism. He had served an apprenticeship in the printing office of the *Norfolk Chronicle* and by dilligent application rose to be editor of that paper, which post

---

[1] The files of the *Truth Teller* form the chief source of information for the facts stated in this narrative. Hence where dates are given, no fuller reference will be given. Complete volumes for about fifteen years may be found in the Library of Georgetown University, Shea Historical Collection.

[2] Biographical sketch may be found in "Catholic Encyclopedia," Vol. I.

he held until he became the promoter of the Catholic cause in 1813. From that time until the establishment of the London *Truth Teller* in 1824, he conducted in turn the *Orthodox Journal* and *Monthly Vindicator,* and the *Catholic Advocate of Civil and Religious Liberty.* He also controlled the London *Catholic Miscellany* and the *People's Advocate,* a sort of political journal. Although Mr. Andrews was a defender of the civil and religious liberty of Catholics, he opposed O'Connell in most of his London papers, strange to say, with unusual vigor.

The other few facts we have regarding the character of William Andrews are learned from his own mouth, on the occasion of a dinner tendered him by his friends and admirers in the great metropolis of England. He came to London in 1812 unknown to a single individual. He was obliged to undergo many sacrifices on account of his religious convictions. In 1806 speculation would have made him a rich man, but he rejected the tempting offer because he felt it would compromise his religious principles. There was something that he treasured more than wealth and distinction —that was his Catholic faith. Fortified with these sterling qualities he was well equipped to battle for the best interests of his co-religionists. A Catholic press was indispensable in the great cause of Catholic freedom. Its friends had been so long accustomed to the yoke of oppression that they had become guilty of supineness. The influence of the press was necessary to stir Catholics to action, in order that they might arm themselves with the privileges to which they were by nature entitled. He recognized that the civil immunities which would come to Irish Catholics by the passage of the Emancipation measure would be of little benefit to them if they were prevented from the enjoyment of those rights by being stigmatized by their opponents as dangerous to the safety of the state.[3]

A similar situation presented itself in America. For years the Federalists had made it serve their purpose to brand foreigners and especially Irishmen, as enemies of our free institutions. Defeated several times in attempts to beguile the people of this country into a policy which would give the Puritan element of the American population an ascendency in Church and State, they at last had to resort to new tactics. Under the obnoxious garb of Federalism they knew they could achieve but little. Hence they discarded that name, formed alliances with other discontented factions in politics, and continued their pursuit of power by endeavoring to arouse religious prejudices against Catholics. This desperate attempt to subvert the principles of government, which guaranteed freedom of conscience to all, was an open challenge to Catholics to cross swords with the enemy.

---

[3]The *Globe and Emerald,* Vol. I.

Catholics had long been trained to suffer these persecutions without a retort. But the time for silence was past. The gauntlet had been thrown down by the ministers of the Gospel, and Catholics concluded at length to accept the call to combat. Their weapons, like those of their enemies, were to be the platform and the press, and before the battle ended Catholics were destined to taste the fruits of victory. Thus, in this struggle to maintain their civil and religious freedom, the *Truth Teller* early became by force of circumstances the mouthpiece of Catholics in New York City.

The first six issues of this periodical, published under the name of W. E. Andrews and Co., contained hardly an item of strictly Catholic domestic interest, aside from a brief notice calling attention to a meeting in the city of those interested in Catholic Emancipation. A discussion of this question and the political activities surrounding it furnish the bulk of the news from abroad in those years which precede the passage of the measure. Thus in the first issue there is a report of the deliberations of the Catholic Association in Dublin, taking up six columns of the paper. Other matters of a general nature appeared. Two columns are given to Cobbett's "History of the Protestant Reformation," and a page to an essay on "The Science and Literature of the Middle Ages." The last page contained a column of original verse and some advertisements, one or two of which have a peculiar interest. Charles O'Conor, the son of Thomas O'Conor, the editor of the *Shamrock,* advertises himself as a Counsellor at Law, 10 Frankfort Street. Joseph Bonfanti had the following ingenious rhythmical advertisement which must have furnished amusement to the people of even his day: "Fancy store, 297 Broadway, opposite Washington Hall. Joseph Bonfanti begs respectfully to inform the public, that he has, at present, an unusual variety of fancy articles, which he is disposing of on very reasonable terms: Among innumerable other useful ornamental requisites he has:

> A wonderful bird the size of a bee
> That flutters his wings as he would on a tree;
> Hops, twitters, and sings on the lid of a box,
> In which he hides quickly when anyone knocks.

> Large elegant timepieces playing sweet tunes,
> And cherry stones, too, that hold ten dozen spoons,
> And clocks that chime sweetly on nine little bells,
> And boxes so neat, ornamented with shells.

> There's keys and there's seals, which are musical, too,
> And snuff-boxes playing some tunes that are new;
> With beautiful dolphins and whales for a bride
> To hang on her bosom with watches inside.

There's rings for the finger and pins for the neck
Of every new fashion the ladies to deck;
In both of which watches that go when wound up
Will tell you the moment to breakfast or sup.

Head-dresses for ladies and combs for your lasses,
Thread cases and needles and round quizzing glasses,
The best of court plaster for scratches and pimples,
Steel, silver, and plated and all other thimbles.

Here's drawing room ornaments whiter than plaster,
A beautiful stuff which is called alabaster;
For beauty and elegance nothing surpasses,
Arranged on the chimney-piece in front of the glasses.

Gold miniature frames and kid gloves in nut shells,
Needle cases, scissors for matrons or belles;
Tooth brushes, pomatum, and nail brushes small,
If I counted till doomsday, I can not count all."

It is probable that these stanzas were composed by Samuel Wood-worth, the author of "The Old Oaken Bucket." After severing his relations with the *War,* a newspaper which he and Thomas O'Conor conducted in 1812, he was reduced almost to poverty. His sons in after years succeeded Bonfanti in this enterprising business.[4]

Fully seven months elapsed before the names of the American editors are found in the first column of the paper. No doubt, they directed the journal from its beginning, but not till after the sixth issue does the paper lose its English flavor. At that time Pardow and Denman realized that they had to take into account the increasing importance and necessity of a well-conducted defense of Catholicism. That the *Truth Teller* had a mission to fulfill is evident from the strong replies to English and American anti-Catholic newspapers. The power of newspaper misrepresentation in 1825 was so alarming as to seem almost incredible. It often became the duty of the editors with the limited ammunition at their disposal, for both were laymen of no theological training, to hold up the conduct and the motives of these vilifiers to the disgust of unbiased minds.

After the sixth issue George Pardow and William Denman are recorded as the proprietors.

In the division of work George Pardow took charge of the business side of this journalistic enterprise, for his early life was given to commercial pursuits. He was descended from an old

---

[4] "Records and Studies," U. S. Catholic Historical Society of New York, Vol. III, Jan., 1903, pp. 115, 130, an article on the *Truth Teller,* by Thomas F. Meehan.

Catholic family of Lancashire. In 1799 he married Elizabeth Seton. He conducted for many years a wholesale hardware and pen business in England. When he emigrated to America in 1823 he also transported his business to New York, where he opened a shop in Maiden Lane.[5] It was in a corner of this establishment that the publication office of the *Truth Teller* was first located. Pardow continued in partnership with Denman until 1830, when he severed his connections with the paper. Until his death in 1847, he took an active part in local Catholic affairs in New York, where for many years he was a trustee of St. Peter's Church. Both he and his wife were buried in the cemetery adjoining old St. Patrick's Cathedral.

The information we have of Major Denman before his arrival on the field of journalism shows that his father was a German, his mother an Alsatian, while he claimed Edinburgh, Scotland, as the place of his nativity. He was born on St. Patrick's Day, 1784. He saw service in the English army and was wounded at the Battle of Waterloo. Denman seems to have been proud of his military career, although in appearance he was anything but a soldier. His dwarfish figure enveloped in a huge military cloak must have been a curious sight to the New Yorkers of his day. He boasted of the rank of major, although as early as 1832 his right to that rank was questioned. The other facts we possess regarding his life and character are so inseparably linked with the *Truth Teller* that the events which made up those years form an integral part of its history and will be told later in chronological order.

In the issue of April 23, 1825, the editor prints another diatribe on the provincial press of England. The language was hardly too strong when one considers the narrowness and bigotry displayed by these foreign papers. The *Blackburn Mail* called the London *Truth Teller* "a Jesuitical newspaper edited by Pope Eusebius." Statements such as these merited a drastic reply, and the *Truth Teller's* editor at times raved so much that correspondents complained that his abuse of the English was too severe.

While these tirades displeased some, others applauded them as justifiable and necessary. If the support that his paper received is any criterion of its popularity, the *Truth Teller* had nothing to fear, for the editor at the end of six months was able to state that his journal had a circulation equal to any weekly in the city. In taking a retrospect of the half year, he was also proud to announce his influence in checking the widespread abuse of Catholicism by the public press.

At the beginning of the year 1826 we have fresh evidence that

---

[5]"Records and Studies," above cited.

the paper was receiving the confidence and support of the Catholic clergy and laity of the United States. The editor informs us that he counts among his contributors many priests of high standing and acknowledged talents. Thus the literary deficiencies of the publishers were often supplied by clever controversial articles written by Father Thomas C. Levins, under the *nom de plume* of Berkeley or Fergus MacAlpin. Many prominent Catholic laymen of New York, such as Dr. William J. Macneven, Thomas O'Conor, and Thomas S. Brady, helped the cause of Ireland and Catholicism by a number of interesting contributions.[6] The fact that the *Truth Teller* never lacked these champions must have encouraged the editors greatly, for these writings added much to the respectability of the journal.

As the paper became more widely known, and more powerful in silencing the illiberal portion of the press in the city, the editors of many journals in and near the great metropolis deemed the communications and discussions in the *Truth Teller* of sufficient importance to reprint them. In doing so they manifested their own liberality of sentiment and assisted the Catholic cause by finding readers that the *Truth Teller* could not hope to reach.

To get, however, a correct idea of this paper we ought also to know some of its defects. The editors were not slow to recognize that many imperfections did exist. This is particularly noticeable after the fourteenth issue of the paper, when the publishers assumed the additional burden of printing, which until that time had been performed by Toohey and McLaughlin, 11 Spruce St.

In the issue of January 7, 1826, "A Lover of Truth," after praising the periodical for the good it had accomplished, made some valuable criticisms, suggesting improvement in the manner of conducting the paper. "Justice," he says, "compels me to add that sometimes you use assertion when argument would be more pleasing, you have once or twice touched upon topics that prudence would whisper 'avoid!' It is almost unnecessary therefore for me to suggest for your future consideration two simple sentences: *'Festina lente.'*..'Always look before you leap.'"

The *Truth Teller* in its carelessness in handling clippings from other papers, sometimes forgot to mention the source from which it drew its information, thus violating the rules of editorial propriety. This oversight sometimes embarrassed the editor. The Albany *Microscope,* in an article entitled "Foul Play," charged the publisher of the *Truth Teller* with willful plagiarism. Such practices of copying were freely indulged in by many journals of the day, but their evil example ought rather to have deterred the *Truth Teller.* The paper, however, soon had the satisfaction of

---

[6] "Records and Studies," above cited.

seeing the editor of the Albany *Microscope* bite the dust.   For the very article, which that paper accused the *Truth Teller* of stealing from its pages, was shown conclusively to have been taken by the *Microscope* from Hunt's London *Examiner*.

Another patron writing during the year 1829 shows that the paper was beginning to betray some signs of a decline in vigor. He says: "I have witnessed with infinite satisfaction the eminently successful endeavors made by you to annihilate the prejudices existing against us here, and to rally round our common standard the friends of Ireland and liberty of every creed and clime . . . While I ascribe to you full merit for the past, allow me not to be understood as unmindful either of the present or the future. Your journal *has* been *good,* and in point of *matter* is passably good *now*.   It has been *better,* and I am persuaded may be effectively *better* still.   Your paper has recently been lamentably incorrect.   I mean in typographical execution. . . .   A little more care and a spice of assiduity in revising your columns would make them far less exceptionable.   Your type, however, is woefully worn and deserves to be allowed to retire from future service."   The *Truth Teller* received these criticisms in good part and beginning with July 4, 1829, it was enlarged from a page ten by fourteen inches to a full-size folio sheet; new type also was procured.

During the month of May the news of the victory for Catholic Emancipation reached America.   This was an occasion of much rejoicing all over the United States.   In Philadelphia, the mayor immediately made the request that the chimes of Christ Church should be rung during an entire day.   He likewise ordered that the bell which first proclaimed the independence of the United States should send out its peal of liberty the whole of the next day.   A Catholic, an Episcopalian, and a Jew mingled their felicitations on the happy event.   Rev. John Hughes preached at a solemn thanksgiving service in St. Augustine's Church.   A solemn *Te Deum* was sung in many cities.   In New York a pastoral letter of Bishop Dubois announced June 21 as a day of sacred thanksgiving and ordered the *Te Deum* to be chanted in the Cathedral.   The Friendly Sons of St. Patrick also rejoiced on this occasion and celebrated the event by a banquet at Niblo's Tavern in Broadway.

While Catholics, Irishmen, and the patrons of civil and religious liberty generally were exulting over the victory achieved by O'Connell, their enemies were not idle.   The triumphs of Catholicism succeeded in alarming and arousing the susceptibilities of a hostile faction in American politics.   The plan of a concerted action on the part of seventy-three ministers attached to the Presbyterian and the Dutch Reformed Churches in New York City to spread their anti-Catholic movement over the length and breadth of the United States soon became manifest. They chose the press as one of their weapons to carry on systematic warfare. A newspaper was established by them in New York City and directed by one Parson Brownlee. The *Jesuit, or Catholic Sentinel,* put into circulation about the same time in Boston, thus characterized this sheet: "It is a paper so notoriously infamous as to reflect disgrace upon the very name it has impudently assumed—a paper from whose profligacy of expression, Satanic baseness, anti-social, anti-Christian spirit, the sensible, respectable, and virtuous Protestants of New York and the Union at large shrink with honest Christian indignation."[7]

In spite of the fact that self-respecting Protestants spurned this paper as injurious to the very cause for which they labored, it nevertheless fanned the passions and prejudices of non-Catholics to white heat. This begins the period of controversy in almost every center of Catholic population in the United States.

To test the credulity of the *Protestant,* and perhaps to furnish a little amusement for himself and his friends, Father John Hughes, of Philadelphia, afterwards Archbishop of New York, wrote in this journal some extravagant communications known as the "Cranmer Letters." The hungry *Protestant* swallowed the bait with avidity and called for more. For about four months Father Hughes manufactured the most ludicrously false accounts about the Catholic Church and its ceremonies that could be imagined. Parson Brownlee himself could not have written better. "Mark," said Father Hughes, speaking of this affair later, "Mark how he bespatters me with his dirty eulogy:[8] 'Our Philadelphia friend communicates his melancholy intelligence in a very evangelical spirit of sensibility and fervor. We trust Cranmer will remember that his letters are sermons of momentous importance and they are now read with intense and increasing interest by a rapidly augmenting host of Protestants of a like spirit. The oftener we decorate our columns with such pathetic appeals and heart-stirring facts, the more encouragement we shall feel to blow the trumpet in Zion and sound the alarm on the Holy Mountain. We hope our correspondent will supply us with a plenty of Gospel ammunition and it shall be discharged so as to produce the desired effect.' "[9]

The time came to throw off the mask, so in the issue of July 3, 1830, of the *Truth Teller,* Father Hughes explodes the whole plot

---

[7] Records and Studies," Vol. III, Jan., 1903, pp. 92, 114, article on the "Revivals of Religious Intolerance."

[8] "Life of the Most Rev. John Hughes," by John R. G. Hassard. New York, D. Appleton & Co., 1866.

[9] *Ibid.,* p. 106.

by a full page exposition, entitled: "Cranmer Converted; or An Address to Those Ministers of the Gospel who have recommended the *Protestant* to the Patronage of the Christian Public." So cleverly was this denouement executed that we shall give it in the language of Father Hughes:

"Gentlemen: In the first number of the *Protestant* it was evident that the editor was prepared to disregard all law except the law of libel. Its friends wished, and its enemies naturally expected, that in conformity with its title it would have proved an honest advocate of Protestantism. Has it done so, gentlemen? Has it not, on the contrary, been a disgrace to the cause? Has it not in six short months sullied your names and covered itself with infamy? Are not the epithets which it applied to the Roman Catholics too vile for the approval of gentlemen, too gross except for the meridian of a fish market? Has it ever contained one dignified paragraph, except those furnished in derision by some Catholic like myself? If the editor is too stupid by nature and want of education, you indeed, could not help that:—but if he is destitute of moral principle, if even the respectability of your names can not raise him to the level of common decency, why will you degrade your profession by stooping and staying below it for *his* accommodation? Your enemies say that you and your sect are impelled by the desire of religious pre-eminence over your fellow citizens of other denominations. They say— and remember the accusation does not originate with Catholics—that being prematurely detected in your plans and seeing but little chance of success whilst the eye of the public is on you, you have hit upon the unworthy expedient of raising the hue and cry against the unoffending Catholics, and representing *them* as the persons who are preparing to tear up the charter of American liberty, which was signed with Catholic ink and sealed with Catholic blood. They say that your object is to send the strong, but perhaps innocent prejudices of the American people, in pursuit of imaginary game, in order that, pending the chase, you may cement the bonds of matrimony between church and state and then regale the weary hunters at the nuptial feast. I hope if ever such a banquet should be spread the guests will be dressed in mourning.

"All this, gentlemen (in which I judge you not), has been said to you, and your recommendations of the *Protestant* have been referred to as proof. It was said that no other motive could have induced you to stake your names and your reputation for a periodical, which, pretending to be religious, violated all the rules of religious charity, truth and social decency. We know indeed from history that men pretending to be ministers of the Gospel like yourselves, and influenced by the same motives which are supposed to govern you, have recourse to means equally or even more degrading to their clerical character. We know in fact that political ambition, fired by the spark of religious fanaticism, is sufficient to make men use the pulpit, and go down to hell for instruments (if instruments could there be found, for the accomplishment of their schemes).

"I trust, however, gentlemen, that nothing of this kind is to be apprehended from you. But, really, there are circumstances which render your motives the object of legitimate suspicion. One of your most zealous but most unwise politicians has declared the wish of the whole to see 'a religious party in Politics.' Another, more ingenuous still, dreading a miscarriage would be the consequence of longer concealment, avowed openly that the church was pregnant with the design, and, like an upright man, advocated the necessity of solemnizing the union, which would make her an honest mother and her children a sacred progeny. Meantime, as small things are not to be neglected, you have all, gentlemen, betrayed an unaccountable partiality for certain texts of Scripture in preference to others, and more particularly for those which say 'Thy kingdom come.' You have all recommended the *Protestant*, and the editor of the paper, since the day you clothed him with the authority of your names, has laughed at all moral as well as official respectability. He seems to think that to have his falsehoods endorsed by seventy-three "ministers of the Gospel" he is privileged to lie in every page and paragraph and line of his polluted hebdomadal.

"Gentlemen, I have read nothing in the annals of knight errantry so chivalrous as your conduct in this matter. They of the Middle Ages went forth generally to realize an image in the mind, a 'beau ideal.' You were love-smitten by the sound of a *name*. But alas! the ardor of your gallantry carried you too far *this time*. The *Protestant* is, in sooth, a pretty name but she has proved a faithless spouse. Send her away, gentlemen, and take the advice of a friend and never marry another as you have married her—in the dark.

"But to speak in plainer language, gentlemen, although I do not suppose that the pride of poor human nature or the shame of inconsistency will permit you, now to withdraw your signatures, still I have too good an opinion of some at least among you to believe that you would ever have signed it, had you foreseen the disgrace in which it was destined to involve you before the public. You would have imitated from policy if not from principle the noble course of many of your reverend brethren who refused to recommend a proposition so violently slanderous. How great is the number of respectable Protestant clergymen who condemn it! And of those who have signed it, gentlemen, with the exception of about twenty (whose names we are sorry to find in the catalogue), what do we see but the clerical scum of the country, men who are a stain on the Bible and a discredit to the black coat; who supply the want of learning by rant, and of piety by preaching up the bad passions of their hearers into hatred against the persons and belief of the Roman Catholics.

"Now, gentlemen, lest your impatience should be excited by the length of this production I must now inform you that the writer of this is the author of those letters in the *Protestant* signed 'Cranmer,' which have attracted so much notice and elicited so much praise. I must be candid, gentlemen, and tell you, like two or three other Catholics of that city, who have been writing for that paper under different signatures, I have woven in as many lies as possible.

"And it is remarkable that the greater the slander the greater the eulogium that was bestowed on me by the editor, and the better Protestant he said I was! Oh, gentlemen, I feel for you when I saw like this man for whose integrity you have pawned your reputation, too stupid to conceal his own knavery or save the bail which had been tendered with so much disinterestedness. He saw in my anonymous communication a number of falsehoods which I rendered obvious and palpable on purpose but they were against the Catholics and he immediately pronounced me a genuine Protestant, and your recommendations entitle him to belief. In this, gentlemen, you pay a dearly bought compliment to your religion.

"But perhaps you ask how my conscience would allow me to gratify, even in jest, the editor's craving for slanderous matter wherewith to season his weekly dish. The fact is that I had a scruple at first—and at last I was obliged to quit lest the hungry expectants would commit gluttony. I imagined myself in the belief that I was writing romance like Dr. Ely in his 'Dreams' and 'Visions of Mercy.' Carter in his 'Letter from Europe,' or Brother Christmas in his account of the Montreal Controversy. I thought, too, I was justified by the example of the missionaries writing to their societies from all parts of the world when their money has run out, and the more so as I did not write for filthy lucre. Thirdly, I knew that you gentlemen and the editor alone would be responsible for any falsehood you might think proper to publish. Fourthly, I was satisfied that no enlightened man would believe a line published in the *Protestant,* except he knew from other sources that it was true, and that no modest women who had read it once by accident would ever read it again by design. Fifthly, I wanted to ascertain whether or not conscience had anything to do with the columns of the Protestant—I found it had not!—I found that from the moment I spoke against Catholics and adopted the signature of the cowardly, cruel, and hypocritical 'Cranmer' I might write anything, however false (nay the falser the better) and it would be published under the sanction of your name. In a word I could not find a line *deep enough* to fathom the editorial depravity of the *Protestant.* It is time now by putting him and you gentlemen and a few of the falsehoods in juxtaposition to see how you stand."

Father Hughes next placed in three parallel columns the editorial comments of the *Protestant* on his communications, Cranmer's letters, and the approval, recommendation, and names of the journal's clerical patrons. How these ministers of the Gospel must have writhed under the powerful criticism of this intellectual Hercules! The *Protestant,* smarting with indignation and shame, attempted to pronounce the long article of Father Hughes in the *Truth Teller* a forgery of some Catholic priest in New York City, but these vile slanderers forgot that they were dealing with a skillfull strategist. Father Hughes, provoked by the persistent boldness and impudence of his adversaries, sent a communication to the *Truth Teller* in which he authorized Mr. Denman to close a bet of five hundred dollars with the editor of the *Protestant* or any of the seventy-three ministers: "That there were in the city of Philadelphia alone not fewer than four Catholics who had been in the habit of communicating all manner of suitable trash for its columns."

This silenced the *Protestant* for a short time but its editor could not conceal his chagrin; and to relieve the embarrassing situation wrote a pseudo-communication signed "Cranmer," expecting to turn the tables on Father Hughes. But the latter was more than a match for his opponent. This time the amount stated was one thousand dollars. Once more the *Protestant* was compelled to retreat, the victim of its own folly.

But there is a sequel to this narrative that rivals in interest the main plot itself. The Rev. Thomas C. Levins, writing over the signature "Fergus MacAlpin," was a regular contributor to the *Truth Teller.* His stinging satires written in a pleasing, masterly style must have attracted many readers to the paper. The dialogues and discussions carried on by the "Sheet Anchor Brotherhood" were addressed "To the Seventy-three Calvinistic Parsons of the *Protestant.*" We can easily imagine how strangely Mac-Alpin's wealth of classical learning must have contrasted with the penury of intellect displayed in the sectarian press which he was attacking.

But Fergus MacAlpin was endowed with a fiery nature which sometimes carried him to too great lengths. Never was he more guilty of a false step than at the time these "Cranmer Letters" were being exposed. Starting with "Scrip Seventh" he began a flaying process on the conduct of his brother priest in respect to the *Protestant.* The pseudo-Cranmer letter was so repeatedly attributed by MacAlpin to Catholicus, that the latter was obliged to buckle on his armor again to clash shields with MacAlpin. He wrote the following letter to the editor of the *Truth Teller*:

"Mr. Editor: When ignorance and insolence co-habit they are sure to beget error and obstinacy. Two weeks ago I disclaimed the authorship of a certain letter ascribed to my pen by Fergus MacAlpin. I should be supposed to know whether I wrote it or not. I have already denied it and yet MacAlpin in the *Truth Teller* of last Saturday repeats with obstinacy the assertion and the falsehood.

"I did acknowledge the authorship of these letters in the *Protestant,* signed 'Cranmer,' which attracted so much notice and elicited so much praise. In making the acknowledgment I knew what letters were (and the *Protestant* knew what letters were not) comprehended in my reference. Fergus MacAlpin knew neither and his ignorance would have justified his silence but it can be no excuse for his bold and repeated assertion of what is untrue. He copies the passage, however, points it out for public reprobation, declares it was written by a Catholic of Philadelphia, and then begins to ask questions and ask them as he tells us 'seriously and sadly.' The editor of the Protestant knew that I never wrote the passage in question nor the letter from which it was taken, and he was very safe in tempting me with the following challenge in the *Protestant* of July 24th, page 298: 'We dare the Arch-deceiver who claims to be our correspondent, in his own name publicly to own, that he is the author of that letter over which Fergus so pathetically whines. A Catholic with all his effrontery will not thus entrap himself.'

"Thus the *Protestant* dared me to acknowledge it and I not only declined but I extracted the passage and had it published in the *Truth Teller* two weeks ago together with my positive declaration that it formed no part of my letters to the *Protestant,* the first of which was published on the 27th of February.   After all this MacAlpin says in the *Truth Teller* of last Saturday in his usual dogmatic and unmannerly strain: 'It did not emanate from the Sheet Anchor Brotherhood; you are its parent.' I am neither its parent nor author.

"Thus I am necessarily placed before the public at issue with Fergus MacAlpin.   There must have been a departure from the truth on one side or the other.   Here then in self-defense I must again have recourse to that tangible kind of reasoning which even the unprincipled editor of the *Protestant* could not abide.   The argument I now make use of is, perhaps, the only one to which neither MacAlpin nor the public will be insensible.   It is simply an appeal to the purse; and I predict that its operation will be like that of an arrow aimed at the heel of Achilles.   I challenge him to meet me with a bet of one thousand dollars (no matter where I get it for the occasion) that the falsehood is on his side and not on mine, the forfeit to be given to the orphans in Prince Street.   He is a man of great liberality and if he proves himself as correct in his statement as he has been bold, obstinate, and unqualified in making it, he will have saved his reputation and effected an object dear to the philanthropist.   Even if this should be at his own expense he will soon make up his loss (if loss it can be called in such a cause) being, as I am told, proverbial in his habits of domestic economy.   But if he shrinks from this proposition, and yet refuses to make an apology, then shall I leave him to abide the sentence which the moral feeling of an impartial public will pronounce on him."

This spirited reply on the part of Father Hughes to the bitter and senseless tirades of MacAlpin broke the back of the controversy.   Father Levins wanted to have the satisfaction of a drawn battle and continued his assaults on Cranmer.   But at this juncture a weary spectator signing himself "Catholicus Ipse" entreated the two assailants to cease their war of words and to make peace.   "Never again," he concluded, "let the pens of Fergus MacAlpin and Catholicus be dipped in the gall of bitterness."

Another intellectual bout of an entirely different nature occurred about the same time between the editors of the *Truth Teller* and the *Irish Shield,* a bombastic newspaper edited by George Pepper. This hot-head had not been long in New York when he tried to make himself hail-fellow-well-met with the exiled United Irishmen there; but failing in this and feeling sore in his disappointment he endeavored to belittle the services and the sacrifices of these patriots.   The *Truth Teller,* on the other hand, had among its contributors and patrons Dr. Macneven, a man of great prestige among the Irish Catholics in New York.   It grieved Pepper very much to see such influential Irishmen giving their patronage and their talents to the support of a paper conducted by two Englishmen. In fact, the history of the *Irish Shield* reveals that from the very moment of its existence it intended to declare war on "a faction who from interested motives enlisted themselves under the standard of a despicable pair of English hypocrites, and ignobly sacrificed Irish feeling and Irish sympathy at the shrine of venality."[10] This testy scribe hoped to divert the patronage of the *Truth Teller* merely to satisfy his self-interest. In fact he boasted that he had already made profit out of his enmity.

In this clashing of interests the firmament was soon to be rent by a storm of invective like to the continuous crash of an artillery engagement in battle. At a meeting of the Catholic Association of New York, Pepper seized the opportunity to declare war also on the United Irishmen. The discussion was centered about the appropriation of funds of the society towards the erection of a suitable monument to the memory of the late Thomas Addis Emmet. In the course of his remarks Pepper lauded O'Connell and very unjustly reflected on Emmet. This led to a strong expression of feeling by Dr. Macneven, Emmet's bosom friend and compatriot. In this warm debate, in which many took part, the editor of the *Shield* was worsted. To tease and torment him still more the editor of the *Truth Teller* doubted the originality of a history of Ireland which Pepper was publishing in the *Irish Shield*. Mr. Denman ironically insinuated that perhaps Macneven had given Pepper some aid. This so infuriated the editor of the *Irish Shield* that he expressed his feelings in the following caustic remarks: [11]

". . . Did you, Dr. Macneven, we respectfully but fearlessly ask the question, ever dictate, correct or suggest a single sentence of our 'History of Ireland.' Did you ever assist us in the composition of a solitary article in the *Irish Shield?* Did you at any time favor us with the loan of any work on the composition of a solitary article in the *Irish Shield?* Did you at any time favor us with the loan of any work on the history, biography, or antiquities of Ireland since the first number of this periodical was published? We put these interrogatories to this respected gentleman in order that his candid and unqualified negative answer may stamp the lie on the base and groundless insinuations of that literary impostor, the Yorkshire sergeant, who holds the felonious scissors of the dying thing of trash called the *Truth Teller,* and silence the echo with which some of the grogstore compeers

---

[10]*Irish Shield and Monthly Milesian,* Vol. I, 1829.
[11]*Irish Shield and Monthly Milesian,* Vol. I, 1829.

of this caitiff hypocrite have propagated them. Now we are 'armed so strong in honesty' and so confident of the entire originality of our history, that we defy any man who reads it to point out a single furtive sentence in the whole contexture of fifteen chapters. Let them, if they can, convict us of plagiarism. We want no stolen plumes in our cap—we disdain to dupe the credulity of our countrymen by arrant hypocrisy, for we feel we have talents that require no props from a disowned American hireling like that spiritless creature who is the jackal of the illiterate English scissors holder of the Lie-Teller whose Midas ears this background scribe ignobly conceals in a garland of nettles and hemlock from the sight of the public.

"But the ignorant and deceptive *Truth Teller* has run its race of duplicity and dullness; it can no longer gall Irishmen—for it totters on the verge of the grave in which it will fall, with the concurrence of every Irishman who prizes sincerity and genius and who hates the double dealing of vulgar Englishmen who have no talent to make it effective or useful. What! are we to suffer the bulls and blunders of a Yorkshire *shrimp* who was taught to spell by telegraph and write on sand by Joseph Lancaster, to be fastened on the literary reputations of our country? No, forbid it patriotism, forbid it justice, forbid it national sympathy! There is not a ray of Irish mind dawning on the wretched editorial trash of the dark and insipid *Truth Teller*.

"Let no one say that which is not true, that we now come forward when the few days of the *Truth Teller's* inglorious existence are numbered, when the doom of the despicable 'thing,' to use a favorite phrase of Cobbett, is decided, to push it into the grave. Our readers will recollect that we have uniformly denounced the effrontery and impudence of 'a pair of Yorkshire adventurers' who, without the least share of education or talent, succeeded, by the imposition of bare-faced plagiarism and the vulgar scribbling of the background Yankee, in palming their wretched 'thing' or 'shreds and patches' on our countrymen as an Irish paper, and in this, hoodwinking their good-natured credulity. It was no motive of envy— envy indeed! Would an uneducated English peasant like the mock editor be worth even the contempt of our envy? No; our aim in decrying and derogating the miserable and illegitimate bantling of hypocrisy was to cleanse and expurgate the literary character of our country, which was so unjustly contaminated by being coupled with a worthless paper like the *Truth Teller,* in whose ignorant columns there was for the last two years no Irish pen.

"If a literary Irishman had any control over its editorial management, would he insult Irish feeling as the Sergeant has done by insertion of police reports of the most prejudiced London papers—distorted reports which exhibited some of our countrymen, and women, too, in the most grotesque caricatures of exaggerated burlesque? Witness 'Biddy Murphy's' red petticoat and 'Emancipation Courtship,' which appeared in the nicknamed *Truth Teller* some time ago. This might be sport to the addle-pated scissors-holder, and to his half-lettered underling, but it was a gross and irritating insult to the sensibilities of Irishmen, and we know that some hundred of them have indignantly resented it, as they ought. We rejoice that we have at last opened the eyes of our countrymen to the duplicity by which they have been hoaxed—that we have boldly and fearlessly torn off the mask from the ugly visage of Saxon hypocrisy. 'Why, Pepper!' exclaimed some of our Yankeefied countrymen who value American pelf more than Irish patriotism, 'why are you continually cutting up the *Truth Teller?* They never attack you!' 'Why?' replied we. 'Because arrant imposition deserves exposure. Attack us, for sooth!—verily, they were not able.' Who, gentlemen, could the scissors-holder of the *Truth Teller* procure in this city that has the courage or ability to enter the lists of controversy with us? Would Mr. Sampson, would Dr. Macneven, enroll themselves on the recruit list of the English Shrimp? Oh, no; Irish pride and Irish genius spurn this degrading supposition. Then let it be known that the boasted forbearance of the Sergeant was but the pusillanimous forbearance of the fox in the presence of the lion. He could procure no one that was fool-hardy enough to encounter us. Ah! well the cunning Saxon knew that if any of his friends, either a mock-doctor or a soi-disant alderman, came in contact with us, that we would have made him sacred to ridicule during his natural life and impressed on his front, with a pen of fire, the figure of an ass as a suitable emblematic symbol of an unlettered-mind.

"We do not wish that the free and candid language in which we have spoken in the beginning of this article of Dr. Macneven should be construed out of its proper meaning, which is far, we solemnly aver, from any servile desire of propitiating his friendship by any unbecoming condescension, and as remote as the poles from the intention of retracting a single syllable of the opinions which we glory in having expressed of the relative comparative merits of our great and illustrious countryman, O'Connell, the very living personification of Ireland, and the Rara Avis of questionable patriotism, the late Thomas Addis Emmet, the repudiator of the land of his birth.

"On this subject we would be proud to have a public discussion with the Doctor, to grapple with him on its merits, as we assure him that, however superior he might be to us on other grounds, in this fair light his classic thunder will lose its lightning and his logical pen its Gorgon terrors. The interest we take in O'Connell's fame would arm us with new powers. As a scholar conversant with poetry and eloquence of Greece and Rome, and as a physician, chemist and physiologist, Dr. Macneven is acknowledged by the concurrent voice of Europe and America to stand in the first rank of eminent distinction. But as an English writer of the present day his style, which Longinus would call cold and critically correct, is a little sullied and dimmed with the antiquated dust of the old school. He does not combine in composition the logic of Locke with the magnificence of Dr. Johnson. The elegant graces of poetic eloquence never adorn his diction with the luxuriant flowers of imagination. The chain of his arguments is strong and massy, but it is a chain of rusty iron. We admire the base and shafts of the Doric columns of his syllogisms, but when we raise our eyes to the entablature we feel disappointed at the dearth of ornament, and the total destitution of sculptural embellishment.

"Before we conclude this article we think it proper to state the origin of the coolness now subsisting between the amiable gentleman and us is to be dated from the first night of the meeting of the Catholic Association in this city, when he, with the assistance of his partisans, rejected a resolution of thanks to Daniel O'Connell which we offered on that occasion. This, with the appropriate censure which we then passed on the reprehensible and iniquitous vote to the Emmet monument, is the head and front of our offending."

Swift on the wings of impassioned thought the editor of the *Truth Teller* swept to his revenge. The coup-de-grace was soon to follow. He decided to curb for all time the arrogance of his adversary who had persistently attempted to filch from him his fair name. He immediately began a suit for libel against Caleb Barlett, the proprietor of the *Irish Shield*. The defendant realized that the editor of his paper had involved him in difficulties from which he could not easily escape. The case was so obvious that Bartlett pleaded guilty and did not attempt to verify any of the charges contained in the libel. He asked the mercy of the court on the grounds that he himself was not the writer and did not know of the publication until his attention was called to it. He also stated that the *Truth Teller* had in some measure provoked the assault, by republishing an article originally appearing in the St. Louis *Beacon,* which censured in severest terms the *Irish Shield* for its frequent and gross attacks on the character of Thomas Addis Emmet, Dr. Macneven and other distinguished men of '98. The case was conducted on the plaintiff's side by Charles O'Conor, who succeeded in obtaining for his client a verdict of four hundred dollars and the costs of the suit.[12] The victory for the *Truth Teller* was complete. Pepper afterwards admitted that he "was forced from New York City by his enemies, who claimed to be advocates of Irishmen yet robbed the support from one on whom a large family depended." He even complained that they persecuted him after he moved to Philadelphia, but it must be added that he too continued to molest the editor of the *Truth Teller* with his favorite epithets "Shrimp," "Sergeant," and "Scissors-holder."

Much of the antagonism between Denman and Pepper can be traced to their opposite views in politics. The *Truth Teller* in 1832 informs us that an "Irish bolt" was being formed by the scheming "Federalists." It seems that the United States Bank party had approached Denman in hope of purchasing his influence with the Irish voter, but it failed utterly. They were more successful with the editor of the *Irish Shield*. This sycophant once more took up his pen to belittle the "English Sergeant." The following curious editorial reply in the *Truth Teller* sums up the political situation as it affected Irishmen and portrays the personal attitude of the two warring editors:

"The *pretended* friends but the *real* enemies of the Irish patriots, those who would link Macneven to the car of a Clay, Sampson to that of a Grainger, and the son of an Emmet to that of the party which through its accredited agent in London protested against the grant of permission to Irish republicans to emigrate to the United States, in conquence of which protest the virtuous and talented Thomas Addis Emmet was doomed to spend more than four years of his valuable life in the cold and dreary fortress of Fort George—those pretended friends but real enemies of the Irish patriots attack us with violence, malignity and falsehood for no other worldly cause than that we are and acknowledged ourselves to be the *real* friends of the Irish people. We are called an Englishman—what a crime! a sergeant—what a disgrace! and are charged with the crime of drilling the Irish. And what of all this? What has our place of birth or our profession to do with the question? We are indeed of English birth and so was a Chatham; we were not

---

[12]*Truth Teller,* Vol. V., 1830.

and we are not a sergeant; and had we been such we would not disown it, for we know no disgrace attached to the office; and must doubt the republicanism of the editor who would stigmatize us as such. We are charged with the high crime of drilling the Irish. We are laboring to *prevent* their being drilled. Who, let it be asked, drilled the Irish, or, rather, endeavors to drill the Irish at Philadelphia? The drillers at Philadelphia may rest assured that their efforts will prove a downright failure; the *federal sergeants* after all their boasts will find themselves without recruits on the day of battle. Irishmen will not be drilled—they will not desert their principles—they will not be set apart for the purposes of a faction—they will vote for liberty and for America. On the day of election they will vote with Americans, with the Democratic Americans—and for the Man of the people."

Once in the political arena, the *Truth Teller* found it hard to withdraw and, taken up with party cares, it neglected its mission as the champion of Catholic interests. The paper soon became tainted with trusteeism, which alienated the clerical support that the journal had until that time enjoyed. Catholic newspapers conducted with greater conservatism and respectability became its rivals for patronage, and before this competition its prestige dwindled almost to nothing. In March, 1855 Denman, wishing to retire, offered to sell the paper for five hundred dollars, to the owners of the *Irish American* but the prospective purchasers thought to effect a compromise by offering the editor five dollars a week for life. Little did they think that "Major" Denman was destined to outlive all his day and generation. He died an octogenarian on September 12, 1870. The compromise payments of fifteen years amounted to four thousand and thirty dollars. The *Truth Teller* closed its long and eventful career shortly after its purchase by the *Irish American* and an existence of almost a quarter of a century.

CHAPTER VI

The history of the *Irish Shield* is already more than half narrated when we have told of its rivalry with the *Truth Teller*. Its full title, when published in New York City, was the *Irish Shield and Monthly Milesian*.[1] It was started very likely in June, 1828, for we are told in the opening remarks of the January issue of 1829 that seven numbers had already appeared. During its first years the periodical should be properly regarded as a magazine, since its aim was to present to its readers essays on the history and literature of Ireland and occasionally a bit of dramatic criticism. In addition to these particular features a review of the proceedings of the Catholic Association in Dublin, Parliamentary speeches on Irish affairs, and a retrospect of Irish politics in general appeared every month.

In the January number, the editor George Pepper began a "History of Ireland," which was the feature in many subsequent issues. This production of his own pen pleased some of his patrons and in April we find a correspondent suggesting expediency of bringing out the *Irish Shield* in the same form weekly. The editor liked the idea and even hoped to act upon it as soon as patronage would allow. Caleb Bartlett, however, who had purchased the journal in February decided that it should continue as a monthly. The magazine certainly must have been a drain on his resources during its brief existence in New York, since there were only six subscribers who paid for the journal in advance. One of these being Dr. Macneven, as the editor informs us.[2]

At the end of the year the *Irish Shield* found that it could not thrive on such patronage. Moreover, the suicidal policy of persistent attack on a paper whose purpose was so different from its own, had not found many sympathizers among Catholics. In his journalistic sprint for favor Pepper overstepped the bounds of editorial propriety by his inflated rhetoric and becoming winded in the race, attempted to foul his rival by defamation of character but was penalized for his conduct. Caleb Bartlett, the victim of his editor's folly paid the fine of four hundred dollars and costs, dismissed the editor, and retired forever from journalistic enterprises, a sorry but also a wiser man.[3]

---

[1]The principal references for the history of this paper are the files of the periodical itself.

[2]*Irish Shield*, December, 1829, Vol. I.

[3]The *Truth Teller*, Vol. V, 1830.

Pepper was forced to leave New York and went to Philadelphia, where he started a weekly journal of quarto size called the *Irish Shield and Literary Panorama.* His experience in New York had not taught him a lesson, for on page thirty-seven he makes another attack on William Denman. For a while he conducted the paper on his own responsibility, but the patronage remained so limited that a meeting of the Irish of Philadelphia was called in its interests. At the meeting resolutions were passed approving the literary style and method of conducting the journal. A committee was also appointed for each ward and district to solicit subscriptions. Another meeting was called about February 15, 1831. Among a score or more of names we find Bishop Conwell and Mathew Carey. This committee was asked to prepare a circular with the view of increasing the *Shield's* patronage.[4] However, in May we again find the editor in the same desperate straits. This time four wealthy Irishmen of the city undertook the responsibility of publishing the *Irish Shield* regularly for a year. This allowed the editor more time for his literary pursuits, and on July 1 of the same year the journal became folio size, dropping the latter part of its title.

In 1832, the paper again changed its name becoming now the *Patriot and Shield.* In August, we learn that Pepper disposed of it and immediately started another called the *Republican Shield and Literary Observer.*[5] These later journalistic efforts, however, were practically the same in purpose as that of the *Irish Shield.* Their sentiment may be summed up in the quotation that appeared under the title of the first numbers of the *Irish Shield :*[6]

> "Whate'er may be our humble lot,
> By foes denounced, by friends forgot,
> Thine is our soul, our sigh, our smile,
> Gem of the Ocean, Lovely Emerald Isle!"

It is to the credit of George Pepper that he always tried to give a fair account of his native land. At one time he would paint for his readers pictures of Erin's churches and abbeys. At another he would present in patriotic style and heroic mold the achievements of her brave and illustrious sons. He deified the great Irish Liberator by the encomiums that he bestowed on him. Aside from the interests of Catholics in Ireland, however, there is not a word in defence of Catholicism in America. Indeed, a correspondent once attempted to enlist the editor in the cause of Catholic truth, but he replied that while he was always ready to repel any calumny that might be aimed at Irishmen, yet he felt it prudent

---

[4] The *Catholic Intelligencer,* Boston, 1832.
[5] The *Irish Shield,* Vol. I, 1829.
[6] The *Irish Shield and Literary Panorama,* Vol. II.

to abstain from questions of religion. He thought that the treatment of such subjects was more in the province of the Boston journal called the *Jesuit or Catholic Sentinel.*

On these accounts we must regard the *Irish Shield* as having no positive sway on the fortunes of Catholics in the United States. The editor's influence was, if anything, negative, since he attempted to dissipate by his senseless tirades the powers of a paper which regarded the protection of Catholic rights a sacred duty.

The reasons for the repeated failures of this paper may be traced to several causes. The subscription rate of three dollars and a half for an octavo size monthly of thirty-two pages was almost too large for a people who wished rather to have the full fresh details of Irish affairs, as represented by weeklies, than stale boiled down retrospects of a magazine. Again, the turgid style of its editor must have repelled more readers than it attracted. Then too, after the paper's establishment in Philadelphia, a tincture of politics generally flavored the already unsavory dish, so as to make it unpalatable to those who differed in views from its eccentric editor. Finally, during its first years in that city, the journal had not a printing office of its own; this was indeed a serious drawback. Its place of publication in 1830 was 22 Strawberry Alley between Market and Chestnut Streets.

We have now to bid adieu to George Pepper, the editor of the *Irish Shield* and its progeny, but let us not sink him into oblivion, as he has yet a part to play in the early Catholic journalism of this country.

CHAPTER VII

The Irish Advocate

Another rival of the *Truth Teller* called the *Irish Advocate*[1] sprang into existence in New York on May 1, 1831. In the prospectus that its editor presented there is an insinuation to the effect that the invader intended to win the excellent patronage which the *Truth Teller* was then enjoying. In its race for favor the newspaper claimed not to enter as an antagonist, but as a fair and honorable competitor. Yet in the course of events, it soon became apparent that its jealous editor betrayed at times in his conduct the same picaroon instincts for detraction that characterized the aspersions of the *enfant terrible* of the *Irish Shield*.[2]

The *Advocate*, like all other Irish journals in America, realized that the influence of the press was a powerful instrument for the establishment of the wholesome principles of civil and religious liberty. Consequently, the periodical laid great stress on these facts, since their propagation had hitherto produced favorable results for Ireland. The purpose, then, of the *Irish Advocate* was to widen that sympathy in behalf of the oppressed sons of Erin. Accordingly, the journal thought that the best means of accomplishing its end would be a truthful recital of the injuries and sufferings as well as the miseries inflicted upon the Irish people by Saxon tyranny.

The resentful feeling that characterized the prospectus of the *Irish Advocate* can be taken as a type of that which appeared in most of the early Irish periodicals. It states:

"Among the nations of Europe not one is there on which the eyes of the people of this country are fixed with deeper interest than that on whose affairs the *Advocate* is more particularly intended to record,—unfortunate persecuted Erin, the home of the fathers, the kindred, the birthplace of many of our best citizens, the cradle of letters and of Christianity in Western Europe, of whose former greatness not even a withered vestige has escaped the ravages of the despoilers save the spirit of her sons. A great crisis is, however, at hand in that unhappy country. Her people feel too sensibly their injuries to submit longer to the stranger's rule. They

---

[1]The files of this paper are exceedingly scarce. The little information we have concerning the periodical is obtained from contemporary journals, especially the *Irish Shield* and the *Truth Teller*.

[2]The *Irish Shield*, Vol. III, No. 2.

are united and determined; and unless their grievances be speedily redressed, the long slumbering sword of retributive justice will leap from its scabbard to avenge the wrongs, the injuries, and the injustice of centuries."

The editor of the *Irish Advocate* was John McLaughlin, a printer whose name is to be found connected with a number of Irish periodicals. The firm of Toohey and McLaughlin printed the first fourteen issues of the *Truth Teller*. Again, after the *Advocate* failed we find John McLaughlin the printer of the *Green Banner*. He was an earnest Catholic ever desirous of correcting the misrepresentations made by the Church's enemies in America. Living at a time when religious antagonisms against Catholics raged like an epidemic, he was stimulated towards devoting some of his efforts to combat the attempts made almost hourly to assail and to misstate her doctrines. One of the chief concerns of the paper was to defend and explain Catholic teaching, and, since the journal was chiefly published for Irish patrons, special attention was given to dispel the illiberal and erroneous opinions which were eagerly circulated by those hostile to the Irish in America.

The paper also took pains to enrich its columns with entertaining and instructive essays on politics, literature and the arts. It was, perhaps, more cosmopolitan than any of the Irish papers which preceded it, for the editor aimed at making it "a weekly messenger with a pack of news from all nations lumbering at its back." With a view of establishing a permanent patronage he devoted part of his paper to a "Business Record" in which the names, the business and the location of each of its subscribers were inserted without extra charge. Another means of securing circulation was the offering of one copy of the paper gratis to each person who would procure five other subscribers. The price charged for a yearly subscription was three dollars. The *Advocate* was published every Thursday on a large imperial sheet of quarto size. The printing, publishing, and editing were all done in the same office at No. 3 Chatham Square.

CHAPTER VIII

The Irishman and Charleston Weekly Register

Another ephemeral journal, first published in 1829, at Charleston, South Carolina, had an uneventful career. There is nothing in its prospectus to indicate specifically that it intended to champion the cause of Catholics, but as it was conducted by an Irish Catholic, we may safely assert that their interests were not neglected. The periodical is described as a "weekly, political, literary, and commercial journal, published every Saturday, by William S. Blain, at 26 State Street, Charleston."[2] The title during the year 1829 was the *Irishman and Charleston Weekly Register*[1] but this was changed the next year to the *Irishman and Southern Democrat*.

Judging from its prospectus, for the files of this paper are not at hand, we observe that it was very comprehensive in its aims. Its purpose like that of all Irish journals of that day consisted in safeguarding for Irishmen the principles of civil and religious liberty. It vindicated the rights of that people by repelling the constant assaults of their traditional enemies the Federalists and of that party's various alliances. To defend the Constitution from innovation, to keep Church and State forever separate, to preserve the purity of the elective franchise, to elevate civil and moral virtues, to safeguard religion, and finally to uphold the majesty of the law were the means by which the editor hoped to perpetuate the sacred principles of freedom.

That such a paper was needed in the South to assist the efforts of the *United States Catholic Miscellany* is shown, when we examine the spirit of the sectarian press. Journals like the *Southern Religious Telegraph* bedizened their pages with columns of sardonic clap-trap about the "invasions of popery" and its "danger to the Republic."

The *Irishman* was still in existence in 1831[3] for the city directory of that year was printed at its office. This paper to increase its patronage used the device the *Irish Advocate* in New York, started about the same time. Those who procured six subscriptions for the journal obtained a copy gratis. The subscription price was three dollars a year in advance.

---

[1] The little information we have about this periodical is obtained from the prospectus published in the *Jesuit*, the *United States Catholic Miscellany, Truth Teller,* and other contemporary journals.

[2] William S. Blain was the agent in Charleston for all the Catholic newspapers then published.

[3] I have seen in the Library of Congress a directory of the City of Charleston with the imprint of "William S. Blain, Office of the *Irishman and Southern Democrat.*"

49

CHAPTER IX

The Green Banner

The *Green Banner* was a creature of circumstance. Its editor
was the Rev. Thomas C. Levins, better known under his *nom de
plume,* "Fergus MacAlpin."[1] The editorial address in the first
issue of October 3, 1835, would indicate that the publication of
this paper was an expedient forced upon him by trouble with his
Bishop, the Right Rev. Dr. Dubois.[2] For some time the relations
existing between his ecclesiastical superior and himself had been
strained. A hasty and disrespectful reply was followed by the
suspension of this talented but quick-tempered priest.[3] In spite
of his failings, however, Father Levins did not lack friends in
New York, but they made of this sad circumstance an excuse for
entering into conflict with the Bishop.[4] While under censure
Father Levins was also employed as an engineer, for which profession he was admirably suited on account of his excellent knowledge of science and of the higher mathematics.[5]

Proficient as he was in this line of work, he yearned to be reinstated in the good graces of his bishop, and to be once more occupied in a defence of his religion, from which in the midst of all
his difficulties he never for a moment swerved. He writes about
this harrowing situation in the first issue of the *Green Banner:*[6]

"It has been a usage and still is to take leave of our friends,
or to use a school phrase to speak a valedictory, when making
our exit from a profession, in which years have been employed. Abrupt departure under such a circumstance would
indicate both a heartless insensibility and a disrespectful ingratitude. If after ten years' toil in the station of my choice—
and I trust it will not be considered affectation to say I have
done the state some service—I have not in place greeted my
friends with a farewell, the omission, it is hoped, will not be
attributed to me. The authority of a venerable friend was
interposed to prevent the observance of the usage,—wisely
judging, no doubt, that my indulgence in pathetic effusion
and heartfelt excitement might induce aches and pains from
which a frame, too nervously sensible and too feathery struc-

---

[1]See the files of the *Truth Teller* for 1827 and the years that follow.
[2]The *Green Banner,* Vol. I, No. 1, p. 2.
[3]"Historical Records and Studies," Vol. III, p. 49.
[4]*Ibid.,* p. 49.
[5]*Ibid.,* p. 49.
[6]The *Green Banner,* Vol. I, No. 1, p. 2.

tured, would not soon recover. Conscious of the integrity of my venerable friend's conscience, convinced that his charity is a seraph's illustration of the Gospel, and revering the source from which the authority interposed emanates, I submit and since have endeavored under the guidance of a sacred counsel to possess my soul in patience.

"My new profession is embraced under the auspices of many friends, esteemed and valued, Protestant and Catholic, American and Irish."

Father Levins had all the qualities that go to make a successful journalist. Having studied at Clongowes and Stonyhurst under the ablest scholars, he came to this country in 1822, and for three years was a professor in Georgetown College.[7] Afterward he severed his connections with the Jesuits, and at the suggestion of the Rev. Dr. Power of St. Peter's was adopted into the New York diocese by Bishop Connolly on March 13, 1825. In the field of theology he showed remarkable talents, and as a controversialist he displayed rare dialectic ability.[8] In the earlier years of the *Truth Teller* he successfully refuted Dr. Hobart, Bishop of the Protestant Episcopal Church in New York. Soon afterwards, he assisted Dr. Power in a disputation provoked by Parson Brownlee, who was so badly worsted in the encounter that Protestants besought him to retire from the arena to make room for someone more experienced in the practice of polemical discussions.

Besides being a champion of the Catholic cause, Father Levins was well versed in all branches of mathematics, natural philosophy, geology, and mineralogy.[9] All this rich fund of knowledge contributed to make the *Green Banner* a journal more elevated in tone than any of the Irish newspapers which had preceded it.

The purpose of the periodical was "to recreate, to instruct, and to enlighten."[10] In this Father Levins was eminently successful, for his paper introduced splendid articles in criticism and the other departments of belles lettres. Sometimes these literary efforts were original, at other times they were selected from leading English journals. He also interested his readers with narratives of life and adventure, choice anecdotes, occasional happy sallies

---

[7] "Historical Records and Studies," cited above, Vol. III, p. 49. See also written diary in *Georgetown University Archives*.

[8] "Historical Records and Studies," cited above, p. 49. See *Truth Teller* in 1827. Controversy with Bishop Hobart. See also *Truth Teller*, 1829 to 1833. Controversy with Dr. Brownlee, also Father Levin's attacks on the *Protestant*, a weekly newspaper of New York.

[9] "Historical Records and Studies," cited above, p. 49. See also files of the *Green Banner*.

[10] Prospectus of the *Green Banner* published in the first numbers of the journal.

of humor, and when enemies merited reproach his pen was trenchant with satire.[11]   During the whole of the year 1836 he moored the "Sheet Anchor Brotherhood" in their accustomed place and attacked again the camp of the philistines, the "Seventy-Three Calvinistic Parsons of the *Protestant.*"   Some of these ministers of the Gospel, attracted by the pecuniary success of Miss Reed's "Six Months in a Convent," undertook to write a viler and coarser work which they called "The Awful Disclosures of Maria Monk."[12]

The scandal-mongers and unscrupulous plotters enticed this Magdalen from an asylum in Montreal, where she had been placed by her mother, to begin a life of shame in New York. "The Disclosures" represent her as an escaped nun from the Hotel Dieu, where she had not only experienced the greatest cruelty and harshness, but had witnessed open immorality and even murder. Harper Brothers were the publishers of the work. This firm, lured by the profits which would come from a composition that pandered to the morbid curiosity of prejudiced minds, undertook to issue the book, but shamed at the very coarseness of slanders contained therein, they published it under the name of Howe and Bates.[13]

The voraciousness of the *Protestant* and other sectarian journals for calumnies of this sort was equalled only by their ferocious greed. Indeed, these conspirators fought among themselves for the lion's share of the lucre.[14]   Well might we say of this association of ministers what the prophet of old told the priests of the synagogue. "Her princes in the midst of her are like wolves ravening the prey to shed blood and to destroy souls and to run after gains through covetousness."[15]

William L. Stone, the non-Catholic editor of the *Commercial Advertiser,* succeeded in destroying this wicked plot against Catholics by paying a visit to the Hotel Dieu. He pronounced Maria Monk an "arrant impostor." Mr. Stone, by his conscientious investigation in behalf of truth, was greeted by a storm of derision by a number of insolent and disconcerted journalists. The most violent of these attacks emanated from the *Protestant* and the *Quarterly New Haven Christian Spectator.* He was made the subject of ridicule in a poem entitled "A Vision of Rubeta."[16]

---

[11]See the files of the *Green Banner.*

[12]The *Green Banner,* Vol. II.

[13]The *Green Banner,* Vol. II, 1836. Also see "History of the Catholic Church," by John Gilmary Shea, Vol. III.

[14]*Ibid.*

[15]Ezech., Chap. XXII, v. 27.

[16]"History of the Catholic Church," by John G. Shea, Vol. III, see footnote, p. 512.

The editor of the *Green Banner* throughout this trying situation wrote column after column in which he exposed the editorial depravity of the *Protestant*. He stigmatized the band of Calvinistic ministers who would stoop so low as to receive a fallen woman as the accomplice of their infamous fraud. He praised the action of the Protestant editor of the *Commercial Advertiser* who in spite of the gibes of intriguing miscreants condescended to become a living martyr for the cause of truth.[17] Another person whose conduct was equally commendable was the editor of the New York *Mirror*. He received a copy of "The Awful Disclosures" and was at a loss to understand the motives of the publishers in sending the book to him. He read one chapter and then put it into the fire.[18]

The name *Green Banner* indicated that it had another mission besides those already mentioned, namely the cause of Irishmen. In fact, the editor made the interests of the Emerald Isle one of the leading features of his weekly.[19] The motto he chose for the paper was very appropriate. The following words found under the title were taken from Shakespeare's "Henry VIII":

> "Be just and fear not,
> Let all the ends thou aimst at be
> Thy Country's, thy God's, and Truth's."

A brief analysis of the first number of this periodical will furnish us with some of its interesting details. The paper comprised eight pages of well-selected matter. The plan adopted by the editor was to devote the first page to studies in literature. Then followed a column or two called "The Voice of the Press." Here was found in a nutshell the best thought on important affairs in England and on the Continent. Discussions of the British Association of Science, held at Trinity College, Dublin, frequently appeared in its issues. Almost a whole page was devoted to miscellaneous writings. An original essay, entitled "Bores of My Acquaintance," is to be found in the first number. Here the editor portrays in a humorous vein the chief characteristics of the "inquisitive," the "story telling" and the "quoting bore." A digest of news taken from Irish journals, a discourse by Bishop England, and some Irish songs and ballads complete the number.[20]

The paper was published every Saturday on a folio sheet of medium size. No doubt the journal had many patrons, for the editor informs us that the stream of immigration from Ireland and from the Continent was so great since he came to the diocese

---

[17]*Ibid.*, Vol. III.
[18]The "Catholic Diary" for the year 1835.
[19]See prospectus of the *Green Banner* in Vol. I.
[20]The *Green Banner,* Vol. I, No. 1.

that five new churches had been built within a decade.[21]   In 1837, due probably to failing health, Father Levins ceased to publish the *Green Banner*. The censures that had been imposed upon him by Bishop Dubois were lifted by Bishop Hughes, and he was placed in charge of St. John's Church, Albany, but his constitution was already shattered and his eyesight so seriously impaired that he resigned his pastoral charge November 22, 1841. He died of paralysis May 5, 1843.[22]   The *Freeman's Journal* states that an immense concourse of people was at his funeral. Thus closed the life of one who was in his day the soul of pioneer journalism.

---

[21]The *Green Banner,* Vol. II, No. 6, p. 46.
[22]"Historical Records and Studies," cited above, p. 49.

CHAPTER X

Spanish Publications of Very Reverend Felix Varela

Under the strange appellation, *El Habanero* (The *Havanian*)[1] there appeared in 1824 the first Spanish Catholic magazine published in the United States. This periodical was not professedly Catholic, but since it contained articles on ecclesiastical subjects and was conducted by a Catholic priest, the journal may with propriety be classed as one of the contributions to Catholic periodical literature.

The first three numbers of this magazine were published in Philadelphia, and printed at the office of Stanley and Bringhurst, then situated at No. 70 South Third Street. Four more numbers appeared at irregular intervals before the journal was finally discontinued. These latter were published in New York. Number four was printed in 1824 at the French, Spanish, and Italian Printing Office, then situated at No. 44 Maiden Lane. The fifth and sixth issues appeared in 1825 and had the imprint of Gray and Bunce. These six numbers constituted the first volume. The last issue of the magazine, No. 7, was published in 1826 by John Gray and Company.

In order that we may acquire a proper appreciation of the contents of *El Habanero,* a brief biography of its editor is pertinent, because the Very Rev. Dr. Felix Varela subsequently became one of the most brilliant lights in Catholic journalism. In 1823 he came to the United States, but it is his career prior to this date with which we are now particularly concerned.

Father Varela was born in Havana, Cuba, November 20, 1788. His primary education was entrusted to the Fathers of the Order of St. Jerome in Belen; his collegiate years were spent in the Royal College of St. Charles and St. Ambrose. Here he completed the humanities and philosophy. Thence he passed into the seminary of the same college to pursue his ecclesiastical studies and at once attracted the attention of his professors by his superior talents both in philosophy and theology. His spiritual life was also of a high standard. The Rev. J. F. O'Neill, of Savannah, in an excellent panegyric delivered in St. Augustine, Fla., on the occasion of the laying of the corner stone of a chapel, dedicated to the memory of Father Varela, states that "his moral char-

---

[1]The main facts respecting early Spanish periodicals are obtained from "Vida del Presbitero, Don Felix Varela," by J. I. Rodriguez, New York, 1878, pp. 226-254. See also *Amer. Cath. Quarterly Review*—an article in English, by the same author.

acter was without stain, his piety fervent, his devotion sincere and sustained." At the college which was attached to the Cathedral of Havana, he received in 1808 degree of Bachelor of Theology, and in a competitive examination for a professorship in the same school, he gave a most brilliant exhibition of his talents and learning. In 1811 he was raised to the priesthood, and thenceforth his intellectual and spiritual progress was remarkable.

The first philosophical work published by Father Varela was written in the Latin language and according to the scholastic method. This was soon followed by a more elaborate work, in which two hundred and twenty-six propositions relating to all branches of science—metaphysics, logic, moral philosophy, physics, chemistry, astronomy, etc., were presented and briefly discussed. At the request of the Archbishop of San Domingo he printed in the same year two volumes in Latin, which were to be used as textbooks in the ecclesiastical seminary of that island. This work was entitled "Institutiones Philosophiae Ecclesiasticae ad Usum Studiosae Juventutis." The books were almost exclusively devoted to logic and metaphysics, and in 1813 they were supplemented by a volume on ethics. In 1814 there appeared a philosophical treatise in Spanish entitled, "A Recapitulation of the Doctrines both Metaphysical and Moral taught in the College of San Carlos."

These were but the beginnings of Father Varela's labors, but they serve to illustrate his scholarship. When he commenced to write he was only in his twenty-third year. In 1817 he was admitted as a member of the Patriotic Society, an organization whose deliberations are a brilliant record of the intellectual progress of Cuba. On the occasion of his reception into this learned association he delivered an address, "The Influence of Ideology on the Life of Society and the Means of Popularizing Sound Notions in this Branch of Human Learning." Because of his zeal for the instruction of youth, he was soon appointed to fill the most responsible position on the Committee of Education, one of the most important departments of the Society.

No efforts were spared by the Patriotic Society to keep Cubans abreast of the times in the important affairs of government. For about a decade the struggles between the King of Spain and the Constitutionalists had been continuous. Constitutional government had been introduced into Spain in 1812. A few months prior to the return of Ferdinand VII in 1814, after the decisive victory of Wellington at Vittoria, the Cortes declined to recognize the king until he had sworn to support the constitution promulgated at Cadiz in 1812, and had approved all measures passed by the Cortes since that time. But Ferdinand, once in power was not influenced by the Constitutionalists, and he banished from Spain all who had served Joseph Bonaparte. A strong revolutionary party, headed by Quiroga and Reigo, took up arms. In 1820 they caused the Constitution of 1812 to be again proclaimed and ordered the Cortes to reassemble.

This political revolution had also its effect in Cuba. The Patriotic Society, feeling that the days of absolute monarchy were numbered, endeavored to enlighten the people of the island by instructing citizens in the principles of constitutional government. They sought the permission and consent of Bishop Espada of Havana to establish in the Seminary a chair of constitutional law. He appointed Father Varela as the professor, who, however, accepted the position with some reluctance. When the course opened in January, 1821, Father Varela had ninety-three scholars and a large, attentive, public audience. This occasion was marked by an excellent inaugural address which profoundly impressed his auditors. During the year he published a book entitled "Observations on the Constitution of the Spanish Monarchy."

Father Varela had so won the confidence of all classes in the island, that he was elected to represent Havana in the Spanish Cortes. The following year, April 9, 1821, he left Cuba and little thinking that he never again would see his native land, he bade farewell by letter to his many friends in the Patriotic Society. As soon as the Cortes had reässembled, the Royal Guard was again up in arms, but it had not sufficient strength to crush the Constitutionalists. At this juncture the powers of Europe interfered. The Holy Alliance, then sitting in congress at Verona, ordered that a French army should enter Spain to place Ferdinand once more in absolute control.[2] By this intervention on the part of the French Government the rights of every member of the Cortes were proscribed and all were condemned to death.[3] Fortunately, however, Father Varela escaped and made straight for English territory. He sought protection and shelter at Gibraltar, and when the opportunity came, secretly set sail for America, landing in New York on December 17, 1823. He soon proceeded to Philadelphia where he at once began the publication of *El Habanero*. With these few details regarding the life of this illustrious priest, the contents of the little magazine become more intelligible.

The first number, of which the principal article was "Considerations on the Actual State of the Island of Cuba," treated both political and social problems. Other important essays in this number were "Conspiracies and Secret Societies," which were no doubt but more detailed treatments of the first article. The sec-

---

[2] "Encyclopedia Britannica," 11th ed., article, "Ferdinand VII."
[3] *Ibid.*

ond issue contained matters of great interest to the scientist, such
as the temperature of sea water at great depths, action of magnet-
ism on titanium, the production of sound and its velocity according to various physicists, and other scientific researches too numerous to mention. In the next number Father Varela published an essay entitled "The Ecclesiastical State in the Island of
Cuba." Another article shows that he was becoming acclimated
in his new home for he chose as a theme "The American's Love of
Independence." In the same issue we find a letter addressed to a
friend in Cuba, probably a member of the Patriotic Society, because the writer is endeavoring to clear away doubts that had
arisen involving the question of ideology. Another article speaks
of the political unrest existing in the island. Revolution in general is discussed, then revolution which might be formed by the
inhabitants themselves, and finally revolution which would be set
on foot by the invasion of foreign troops. Six pages are taken
up with a dialogue that took place between two Spaniards in
Philadelphia, one a partisan for Cuban Independence, the other a
defender of the Colonial regime. Three other items may have
some importance to the student of history or of politics. The
first is a short essay called "French Politics with Relation to
America." The second piece of information deals with the
"Secret Instruction given by the Duke of Ragusa to Colonel Gela-
bert in Paris." The third article speaks of "Instructions given by
the French Cabinet to Mr. Chassenas, envoy to Colombia." There
are also some reflections on the "Situation in Spain."

When the magazine appeared in New York, the very first article
showed that *El Habanero* had in the meantime suffered persecution at the hands of its enemies. In the fourth number the editor
raises many questions on the Cuban situation. The titles are
clear indices of the trend of public opinion in Cuba. "Is it necessary for a political change in the Island of Cuba, that troops be
expected from Colombia or Mexico?" "What ought to be done
in case of invasion?" "Is invasion probable?" "Is there Union
in Cuba?" "What would be the consequence of a surrender of
Fort San Juan de Ulloa?" After proposing all these questions
and discussing them briefly, the editor sums up the whole situation by giving his reflections on the troubles which are likely to
arise by not attempting a political change.

This short examination of *El Habanero* makes very clear the
direct purpose and scope of this magazine. It aimed at mould-
ing a public opinion among the Cubans concerning the best form
of Government for the people. No doubt the island was very
much disturbed by the vicissitudes experienced by the monarchy
in Spain. Living in an age when almost every ruling power was
in the process of transformation, many Cubans naturally hoped

that the time had come to throw off the yoke of absolutism and to emancipate the Island from Spanish tyranny.

Father Varela, because he was a refugee and a member of the late Cortes, so mercilessly persecuted by Ferdinand VII, and because he was laboring for the emancipation of Cuba, had to proceed stealthily in the work of propaganda. The magazine on that account was purposely made small. Each number of *El Habanero* was a booklet duodecimo in size containing twenty or thirty pages of matter. Because of its size, it could be sent through the mails very conveniently without attracting the attention of the postal authorities in Cuba.

The effect which this journal produced on the minds of intelligent Cubans was marvellous. The favor with which they received it was proportionate to the great annoyance which it caused to the Governor and a certain privileged class, always inferior in number and capacity, but always "monopolizing and oppressive." Their selfishness and ambition were dire influences on the destinies of the country. In their efforts to prevent the development of the prevailing public spirit of the island, they resorted to the habitual means of prohibition and persecution. So united were they under such circumstances that they misled public opinion and corrupted the judgment of the Cubans. There were not wanting sycophants who consented to prostitute their pens in an evil cause, so that they might buy favor or obtain money. One was found, who attempted to write a commentary on the articles appearing in *El Habanero*. This was printed at the press of the Governor of Cuba in year 1825.

Failing to produce the desired effects on the Cuban mind, the enemies of Father Varela called the attention of Ferdinand VII to the articles in the magazine, and the king issued a royal order prohibiting the circulation of *El Habanero* in Cuba. The edict was without results; the periodical continued to spread its light from day to day in the minds of the Cubans. The enemies of Father Varela now decided to free themselves of this menace to their political security. One of their number was ordered to set out for the United States with the commission to assassinate him. This fact Father Varela mentions in one of the numbers of his magazine in the following language:

"Meanwhile the political negotiations take on this aspect, that in Havana alone is there an attempt being made to persecute the author of these articles. I resolve to face the attack stated in the notice,—which informs me that in consequence of the effects produced by the second number, a subscription has been started to pay assassins, who are already hostile, and who are setting out from the Island of Cuba with no other object in view than to murder me. The notice is given by persons concerning whose veracity there can be no question. And moreover, there are things antecedent which confirm the information."

Friends of Father Varela both in Cuba and in the United States became alarmed when they read this communication. Their anxiety was increased when there arrived in New York City a person coming from Havana, commissioned to carry out this dreadful crime. Father Varela's friends begged him to take some precautions, to hide himself, to retire into the country or to take some steps to place himself in safety. The most they could get the good priest to consent to, was to permit them to communicate their alarm to the mayor of the city and to the chief of police. For some reason the would-be-assassin was struck with fear or compunction, for he soon re-embarked for Havana. These events happened during the month of March, 1825.

The seventh and last number was edited in 1826, almost a year after this exciting episode. No reason was then given why the magazine was discontinued. Very likely the more sacred duties of the priesthood at this time kept Father Varela occupied; he had recently been adopted into the New York Diocese by Bishop Connolly, who recognized in him the talents of a theologian and a philosopher, and the zeal and virtue of a truly religious man.

Father Varela from this time on figured conspicuously by his contributions to Catholic journalism. In 1829 he wrote for a magazine called *El Mensajero Semanal,* conducted by Señor Saco in Philadelphia. This periodical was soon afterwards transferred to New York City. We have the words of this layman himself, that Father Varela was more than a mere contributor: Señor Saco says "The worthy Varela and myself edited at that time *El Mensajero Semanal."* These words seem to indicate at least that the magazine was under the direction and counsel of the priest. The periodical lasted until January, 1831, two volumes. An imperfect collection, probably the only one extant, was found in the library of Señor Don Leonardo Del Monte.

A summary view of the other editorial labors of Father Varela will show that his pen was never idle as long as truth was assailed and the teachings of the Church were misrepresented. Señor Valerino states that this zealous priest felt bound in conscience for his religion, his honor and his office to become the annotator of a paper called the *Protestant.* On this journal and others of its ilk all the artillery of the Catholic press was at some time turned, on account of the unprincipled warfare which these papers carried on against the Catholic Church. The *Protestant,* the chief organ of the Protestant Evangelical Association, and the worst of these ribald sheets, required a special, vigorous, systematic opposition on the part of all contemporary Catholic journalists. Father Varela started the cannonade in 1830 with a publication called the *Protestant's Abridger and Expositor.* Six numbers of this Catholic periodical were edited with the sole purpose of exposing the falsehoods and fabrication of that paper, which might have been more appropriately called the Devil's Advocate, since it was, like Satan, "the father of lies."

After the *Protestant's Abridger and Expositor* was discontinued the opponent sent a challenge to the *Truth Teller,* then the only Catholic newspaper in New York City, inviting the Catholic clergymen of the metropolis to defend Catholic doctrine in a number of controversial articles to be printed in both papers. The challenge was accepted and the intellectual duel commenced. Father Varela's skill in theology and philosophy as well as that of his colleagues, the Very Rev. Dr. Power and Father Levins, was never seen to better advantage. The boldness and self-sufficiency with which Dr. Brownlee and the other theological tyros embraced the controversy contrasted bitterly with the confusion and utter helplessness with which they retired from the combat.

Father Varela was also a frequent contributor to the columns of the New York *Register and Catholic Diary* during those trying[4] times, when the absurd and fictitious stories about "Louise, or the Canadian Nun," "Rebecca Reid's Six Months in a Convent," and "The Awful Disclosures of Maria Monk" were polluting the pages of many Protestant weeklies. About 1836, when the New York *Catholic Diary* ceased publication, Father Varela started a paper called the *Catholic Observer* but as nothing definite is known of that project we may naturally conclude that the journal soon met with failure. Two other efforts of this priest's untiring zeal to propagate the Catholic religion are recorded elsewhere in this history of Catholic journalism. These periodicals are the *Children's Catholic Magazine* and the New York *Catholic Register* which appeared in 1838 and 1839 respectively.[5] Finally another monthly magazine, the *Catholic Expositor,* begun under the joint editorship of Father Varela and the Rev. Dr. Charles Constantine Pise, was published in New York.[6] But as this narrative relates to only Catholic journalism down to the year 1840 inclusive, the many interesting facts in regard to this periodical will be told in another work.

In 1846 Father Varela's health began to fail and he departed

---

[4]See history of the New York *Register and Catholic Diary.*
[5]See history of these two periodicals.
[6]"Historical Records and Studies," Vol. XIX, pp. 52, *et seq.* Article by Thomas F. Meehan: "The Centenary of American Catholic Fiction."

for Florida where he died February 18, 1853.   In the cemetery of
St. Augustine his remains repose in a chapel, built to his honor by
the lovers and admirers of one, "who was a holy and learned
priest, who spent his whole life in the service of God and men,
and who was at all times a perfect model of apostolic zeal and
boundless charity."

CHAPTER XI.

One of the most daring conspiracies to subvert the principles of Catholicism in the United States sprang up in the city of Philadelphia. The innovators, claiming to be Catholics at heart but in reality a band of turbulent renegades, attempted to bring about a general schism in the country, whereby they sought to make of the clergy a set of hirelings to be employed and dismissed as it suited their pleasure.

The catspaw of these so-called reformers, whose conduct convulsed the Church in Philadelphia for upwards of a decade, was a malcontent priest named William Hogan. He rode on the whirlwind of popular favor and was blown hither and thither by the storm of heretical doctrine. An examination into his previous career shows that at one time he contemplated renouncing his Catholic faith and had expressed a desire to enter the Protestant Episcopal Church.[2] Shortly after leaving Ireland he settled in Philadelphia, where his irregularities soon attracted attention. When Bishop Conwell was appointed to Philadelphia, one of his first episcopal acts was to place the contumacious priest under suspension.

The trustees and the wealthier portion of the congregation of St. Mary's Church, Hogan's partisans, considered this a high-handed act of injustice. Assuming the role of dictators, they attempted to hector the new bishop, and failing to intimidate him, they arrogated to themselves the authority of choosing their own pastor and reinstated Hogan. Not content with stirring up sedition in St. Mary's Church, these belligerents were prepared to spread anarchy into every diocese in America.

On June 18, 1822 they issued an "Address of the Committee of St. Mary's Church of Philadelphia to their brethren of the Roman Catholic faith throughout the United States of America on the Subject of a Reform of Certain Abuses in the Administration of our Church Discipline." In this broadside the trustees state:

> "Owing to the arbitrary and unjustifiable conduct of certain foreigners sent amongst us by the Junta or Commission directing the Fide Propaganda of Rome, imperiously call on us

---

[1]For a detailed account of the Hogan Schism see "History of the Catholic Church in the United States," by John Gilmary Shea, Vol. III, Chap. XV, pp. 227-260, Chicago, D. H. McBride, 1890.

[2]*Ibid.,* p. 230.

to adopt some measures by which an uniform system may be established for future regulation of our Churches, the propagation of our holy Faith by nomination and selection of proper pastors from our own citizens, from whom alone ought to be chosen our bishop, without our being compelled to depend on persons sent to us from abroad, who have uniformly shown themselves hostile to our institutions."

Then followed a storm of vituperation that spared no member of the American heirarchy. The address stigmatized the bishops and clergy as "a danger to our religion."[3]

This collision of principles and aims divided Philadelphia into two warring parties, the Hoganites and the Bishopites. The former deluged the city with a plague of pamphlets, each endeavoring to sting the conscience of Catholics into a bitterness and riotousness like unto his own.[4]

Mathew Carey, whose pen should have been as a sword wielded in defense of legitimate authority, was a Hoganite. With the craftiness of a Machiavelli, his thoughts vaulted over all canonical impediments to attain a victory for trusteeism. He was the first layman of St. Mary's to hurl defiance at the Bishop. Much after the fashion of a non-Catholic, he addressed Dr. Conwell as the "Bishop of Pennsylvania."[5] Hogan, himself unstudied in the art of rhetoric, sullied not only his reputation but that of all in his profession by his doltish display of mock-heroics.[6]

The combat grew apace when Hogan, now under suspension, attempted to exercise his ministry against the express commands of his bishop. The condign punishment of excommunication was meted out to him for his rashness and obduracy. A fresh storm of pamphlets more virulent than any which had yet appeared was thrust upon the public as a result of this action. Many strong protests were written by Catholic clergymen who defended the bishop's course.

The question no longer was made the concern of the Catholic body alone. The trustees, by enlisting worldly sympathy, introduced into the arena a band of literary tyros who were absolutely ignorant of the teaching of the Catholic Church, of her canons and her discipline. One, the editor of a paper called the *Balance,*

---

[3] *Ibid.,* p. 237.

[4] Finotti, "Bibliographia Catholica Americana," pp. 137-172.

[5] *Ibid.,* p. 140; also Shea's "History of the Catholic Church," note, p. 231.

[6] "The Works of the Rt. Rev. John England," collected and printed by Rt. Rev. Ignatius A. Reynolds, Vol. V, Chap. VII. In Sect. VIII, p. 141, we have a sample of Hogan's display of English. He shows in that place a lamentable ignorance even of ordinary spelling. Some of his pamphlets are recorded in the *Hoganiana* made by Finotti. See "Bibliographia Cathoilca," cited above.

carried in his issue of January 22, 1822, three scurrilous articles entitled "Churches Militant," "The Dutch," "The Bishopites and the Hoganites." This was followed in the next issue by a series of six sermons contributed by "Lay Preacher."[7] On February 13, he published a forged and ridiculous form of excommunication, filled with all the scurrility of the author from which it was taken. Bishop England thus speaks of the grotesqueness of this scribbling jester:

"On reading this execrable production, we absolutely felt a chill of horror and unvoluntarily asked a friend who was near us, whether there was anything so pestiferous in the air of Philadelphia as to destroy every particle of moral feeling. We scarcely have thought that any person, whom public opinion had entrusted with the direction of the press, could be so debased as to be guilty of so daring a fraud, so shameful and so easily detected, but our astonishment ceased when we recollected the *pamphlets*. Yes, there was the vampire who penned them crawling forth from the graves of the respected dead with his head smeared with gore, his entrails filled with corruption and the air around him fetid and contagious. We no longer were sceptics. The object of the party was to bring disgrace upon the Catholic religion. For this purpose the infidel, the profligate and the vindictive were leagued in a holy alliance—for this purpose the Vinegar Hill boys were enlisted—for this purpose the *Balance* even the *Balance* was subsidized, and one of Sterne's effusions, the compilation of his ingenuity and his—can we call it less than malignity?— was copied from 'Tristam Shandy,' and sent out to the public of America as the official document of one of the dignitaries of the Catholic Church; and the men who consent to, and delight in, and circulate this grossest of libels upon the Catholic Church presume to call themselves Catholics."[8]

This exposure did not have the slightest effect on this ribald journal. During March there appeared "A Letter to Rev. Dr. Cabbage Stock," meaning thereby Bishop Conwell. Another piece of sarcasm written by some benighted rhymester was styled "A Hole in the Wall; or, The Cabbage Stock in Council." Father Harold, who was at this time a zealous Bishopite, was thus complimented for his bold denunciation of Mathew Carey. "Victor Harold was three weeks in labor and at last brought forth a scandalous pamphlet." The bishops and clergy were disgracefully

---

[7]"Bibliographia Catholica," etc., cited above, p. 148.

[8]"The Works of Bishop England," cited above, Vol. V, Sec. II, p. 111. This section gives the forgery contained in the *Balance* of Feb. 13, 1822.

caricatured by this pernicious journal in a series of sketches entitled "A Medley of Characters Well-known to the Public." These senseless pasquinades in which Dr. Conwell was styled "Old Harry Bishop of Philadelphia" and Father Harold was named "Friar Tuck" or "Prior Dominic" filled even the most disinterested spectator with nausea. Even a disgusted "Pro-Hogan Catholic" protested against the filthy language with which the *Balance* filled its columns.[9]

We have just noted that Father Harold crossed swords with Mathew Carey. The latter wished to constitute himself an ecclesiastical court to pass judgment on the Bishop. This attempted usurpation of power began the war of the pamphleteers. Very likely the reply to Father Harold mentioned in the *Balance* had reference to Carey's "Address to the Rt. Rev. Bishop of Pennsylvania" published about February 23, 1822.[10] Father Harold wrote in March and simultaneously appeared another pamphlet with the title "Brief Remarks Addressed to a 'Catholic Layman'" contributed by a Protestant Episcopalian.[11] This was a dignified and effective paper written by an impartial observer. The rejoinder to these two replies appeared on March 28, which pamphlet contained also the more important of Mathew Carey's previous productions. One of these was a spirited address to St. Mary's Congregation entitled "On the Banks of the Rubicon."[12] At the same time this booklet appeared a friend of Carey's wrote a paper, styled "Letter to Rev. W. V. Harold on reading his late reply to a 'Catholic Layman.'" This epistle snorted an air of defiance at the Bishopite. It began with Shakespeare's oft quoted words in Macbeth. "Lay on Macduff and damned be he who first cries, Hold—enough."[13]

Father Harold was somewhat wrought up by this double attack and by their fierce display of invective. He chides his adversaries as "assassins" of character. "A vulgar mind," he said, "finds it easy to utter foul aspersions—for in doing so it follows its natural bent."[14] The heat of the controversy at this stage becomes almost feverish. The frenzied state of Mathew Carey's mind is strikingly shown by the forceful lines of Pope, which he employs in his reply to Father Harold:

> "Curst be the lines how smooth soe'er they flow,
> That tend to make one honest man foe,
> Give virtue scandal, innocent a fear,
> Or from the soft-eyed virgin steal a tear."[15]

<hr>

[9] "Bibliographia Catholica," Finotti, cited above, p. 149.
[10] *Ibid.*, p. 151.
[11] *Ibid.*, p. 152.
[12] *Ibid.*, p. 153.
[13] *Ibid.*, p. 153.
[14] *Ibid.*, p. 154.
[15] *Ibid.*, p. 155.

In this communication Carey already betrays some signs of defeat, for he trumps up charges which he can in no way substantiate.

This exasperation did not escape the notice of the discerning Bishopite. The following lines taken from Horace show that he was a master of repartee: "Anger is a short madness: Govern your passion, which unless it obeys, tyrannizes: curb it with reins (or) with a chain." As if to make the taste of his remarks a little more pungent, he adds a few drops of acid to his wit by flavoring it with the language of Shakespeare's "Tempest." "He's in a fit now and does not talk after the wisest."[16] Father Harold in this pamphlet is perfectly aware that he has annihilated his opponent. He must have felt like the young David in the presence of the great Goliath, for Mathew Carey was a man of no mean erudition. The clergyman was confident though, that under the literary scourge of one more competent than himself he would have fared even worse. "Another," he says, "would have whipped you with scorpions, but I merely put a little wire in the lash."[17]

There were many similar encounters by the champions of the two contending parties. During the latter part of the year 1822 the schism gathered fresh impetus. Two events occurred which contributed to define still more sharply the position of the Hoganites. Pope Pius VII by his Brief "Non Sine Magno" condemned the unfortunate priest for his contumacious conduct.[18] This major excommunication also dealt a severe and decisive blow at trusteeism in America. The brief stated clearly the position of the trustees in respect to their bishop. "Trustees," said the Sovereign Pontiff, "ought to bear in mind that the properties, which have been consecrated for divine worship for the support of the Church and for the maintenance of its ministers, fall under the power of the Church; and since the bishops by divine appointment preside over the respective churches, they can not by any means be excluded from the care, superintendence and administration of these properties."[19]

The highest ecclesiastical court had decided against the schismatics. The supreme court of the State also passed a sentence against Hogan. A summary report of this judgment appeared in Poulson's *American Daily Advertiser*[20] and the *Franklin Gazette*.[21]

---

[16]*Ibid.*, p. 155.

[17]*Ibid.*, p. 156.

[18]Shea, "History of the Catholic Church in the United States," cited above, p. 243. Text of decree in "Works of Bishop England," Vol. V, Sec. XVIII, p. 178.

[19]Translation taken from the "Works of Bishop England," cited above.

[20]Poulson's American Daily Advertiser, 1822-1823.

[21]The *Franklin Gazette*, 1822-1823.

This court bound William Hogan to appear before the Mayor, and in the meantime, until the whole matter would be finally adjusted, advised the followers of the Bishop to refrain from worshipping in St. Mary's Church. The opinions of the three judges are recorded in full by the *Democratic Free Press*. Would that these papers had at all times exercised more discretion in their columns.[22]

During the year 1822 and 1823 when the battle was hottest, the daily journals of Philadelphia vied with one another in catering to this unholy warfare. The following papers were most often employed on the side of the schismatic Hoganites: The *Democratic Press*, the *Aurora*, the *National Gazette*, the *Gazette and Daily Advertiser*, the *Franklin Gazette*, the *American Sentinel and Mercantile Advertiser*, the *American Daily Advertiser* and the *Columbian Observer*.[23] Mathew Carey is said to have been a frequent writer for some of these journals. Six letters signed "Catholicus" which appeared in the *American Sentinel* and *Mercantile Advertiser* are attributed to him.[24] The opinion of Peter S. Duponçeau, one of the counsels in the Hogan trial, based on a wrong interpretation of the *jus patronatus* appeared in the *Columbian Observer*.[25] An article in the same paper by one signing himself "Columbus" endeavored to embarrass Bishop England in his conciliatory efforts to bring a speedy end to the schism. This attempted to poison the minds of his readers against one, who was considered the "Corinthian Pillar" of the Catholic Church in America. During the course of the year 1825 the following communication appeared in the columns of the *Columbian Observer*:[26]

> "To the members of the congregation worshiping at St. Mary's Church and to all others professing liberal principles. The weekly paper edited by the Roman Catholic Bishop of Charleston, S. C., in conjunction with other enlightened men, has been assailed merely because of the liberality of principle which it adopted of late. Bishop England has divested himself of much bigotry and espoused the cause of the trustees of St. Mary's and of the minister of their appointment—the people's appointment—in opposition to the tyranny of antiquated abuse and the narrow views and violent clamor of the sticklers for that tyranny. For this exertion of mind over slavery to traditionary authority—an exertion resembling in

---

[22]*Democratic Free Press,* 1822-1823. Many of the papers mentioned above have been consulted in the Library of Congress.

[23]Finotti in his "Bibliographia Catholica Americana" refers briefly to the part played by the daily press.

[24]Files of these papers may be found in the Library of Congress.

[25]Finotti, cited above, p. 162.

[26]*Ibid.,* p. 162.

its principle our own glorious Revolution, and likely (if supported) to assist the march of evangelical liberty; his reward has been the *secession* of thirty-five of his subscribers in one day in this enlightened city!

"In his last number the intrepid prelate discloses this fact (as explicitly as his peculiarly embarrassing circumstances would permit) to you for support. You will not, you must not disappoint him, for you have too much sagacity not to perceive how much may be effected by fostering what is yet only a spark, but may yet be kindled to a bright and steady light. America will not coerce; but is she not bound to enlighten? Only suffer the journal now claiming your help, to become the victim of the tyranny, which smothered the intellect of Europe for fifteen ages, and has since impeded its progress to the fullness of reanimation, and you will have sacrificed the surest means which Providence has yet offered in our day to give success to a cause embracing the universal improvement of man. To add anything more might seem to imply a diffidence of your claim to the character of the first of nations—'Columbus'."[27]

The unscrupulous plotter was treated to the following tart reply by the Bishop of Charleston:[28]

"What the party of the writer may be we know not and we care not; but we take the first opportunity of distinctly avowing, that he has been guilty of a gross misrepresentation of the bishop of this diocese and of the editors of this paper. If we could indulge in conjecture we would *not,* at once and unhesitatingly attribute to a partisan of the schismatical party this libellous production. If it was written by an opponent of that party, it was an indiscreet and criminal effort to malign us for not going full length which he would desire. If it was written by an advocate of the schismatical party, it was a vain and foolish effort to draw us by our passions into a dereliction of our principles. We may desire to repress the warmth of the partisan who espouses the cause of truth, but we trust we shall never be found on the side of infidelity, which is miscalled liberality, ignorance which profanes history, and the lawlessness of congregated despotism, which in destroying order boasts that its licentiousness is but the legitimate exercise of liberty. We neither seek nor desire the

---

[27]"Works of Bishop England," Vol. V, cited above, Sec. XXVI, p. 199. See also files of the *Columbian Observer* for the year 1825.

[28]"Works of Bishop England," Vol. V, Sec. XXVI, p. 200. See also files of the *United States Catholic Miscellany,* 1825.

support of those who would support schism; and we love and respect America too much, to aid in tarnishing her glories by veiling that truth which the writer assails."

No doubt the heat of the battle had made the bishop's followers as bitter and radical in their views as even the Hoganites themselves. The conciliatory measures adopted by Bishop England were misinterpreted by them, and we have learned that some withdrew their patronage from the *United States Catholic Miscellany,*[29] the oldest and at one time the only defender of Catholic doctrine in America. Concerning the attitude of these bishopites, Dr. England states:

"To them, should they vouschafe to look at our paper, we would suggest that a little prudence would be useful with their zeal. They are not known to the public and we may therefore address them freely. Some of them were formerly as warm against a good bishop as they are now in favor of a bishop, in respect for whom we do not yield to them, nor to his greatest sycophants. We not only respect his order, but we sympathize with him for his sufferings; and though we may respectfully differ with him in some *modes* of proceeding, we are convinced that there is not in America a bishop more ardently attached to the interests of the Church than is Doctor Conwell. Do the good Catholics, who have withdrawn their names, think that $140 a year will cause us to change our principle? They do not know the conductors of this paper. Do they desire to put it down? To us it would be a serious relief. But it neither depends upon Philadelphia, nor upon Charleston, nor upon any one city, nor upon any one state, nor upon any one diocese of the Union to extinguish or maintain it. The *Miscellany* is the paper of the Catholics of America—it is not the tool of any division of that now uniting phalanx.

"The anonymous advocates of episcopacy have been worse than insulting, more gross than scurrilous to the Bishop of Charleston. He is also styled the conductor of this paper; it is called *his Miscellany.* We thought it was the *Miscellany of the United States.* We heretofore considered it the *Miscellany* of the archbishop and of every bishop of the Union. Any article sent by a prelate for insertion, we looked upon as under no control, and we have still the same impression of duty. Whatever the judgment of the Bishop of Charleston, or that of the other editors (for he is one who has given his labor, together with others, to its pages) may be, he has no

---

[29]See reference in communication to the *Columbian Observer* quoted above.

control and we claim no control, over any article sent for insertion by a bishop. Thus it is Dr. Conwell's *Miscellany* just as much as it is Dr. England's. 'Tis true, the archbishop and a most respectable priest of his diocese and many respectable laymen of his city and its vicinity, have advanced money to support it. But Dr. England has certainly whatever claim the expenditure of $300 or $400 can bestow, together with a very ample contribution to its contents; yet if he tomorrow swerved from Catholic discipline, he would find the *Miscellany* secured from his domination, and at the service of the heirarchy of America.

"Whether the statements of the *Miscellany* respecting the schism at Philadelphia are accurate or not; whether the opinions expressed are correct or otherwise; of one principle the readers of this publication may rest assured: no patronage shall corrupt, no secession shall dismay its conductors. They desire to publish for general instruction, not for the gratification of a party. They bow to the authority of the Church in all matters of faith and of discipline—to every bishop of that Church, to the Bishop of Philadelphia as well as to the Bishop of Charleston they bow with respect, and they hold in communion; but, whilst they disclaim all or any connection with the authors and the abettors of schism in the city of Philadelphia, they will entertain and express, with that freedom which is their right, and that deference which is their duty, those opinions which it is their privilege to form and to publish. The good people of Philadelphia who have seceded from us have probably, ere now, discovered their mistake. But if our agents and friends continue to act as they now do, the *Miscellany* can spare ten times thirty-five subscribers and still continue to publish."[30]

Besides the virulent attacks on Catholics contained in the daily press, there were two weekly papers conducted by Hoganites which defended the position of that party with all the ability of which they were capable. These journals were called the *Catholic Herald and Weekly Register* and *Erin*. Of the former we know very little as there are but a few numbers extant. It was the chief organ of the schismatics and was conducted by E. F. Crozet. It is significant to remark that both these papers were started after the Pope's Brief "Non Sine Magno" was promulgated. The witch's cauldron in "Macbeth" was not filled with worse ingredients than was found in the *Catholic Herald*. So blasphemous was the tone of this journal about Catholic matters

---

[30] "Works of Bishop England," Vol. V, Sec. XXV, p. 195-6. See also files of *United States Catholic Miscellany*, 1825.

generally, that it must have at times shocked the slumbering consciences of the stubborn Hoganites. The first issue appeared on November 30, 1822.[31] Three numbers of this paper are extant, and these are, perhaps, the only ones that were ever published.

Erin has been described by some one as "an angel's name with a devil's tongue."[32] When this journal began its brief existence in September, 1822,[33] it gave promise of being a respectable journal. There was nothing in its prospectus to indicate that it was soon to soil its pages with the most disgusting filth that the scurrilous brain of a Hoganite could create. In fact, the prospectus states that "no sect shall be abused, no personal feelings shall be outraged." Like every other Irish paper that appeared before or after it, this journal claimed to be a defender of the liberties of Irishmen. And indeed its editors would have found enough to do to remove the prejudices that existed against Irish immigrants instead of aiding a set of Jacobins to dissipate the little freedom that Erin's sons enjoyed.

In the first number of the year 1823, the paper begins its imprudent policy of defending the Hoganite faction.[34] While claiming not to be the partisan of either party, in reality it became the mouthpiece of Hogan himself.[35] It quotes an excerpt from the letter of his that rivals in vulgarity and indecency anything that could be found in any of its Protestant contemporaries. Here the Bishop of Philadelphia is accused of an unspeakable crime. In the issue of March 12, two months later, it had to record that Catherine Navis, the shameless defamer of the innocent bishop, had absconded before a second hearing in the Court of Justice Palmer. On March 22, the text of a measure presented by the schismatics to the Pennsylvania Legislature appeared. This is familiarly known as the "Catholic Bill." On April 5, an item is found regarding the election of rival boards of trustees.

Until April 20, *Erin* was conducted by Hart and Company. On that date the partnership is dissolved, Hart becoming sole editor. The publisher and printer from that time on was Thomas Town, no doubt a strong Hoganite, as many Hogan documents bear the imprint of this office. The editor found this course necessary that he might be able to give more time to editorial work. Under the new management we find more discretion. On May 17, the editor informs us that he has refused a vile article written against the Bishop. The previous conduct of *Erin* had,

---

[31] Finotti, "Bibliographia Catholica Americana," p. 160.

[32] *Ibid.*, p. 162.

[33] In the *Aurora* of August, 1822, the prospectus of *Erin* may be found, stating that the paper will commence publication in September.

[34] *Erin*, January 1, 1823. Files of this year in the Library of Congress.

[35] *Ibid.*, p. 2.

however, imperilled its existence. On July 26, filled with many regrets, Hart retired from the editorship; but the mischief had been done. His last words to the public are: "As regards the question respecting the right possession of St. Mary's Church, I can only say that if at any time anything offensive has appeared in this paper, it was before I had the sole management and against my expressed opinion."

From this time *Erin* was conducted by Thomas Town, but it did not long survive the unhappy career of its former editor. On October 18, it contains a notice to the effect that the proprietor "offers for sale the *Erin* newspaper with or without the printing material." But the loathsome thing could find no purchaser. On October 25, the editor states: "The repeated solicitations to subscribers to comply with the terms of the paper not being attended to, and the necessity of the publisher to have them complied with, has compelled him to strike from his list of subscribers a large number of names, the residue of which does not warrant him to continue the publication of *Erin*." Thus did this semiweekly, after it had struggled just one year, perish "unwept, unhonored and unsung."

When the schism began, there was not a Catholic press in existence. In 1822 the *United States Catholic Miscellany* was commenced in Charleston, South Carolina. The zealous efforts of Bishop England were continued in behalf of Catholicism in spite of the most insulting attacks on the part of the Bishopites themselves. Another editor who worked hard to smooth away the difficulties that beset the Church in Philadelphia was Thomas O'Conor, who revived the *Shamrock* in New York about the middle of the same year.[36] Encouragement was also received by Catholic contributors to the Baltimore *Federal Gazette*. Charles Carroll of Carrollton, in an attempt to conciliate the Hoganites, was grossly insulted by them.[37] There was one drawback to all these journals; they were far from the scene of battle and hence were not always in touch with the tactics of the enemy.

Against this formidable array of discordant and biased journals and pamphlets, what had the Catholic Church to oppose save God, truth, and the justice of its cause! Against this hostile phalanx, one lone journal battled for supremacy. This paper was the *Catholic Advocate and Irishman's Journal*. The character of its first appeal shows that it was armed for warfare. "The object of the present paper," the editor states, "is to defend our ancient and holy religion from the pestiferous breath of heretical innovation, to cling to the same faith and the same hope in which our fathers

---

[36] Finotti, "Bibliographia Catholica," p. 162.
[37] *Ibid.*, p. 162.

lived and died, and not to be led astray by the wicked machina-
tions of base and irreligious intruders. Here we need not mention
more explicitly to what party we belong. No, we shall ever support our bishop, our country, and our faith." The paper appeared
for the first time on Saturday, February 22, 1823, and after a
few issues ceased publication.

CHAPTER XII

The United States Catholic Miscellany

The first strictly religious journal established in this country in defense of Catholic doctrine was the *United States Catholic Miscellany*, which first appeared at Charleston, South Carolina, on June 5, 1822. One may easily understand the need there was for such a paper when one considers that Catholics in the newly founded Diocese of Charleston were very few in number, and were scattered over a territory embracing the three great States of North Carolina, South Carolina, and Georgia. At the period of the Revolution, hardly a member of the Catholic Church could be found in that whole extent of country, and the people who inhabited the land were in absolute ignorance of its doctrines and practices.[1]

The first settlers were almost exclusively English immigrants, who carried with them into this wilderness a hatred of the Church of Rome. Their children gathered all their information either at the family hearth or from newspapers published in England. "America was supplied from the mother country," say Bishop England, "with abundant addition to the original calumnies; every plot, every explosion whether of a mine of gunpowder or of a meal-tub, was said to be the villainy of 'papists.'" After the revocation of the Edict of Nantes, numbers of Huguenots left their native land and came to the Carolinas filled with a deep sense of the injuries that they had suffered at the hands of the Catholic king. The early English as well as the French settlers were people of means, and with their opulence they carried a certain spirit of independence and a peculiar immobility of both opinions and conduct. It was deemed useful and almost necessary to encourage the immigration of a less wealthy class, who were to assume the role of a border barrier against the attacks of the Indians. These hardy men from Ireland were from Ulster and hence brought their "Battle of the Boyne" prejudices with them into the land of their adoption.

Georgia was circumstanced much like the Carolinas, but in addition was often engaged in border warfare with the Spanish Catholics of Florida. Bishop England described the average Georgian as one, "whose imagination had been filled with a horror and contempt for 'Popery,' and who slept on his arms to be continually

---

[1] Bishop England's Works," Vol. III; "History of the Diocese of Charleston," pp. 246, *et seq.*

prepared against treacherous incursions of bloody and faithless Papists banded together for his destruction."[2]

About the beginning of the century, and shortly after the Rebellion of '98 in Ireland, Irish Catholics wandered into the Carolinas. They were principally adventurers and were so poor and ill-instructed that they were heartily despised by their wealthier neighbors. Some ruined Catholic refugees from the Island of San Domingo, together with their servants, also made the Carolinas their home. Here, then, was the unpromising field of labor which was to occupy the best efforts of Dr. England, the first Bishop of Charleston.[3]

That this intrepid and invincible champion of Catholic truth was equal to the magnitude of the task placed before him is borne out by every work which he took in hand. Not a single press had ventured before his time to stem the tide of prejudice that was rolling upon the feeble and defenceless body of the Church in America. Not until the *Miscellany* was established was any systematic effort made to reach the greater part of the American people through the medium of a Catholic newspaper. This pioneer journalist brought with him from Ireland a practical experience as editor. As early as 1809, he had published a monthly periodical, called the *Religious Repository*. The object of this magazine was "to diffuse a spirit of piety among the people and to withdraw them from the perusal of books of a dangerous and immoral tendency." The young writer, with eight other functions already enjoined on him, borrowed money with which to take over the control of the Cork *Mercantile Chronicle,* the organ of the Liberal party. It was really in the office of this paper that Dr. England mastered the journalist's art. He was bold in his denunciation of the moral degradation, to which Ireland was subjected during those trying years which followed the Act of Union. He was quick to perceive all the consequences that would flow from the corruption of judges and the packing of juries.[4]

With cool courage and shrewd political sagacity, the patriot priest attacked the policy of the English Government in its maladministration of laws and its inhuman treatment of Irish prisoners. So vigorous, yet so dignified, were his statements of fact that he was placed at issue with Earl Talbot, the Tory Lord Lieutenant of Ireland, who sued him for libel; and after a trial which was a travesty on justice, Dr. England was compelled to pay five hundred pounds sterling. Even before becoming editor of this paper,

---

[2]*Ibid.*

[3]*Ibid.*

[4]"Bishop England's Works"; "Memoir of Bishop England," by William George Read, Vol. I, pp. 4-20.

he was the bosom friend of O'Connell, who became a frequent contributor to the columns of the *Chronicle*. On one occasion the Liberator wrote a scorching article, which almost involved Dr. England in another lawsuit.[5] But when he came to be indicted, the editor was saved by a mere technicality of law, his certificate of editorship had expired on the day on which the article appeared, and no new one had been issued. He thus escaped the clutches of an Irish "Court of Justice."

The young priest continued his editorial labors for some time, but in the course of another decade a wider and more important field of action was opened to him. He received episcopal consecration for the new See of Charleston. He was quick to recognize the needs of Catholicism in America. Among other things he beheld the secular press so filled with absurdities and misconceptions concerning Catholics, that he felt constrained to take up his pen to answer some of these attacks upon Catholic doctrines and practices. The new bishop was certain that if he could disarm the honest prejudices of the landed aristocracy in the Carolinas, whose opinions were like a stone wall, he would soon fight his way into their very hearts' affection. Once the upper classes of society were conquered, but little effort would be required to influence their less wealthy neighbors. He soon realized that these people cared not for verbal denunciation, since they were beyond the sound of his voice. Consequently he hoped to reach them through the medium of the daily press. The *Courier* and the *Mercury,* the two leading papers of Charleston, were held in high repute by everybody and patronized by people of wealth, learning and influence. An opportunity to begin his conquest presented itself, when a violent assault on the Catholic religion appeared in an issue of the *Courier*. Dr. England addressed the editor of the *Courier* by letter, asking for some space in which to make a reply to the calumnies against Catholic teachings.[6]

His request was promptly refused, but the Bishop was not so easily daunted. He applied for advertising space in which to publish his remarks, and thus secured a wedge to open a way into public confidence. Error was attacked in its very stronghold, and the persistent energy of the zealous prelate triumphantly carried the day.[7] But he felt that his position would become precarious, if he courted indefinitely the good will of the *Courier* or the *Mercury,* so he was led to establish the *United States Catholic Miscellany*. The purpose of the journal, as expressed in its prospectus, was to give a simple explanation and defense of Catholic doc-

---

[5] *Ibid.*

[6] "Catholicity in the Carolinas and Georgia," by the Rev. Dr. J. J. O'Connell, O.S.B.

[7] *Ibid.*

trine.[8]   Bishop England was gifted with an admirable tact for marshalling his arguments always to the best advantage.   None of his Catholic contemporaries had his profound grasp of doctrine, nor had they the lofty tone with which he embellished his writings. Possessed as he was of a very high order of talent, and a quick, clear perception of his opponent's weak points, he presented his facts in so lucid and logical an order as to disarm all resistance and convince even the most skeptical. He was called upon by the exigencies of his time to make a defense of the Catholic Faith. But for such a task he possessed the faculty of presenting his ideas in a vigorous, persuasive, yet inoffensive style, which so perplexed his antagonists, that in turn they were compelled to soften the tone of their own writings, and at the end of their controversies with him, they learned to admire his candor, his matchless courage, and his firmness and gentleness of character.[9]

The *Miscellany,* under the editorship of Dr. England, gave to Catholic journalism that powerful stimulus, which enabled Catholics to defend the principles of their religion against the assault of its persecutors. One of the earliest examples of Bishop England's successful efforts to undeceive the public press of certain pet misrepresentations occurred soon after the paper was started. The *Miscellany* took exception to a newspaper report of a sermon delivered at the dedication of a Unitarian church in Washington, D. C. Dr. England, writing under the pen name "Curiosity," noticed the subject as reported in the daily papers. Certain aspersions of the Catholic religion had been indulged in by the preacher, the Rev. Robert Little, and inaccurately written up by the Washington *Gazette.* In consequence, the editor of this paper became involved in a controversy, which drifted into a discussion of the moral character of some of the popes. With calm dignity, the editor of the *Miscellany* defended his position in several issues of the journal, and by a clear statement of facts taught the contributor to the *Gazette* a keener appreciation of truth.[10]

Soon after this disputation was ended, the *Miscellany* had occasion to enlighten a religious paper in Boston, the *Gospel Advocate,* on certain popular misconceptions of the dispensing power of the Pope. The New England paper had often commented with severity on the attitude adopted by the *United States Catholic Miscellany* in respect to the Protestant press in general. The particular incident, however, which placed the two papers at issue with one another, was based on the supposed claim and exercise

<hr>

[8]*United States Catholic Miscellany,* Vol. I.
[9]*Preface to "Bishop England's Works,"* Vol. I.
[10]*Ibid.,* Vol. II, p. 436-472. See also *United States Catholic Miscellany,* Vol. I, No. 4, June 26, 1822, and subsequent numbers.

by the popes of a supreme arbitrary power of dispensing from moral duties and obligations required and enjoined by Divine Law. The ability and success with which Dr. England refuted the misrepresentations of this journal aimed the first decisive blow at that intolerance against Catholics so prevalent in New England.

Not infrequently the editor of the *Miscellany* was called upon to defend his Church within the limits of the Charleston diocese. While on an episcopal visit to the State of Georgia, during the course of the year 1824, he preached an eloquent sermon at Warrenton. His fame as an orator generally attracted many Protestants, and on this occasion there was present in the audience the editor of the *Mount Zion Missionary,* who afterwards felt an inclination to obtain notoriety by challenging the truth of some statements that the prelate then made.[12] For three years, the editors carried on a lively newspaper discussion, in which several important Catholic doctrines were attacked and ably defended. In July of 1824, the *North American Review* published an essay containing some vague and general denunciations of the corruption of the Catholic religion in South America. Bishop England exposed in a series of excellent articles the contradictions and fallacies written by the contributor for this magazine.

Mention has to be made of the intimacy existing between Dr. England and Daniel O'Connell. The latter had a profound respect for the mature judgment of the Bishop and often sought his advice on grave questions of state. The prelate wrote to the Liberator early in 1825 respecting the relief of Irish Catholics in their native land.[13] The affairs of the Emerald Isle were always faithfully recorded in the *Miscellany;* for the editor, while in Ireland, was closely identified with the movement that had for its object, the obtaining for Catholics a religious and civil liberty.

During the year 1826, the Bishop commenced a more active propaganda against the misrepresentation of Catholic doctrine, urged thereto by the writings of the Rev. Blanco White,[14] whose

---

[11]"Bishop England's Works," Vol. II, pp. 400-421. See also *Catholic Miscellany,* Vol. I, No. 25, Nov. 20, 1822.

[12]"Bishop England's Works, Vol. II, pp. 277, *et seq.* See also *Catholic Miscellany,* Vols. II, III, and IV for 1824-25-26.

[13]See *Catholic Miscellany,* 1825.

[14]"Bishop England's Works," Vol. I, pp. 106-347; also *Catholic Miscellany,* Vols. VI and VII for the years 1826-28. Rev. Father Barry, afterwards Bishop of Savannah, who at this time was connected with the publication of the *United States Catholic Miscellany,* states in a letter to the Bishop of New Orleans, that "Blanco White is the name of an apostate Spanish priest, who according to his own acknowledgment fell into Deism and subsequently went to England, where he now professes himself a good Church of England man, the truth of which is sufficiently evinced in his 'Evidences Against Popery.'"—Letter in Catholic Archives of America at the University of Notre Dame.

calumnies were industriously circulated by press and pulpit. In the opening letter of a long series, continued for more than two years, the Bishop shows the ready welcome that awaited every utterance of this apostate Spanish priest. The editor made the following observations:

> "How many volumes of *religious* tracts, how many Gospel and Evangelical and Christian periodical publications teem with misrepresentation and abuse of our creed. Nay, look at the common newspapers of the day, whose editors boast of their liberty, and confirm their claim to the title by most copious and liberal quotations from every British hireling and malevolent infidel; in the midst of all this, how is it possible for us to expect that we shall be held in just estimation by our fellow citizens? It is a duty which we owe to them and to ourselves to attempt our vindication .... I shall begin by examining the charges made by Rev. Joseph Blanco White, because I observe that his work is particularly lauded by the clergy of the Episcopalian, Presbyterian, and Methodist churches of the District of Columbia, and that strenuous efforts are now being made to disseminate the same, for the purpose of adding to the prejudice which unfortunately exists. I know that I undertake a weighty task, but labor does not discourage me. These pieces shall appear in the *Miscellany,* addressed to the Roman Catholics of the United States, and should I find that you approve of them by patronizing the paper, and that they are thought by my Protestant fellow citizens to lead to a better feeling between them and us, and that God shall give me health and leisure, when I shall have done with Mr. White, I have many more to succeed in turn."[15]

With the exciting years that followed, Dr. England became one of the chief champions against that army of turbulent philistines styling themselves the Evangelicals. In their attacks upon the civil and religious rights of Catholics, these ministers of the Gospel were, in the language of Pope,

> "Awed by no shame, by no respect controlled,
> In scandal busy, in reproaches bold,
> With witty malice studious to defame,
> Scorn all their joy and laughter all their aim."

They gloried in licentious style to lash the Catholic as the enemy of civil freedom. Some of the most ridiculous and vulgar phraseology was employed by them in their denunciations of "Popery."

---

[15] "Bishop England's Works," Vol. I, p. 109.

The *Southern Religious Telegraph,* a paper which the Bishop singled out as a specimen of degraded journalism, crowned its infamy by publishing most vicious assaults on the Catholic religion. In one short paragraph the following unpatriotic and un-American sentiments are rather indelicately expressed: "Popery should be noticed in connection with intemperance," "It stupefies the conscience." "It binds the understanding." "It makes the whole man a superstitious slave to the impositions of a crafty priesthood," "The *beast* numbers half a million subjects in the United States," "Popery is a monster forging chains to bind the people." Dr. England began his defense of the Catholics of the United States against the charge of hostility to republican institutions by showing that these agitators were themselves a danger to our civil institutions. The origin and progress of this "Christian Party in Politics," with whom the editor of the *Southern Religious Telegraph* was in league, is accurately described by the Bishop.

"Not only has it," writes the editor of the *Miscellany* in 1831, "continued through a number of its presses to vilify and misrepresent Catholics, but has by some of its publications endeavored to excite against them the suspicions and the hatred of all friends of civil and religious liberty. Not only has it sought by means of associations formed under its auspices and directed by its influence to secure for itself a widespread domination through the land, but has collected vast sums of money and prepared to organize a host of zealots to sweep from the valley of the Mississippi the religion of the survivor of that noble assembly that created the liberty which he enjoys. Not content with the possession of the vast power which it at present holds, it looks forward to the securing of a future monopoly, of a more extensive and absorbing nature, and hesitates not, in triumph of its calculation, to anticipate what it considers the inevitable arrival of the millenium of its glory, when the youth that it now trains up shall with its principles assert their bloodless victory at the ballot boxes. Yet, impatient of the delay, and desirous of hastening the happy epoch, it makes unceasing efforts, at one moment to procure from Congress a fatal precedent in even one act of what it styles Christian legislation; and at another, to render Catholics more odious to their fellow-citizens, or more suspected of being *dangerous to the republic.* Let it succeed in either way and a passage will have been opened, through which it may pour the stream of its power, sweeping away the obstacles that retard, widening and deepening the channel by the impetuosity of its current, until, like so many new feeders, law gradually added against law, shall have caused church after church to disappear; and if then an effort should be made to stop the torrent, if the dam itself should not be swept away, the inundation would spread over the face of the land and overwhelm its inhabitants."[16]

During the course of the year twelve letters appeared in which the Bishop temperately demonstrated the claims of Catholics to civil freedom. With an abundance of facts judiciously chosen he extinguished the flames of intolerance so persistently kindled by sectarian journals. With the strength of a Sampson, he reduced to ruins the temple of Dagon, upon whose altars Dives had placed the idols of mammon and iniquity. With the courage and wisdom of a Solomon, he and his Catholic contemporaries laid the foundations of another and a greater temple, planned by Divine Providence and consecrated to the Triune God—a temple of freedom whose arched roof was the canopy of heaven and whose "long drawn aisles" stretched from ocean to ocean.

The labor of years was required to bring about this result. In the beginning of that Titanic struggle for fuller liberty, the aggressors were crafty and cunning. They left no means untried to procure their own political ascendency and to encompass Catholics with ruin. The activities of the Evangelical Association are thus graphically described by Bishop England:

"The avowal of the saints, then, is that they should have the opportunity of speaking of the dangers to which the republic is exposed by Papists and infidels and anti-Christians, without being charged with the crime of mingling religion with politics! But surely they have that opportunity; neither are they sparing of its use. It is the theme of their declamations by day, and, we may naturally suppose, of their dreams by night. See the distorted countenance,—mark the dark eyeball gleaming its hidden fire,—hear how he thunders from the desk,—the spirit is upon him, and he is voluble in his denunciation. The broad Mississippi rolls majestically along, and its valley spreads to his view; how he describes the abominations of the man of sin! Some monster has appalled him,—he is bewildered—he describes it as a beast of prey ravaging the land. And yet this beast brings chains and fetters to rivet upon the people!!! Alas! what has caused this disorder of the imagination? Yet is he permitted to rave, and he complains of cruel, of impious, of sacrilegious restraint!! The compositor is active, the corrector is vigilant, the pressman labors, the press itself groans. Steam is applied to add to its powers. The young and the old—

---

[16]"Bishop England's Works," Vol. IV, p. 16.

the demure and wrinkled dame, round whose lips not even
Monus could produce the approximation of a smile, goes
forth together with the maiden, in whom beauty and inno-
cence appear blended and personified, to distribute the productions of their exertion: stages bear them through the
country, the churches expect them, the revivals are anxious to
experience their blessed consolation; the city and the field,
the ship and the steamboat, the barrack and the brothel are
all put in possession of the catalogue of abominations in every
variety of shape, size, sermon, story, statement, and supply.
From all these various sources the dollars and the cents are
collected to replenish the coffers of the powerful directors of
this grand and extensive system."[17]

The propaganda of these zealots fomented such discord as had
never yet been seen in the United States of America. In their
fanatical rage, they next planned deeds of violence worse than any
acts perpetrated by the cruelest despotism. Happily, Charleston,
South Carolina, was saved the crimes and outrages that later disgraced Charlestown, Massachusetts. Thanks to the cool courage
of Bishop England which prevented that humiliation to his State.
No effort was spared by the *Miscellany* to turn aside this peril
which, like a mighty volcano, threatened by its belchings the whole
system of republican government. The prelate was also prepared
to resort to arms, should the personal or property rights of the
Catholic citizens in Charleston suffer the least hurt by an infuriated mob. That such steps were necessary is shown by the high
state of excitement that followed the appointment of Bishop England as Apostolic Delegate of Haiti. Base reports and rumors
were circulated with no other motive than to crush out Catholicism by brute force. "This man," it was said, "is an enemy to the
State; he is even now concocting in our midst a servile insurrection; the most brutal and bloody of all revolutions; he is planning
our destruction; our lives and the lives and honor of our families
are imperilled; come, let us root him out, and let his name be no
longer called amongst us."[18]

With public harangues of this sort becoming common, the time
for discussion was past, and the hour for action had arrived. The
prelate organized a band of volunteers whom he himself drilled,
and he held them in readiness the moment an attack would be
made on the convent or any other ecclesiastical institution in

---

[17]"Bishop England's Works," Vol. IV, p. 61. Also see *Catholic Miscellany*
Vol. XI, No. 4 to 15, July-August, 1831.

[18]"Catholicity in the Carolinas and Georgia," by Rev. Dr. J. J. O'Connell,
O.S.B. Chapter II, p. 81.

Charleston.[19] Such, indeed, were the energetic measures that saved South Carolina from shame and disgrace.

The Bishop was about to settle down in the religious peace he had so long labored to establish, when an attempt was made by a political journal to identify the prelate and the Catholic voters of the United States with political conspiracy. The charge was that Bishop England used his influence to throw the Catholic vote against the election of President Harrison. It was also stated that Catholics were in league with European governments in a scheme to overthrow the republican institutions of this country. The matter was taken up by a score or more of journals, and once more the presses groaned with their increasing burdens. Duff Green, the editor of the Baltimore *Pilot and Transcript,* was the leader in this campaign against the rights and privileges of Catholic voters. The occasion of this political assault was the publication of a pastoral letter in which the bishop counselled his flock to favor only such men and measures as would assure an uncompromising adherence to honor, virtue, patriotism, and religion. The prelate was at once denounced in the Baltimore *Pilot* as a meddler in politics. If we wish to search for the real cause of attack, we shall find that the Whig party was badly in need of campaign material and used this subterfuge to secure their success at the polls. Moreover, to Duff Green it was a source of pecuniary profit to challenge the illustrious Bishop to a political combat, for such notoriety would certainly increase the circulation of the *Pilot.*

In the number for October 17, 1840, he sets forth his prospectus, showing that his motive was as we have just now stated; for the topic was to claim the chief attention of his readers for many issues. In this address to his subscribers, he tells in a few words his whole attitude towards the Bishop and towards the Catholic voters of the United States. Green signed his name to the following:

> "The part taken by Bishop England in the pending presidential election, the manner in which his interference in the politics of the country, has been treated by the political press, the influence which their clergy exercise over the opinions of Catholics, especially of those born and educated in despotic governments, and the manner in which both parties have labored to obtain foreign votes, have convinced the undersigned that the political press of this country should examine and freely discuss the means adopted to extend the influence of the Jesuits in the United States, and especially the designs of the Austrian government in the organization

---

[19]*Ibid.*

of a society which, under the administration of *Prince Metternich,* contributes large funds for that purpose.

"The undersigned proposes, immediately after the Presidential election, to enter upon an examination of these and relative subjects and invites the cooperation and support of all who desire to perpetuate our free institutions. He disclaims any purpose of blending religion and politics. He proposes to leave the question of religious faith to be discussed by the clergy and the religious press; but, how far Popery is a civil institution, and how its extension in this country, by means of the emissaries of the most despotic foreign governments, may tend to endanger our liberties is a political question and its discussion appropriate for a political paper.

"The election of General Harrison will, it is hoped, leave parties in a condition favorable to such a discussion. The first step is to assert the danger we are exposed to: the next, to discuss the remedy. Much will have been accomplished by arousing public attention, but one of the most important measures of protection is a modification or entire repeal of our laws of naturalization. The right to become a citizen of the United States is a boon which we may give or withhold at will. If we concede that those who are now in the country should be naturalized under existing laws, that is no reason why we should not repeal those laws and refuse to naturalize others who may hereafter come.

"The undersigned is deeply impressed with a sense of the weighty responsibility he assumes. He is free to confess, that late events have clothed this subject with an importance new and alarming. He enters upon the task, from a sense of duty—inviting and relying upon the cooperation of those whose reading, wisdom, and experience better qualify them to support the cause. He will do what he can. He will at least furnish a free press through which those who will may speak."[20]

The Bishop's editorial labors were now drawing to a close. The last work of the great prelate consisted of a number of letters on the subject of domestic slavery. These were opportune on account of an Apostolic Letter of Pope Gregory XVI, which had been misinterpreted by Daniel O'Connell, the bosom friend of Bishop England. It is possible that the great Irish Liberator little dreamt of the mischief that his sentiments were doing to the cause of Irishmen in the South. Mr. Forsyth, then Secretary of State,

---

[20]"Bishop England's Works," Vol. IV, pp. 69-93. See also *Catholic Miscellany,* Vol. XX, Nos. 10 to 17. Likewise excerpts from Nos. 25 and 27.

believing that the religious authority of the Catholic Church was behind the incendiary appeals of O'Connell, vigorously attacked the Pope's letter and its erring commentator. The Secretary of State was informed, in a series of letters, concerning the Church's real attitude on the question of slavery. Eighteen letters had appeared when their publication was suspended. The Bishop was about to express his own attitude on the continuation of domestic servitude when death interrupted his labors. He wished to see the institution of slavery abolished, but at the time that he was writing, did not think it expedient for the government to pass such a measure.[21]

The *Miscellany* continued under the episcopal control of the Diocese of Charleston, until the ravages of the Civil War put it out of existence. The later files of the *Miscellany* are exceedingly rare. It is doubtful whether a complete set of this periodical can be found in the United States. The salutary influence of the journal continued until the end; for the traditions of its first editor were steadfastly followed after his death. Bishop Reynolds, like his predecessor, used the columns of the *Miscellany* as a means of spreading doctrine. His pastorals and letters on mixed marriages are splendid specimens of composition. Bishop Lynch, the third ordinary of Charleston, was also an experienced controversialist. He successfully refuted the Rev. Dr. Thornwell, of South Carolina College, by his deep learning, strong arguments, and sound philosophy.[22]

Another aspect of the history of the *United States Catholic Miscellany* remains to be told. The story of the heroic efforts of its editors to sustain the paper in the face of most disheartening circumstances is perhaps without an equal in the annals of early American journalism. When it commenced publication on June 5, 1822, it was an unpretentious periodical of eight pages of quarto size. Small as the paper was, the matter was always well selected and therefore had much in its favor to encourage an extensive patronage. Moreover, no distinctly Catholic weekly was in existence for nearly three years after the *Miscellany* was established, hence Catholic subscribers should have flocked to its support. Such was not the case, however, for a complaint was made in October that if all subscriptions were promptly paid, there would still be a loss of some hundreds of dollars. Six months elapsed. The paper had done excellent service in vindicating doctrine, Catholics had been defended against the persistent attack of enemies, historical essays had appeared clearing away

---

[21]"Bishop England's Works," Vol. III, pp. 106, *et seq.* These letters appeared in the *Miscellany* during the years 1842 and 1843.

[22]"Catholicity in the Carolinas and Georgia," cited above, p. 117.

at least some of the misrepresentations of the literature pouring forth from various publishing houses, news had been regularly collected at no slight inconvenience and expense from Europe, Asia, Africa and the West Indies. With all this sacrifice of time, labor and money, the number of subscribers in November, 1822, was only six hundred, not half of whom contributed one cent to aid the pioneer journal. So disheartened were the editor and his assistants at these losses, that frequently there were intimations that the *Miscellany* must discontinue its publication, on account of the too meagre support it was receiving from the Catholics of the United States.[23]

Yet heavy as these burdens and trials were to bear, Bishop England endured them with a martyr's patience. Not infrequently the staff of the printing office was disorganized through inability to employ sufficient labor because of lack of money with which to pay the printer. To avoid embarrassments resulting from this scarcity of help was a problem that confronted the editor, and one could see a bishop acting either as pressman or setting up in type with his own hands the copy furnished but a few hours before by himself or by his assistants.[24]

With each number of the *Miscellany,* the financial condition of the journal became more and more a source of anxiety to its conductor. The Bishop felt that some measures had to be taken to meet the immediate expenses of the paper. He proposed in the last issue of November, 1822, that the publication of the journal should be placed in the hands of an association which should issue shares of twenty-five dollars each. The management was to be entrusted to a committee of five members. This whole plan failed, because only seventeen shares were subscribed for at the close of the year. The editors therefore found it necessary to suspend publication until enough money could be raised. As at least one hundred shares would be required to warrant a fresh venture, Bishop England decided to wait until March 5, 1823, before refunding the shares that had already been subscribed. When that date arrived, a few more dollars had been contributed, but so paltry was the sum that the committee of management determined that the most prudent course was to hold out a while longer.[25]

Not until January 7, 1824, did the *United States Catholic Miscellany* resume publication. In the meantime, five hundred dollars of the Bishop's own money were paid to cancel certain debts that had been incurred in 1822. The new publishers were Messrs.

[23]*United States Catholic Miscellany,* Vol. I, 1822. The files of the *Miscellany* for more than twenty years are preserved in the Library of Georgetown University, Washington, D. C.

[24]"Catholicity in the Carolinas and Georgia," cited above, p. 57.

[25]*Catholic Miscellany,* Vol. II, No. 1, Jan. 7, 1824.

Gray and Ellis, who were also booksellers at No. 9 Broad Street. The paper was now even smaller in size than on its first appearance, but it contained sixteen pages instead of eight. The prospects at the beginning of the second volume were very encouraging. The danger of dissolution seemed at last to have passed.[26] But as the year drew to a close, the treasurer of the Association notified the editors, that notwithstanding the rapidly increasing demands for the paper, their funds had been found insufficient to pay all indebtedness to the printers. The editors, hearing this unwelcome news, would have cheerfully transferred the paper to some purchaser, but no one seemed anxious to assume the control of so perilous a project. Like ship-wrecked mariners, the conductors of the *Miscellany* held their posts in the face of grave disaster, in hope of saving something from the impending ruin.

During the early months of 1825, the *Miscellany* had very little to recommend it to the attention of its subscribers. On account of the lack of proper organization in the staff, the work fell principally into the hands of one editor. Episcopal visitations compelled the Bishop to be away from Charleston for months at a time. He placed Father John McEncroe in charge of the paper and gave him full responsibility during his absence. This priest did not have the experience of his ecclesiastical superior, and besides was handicapped by continual troubles with the publishers. Filled with disgust at the difficulties that seemed almost insurmountable, the acting editor at the end of the year placed the following communication in the *Miscellany*:

"Gentlemen: I feel myself individually bound to offer the following remarks, which I trust will not be considered untimely. On several occasions I have taken an active part in considering the *Miscellany*. Since the early part of last October, I have almost solely had to act both as editor and as agent. The late agent left in July and gave us to understand that he was to return. On that account no other was appointed, which circumstance left the editors embarrassed in many respects. A considerable sum was due to the publishers in the month of October and they seemed inclined to discontinue the publication. I then became individually responsible to them for the expense of the paper till the close of the fifth volume at the end of December. Since the thirteenth of October, I received on the account of the *Miscellany,* one hundred and sixteen dollars. I have paid the printers two hundred and forty-two dollars, and have become responsible for paper to the amount of one hundred and thirty-seven dollars, and

---

[26] *Ibid.*

paid three dollars and a half for postage, which leaves me two hundred and sixty-six dollars and fifty cents out of pocket. . . .

"Yet, Gentlemen, you have reason to murmur at, and I have reason to be ashamed of the many glaring typographical errors in the late numbers; but I must state that the fault was not altogether mine. There certainly appeared a want of sufficient attention on the part of the publishers, probably because they were not fully paid. It frequently happened that papers were not properly made up for the mail, and hence many never came to hand, and several packages were returned from Washington and New York for re-direction and making-up.

"From this great want of attention to the paper, I was often inclined to discontinue the publication until such time as it could be properly attended to. So many duties more imperative on me, and of higher importance in my calling claimed my time, that I was not able to look to the minor details of the *Miscellany*. Notwithstanding these disappointments, I find the number of subscribers increasing, and hence failures are doubly painful. In justice to the publication and to myself I have found it necessary to state the above facts."[27]

Rough and rugged was the path of this editor, but there were those who would add a few thorns to make it more painful. Influences were at work to prevent information intended for publication from reaching the office of the *Miscellany*. This attempt by some of the Catholic clergy to blacklist the only real defender of the Catholic religion in America caused much annoyance to Father McEncroe, and must have been a source of grief to the Bishop. The *Globe and Emerald* noticed these acts of unkindness and ingratitude and was full of just indignation.

"To the disgrace of many of our fellow-countrymen," says the editor of the *Globe,* "the *Catholic Miscellany* has been almost totally neglected both in Philadelphia and New York. While the enlightened Bishop of Charleston, the ornament of his country and the benefactor of his species, has been laboring to dispel prejudices and impart instruction, the objects of his solicitude have turned away from him with foul ingratitude and cringed to strangers, whose ignorance and incapacity and prepossessions render it impossible that they can be faithful organs or enlightened writers. What will be the indignation of the Catholic population of this country,

---

[27]*Catholic Miscellany,* Vol. V, December 17, 1825.

when they are informed that even some of the subordinate clergy have employed the meanest subterfuges to impede the sale of the *Miscellany,* and to substitute the foreign publication we allude to in its place? We could even expose one man, who communicated to the opposing party the contents of a letter confidentially entrusted to him. This may yet form the grounds of an official complaint, and we have yet to learn whether the dignitaries of a venerable Church are to tolerate in their pastors, conduct so highly derogatory to their sacred calling. If the people require and demand instruction, who is more capable of imparting it than the prelate whose genius and attainments are indisputable, whose zeal in the service of religion forms the subject of eulogy within the very walls of the Pontifical Palace, and whose extensive philanthropy and influence in this community eminently qualify him for the duties of public instructor?"[28]

After the establishment of the *Truth Teller,* the New York patronage of the *Miscellany* dwindled to almost nothing. The editors of the latter journal were compelled once more to retire in solitude to lament their losses and to devise some plans for reviving their paper. On July 22, 1826, the first issue of volume six appears. In the meantime, Bishop England had procured a press and some type and established an office in the Seminary, where he employed Jeremiah Dennehy as printer. The editor still had cause for bitter complaint in regard to the persistent efforts of some persons to withhold communications intended for the *Miscellany.* He gives as an instance a pastoral letter of the Bishop of New York, which that prelate directed to be transmitted to the Charleston paper. This information did not come to hand for months.

In the year 1827, the *Miscellany* suffered two severe losses, both occuring within a month of each other. On September 22, the Rev. Godfrey Sheehan, one of the editorial staff, was called to his reward. It is said that this zealous young priest had edited the greater part of the number that announced his death. Before the paper had issued from the press, he was carried off by yellow fever, which was then prevalent in Charleston. On October 20, the *Miscellany* was again draped in mourning, for another voice was still in death. No greater loss befell Bishop England than that of his sister, the angel who had assisted him in his labors and cheered him when he was weighed down with trials and discouragements. She had a wonderful influence on his life. Nowhere was this sway more sublimely exercised than in the conduct of the *Miscellany.* The Bishop's earnest temper sometimes unconsciously infused a sternness into his logic. Her gentleness smoothed away the harshness of his chief controversial articles. Frequently he rebelled at her censorship, but she was never perturbed on such occasions. She would use but a few kind words of persuasion and invariably he yielded to her gentle jurisdiction. Her presence always shed over him a magic charm which was fatal to all opposition on his part. But Miss England helped her brother in many other ways. Her little fortune was spent in relieving the many embarrassments of his poverty-stricken diocese. Her elegant literary taste governed in a large measure the literary department of the *Miscellany* and several of her contributions graced the pages of its earlier volumes.[29]

No impudent remarks were ever seen in the *Miscellany* as long as Johanna England lived, but after her death it sometimes displayed haste in accepting articles, rather hurtful to the progress of the Church in America. An example of this lack of judgment is found in 1829, when the paper published an anonymous letter written by a "missionary," who intended to wound the feelings of the Right Rev. Edward Fenwick, Bishop-elect of Cincinnati. The most objectionable part of this communication was a malicious blow aimed at the secular clergy of the State of Ohio. The correspondent, among other things, states:

> "We count nearly eleven churches in Ohio, five of which would do honor to any country. By a late decree of the Pope regulating the Diocese of Cincinnati, all these churches, with the exception of the Cathedral of Cincinnati, belong to the Dominicans of this State, the Bishop of which and his successors being made by the same decree, signed by the General of the Dominican Order, superiors *ex officio* of the Order in the province. The regulation was intended, and will produce its effect, to prevent any collisions respecting the churches and other property that might otherwise occur between the Bishop and the Religious of that Order, as their spiritual and temporal concerns are and hereby become completely the same. The arrangement was made by concurrent consent and petition of the present bishop and the Dominicans of this province."

The letter caused Bishop Fenwick great distress of mind and he therefore lost no time in refuting its misrepresentations and falsehoods, by addressing the following letter to the editor of the *Miscellany*:

> "Gentlemen:—It is with pain I have observed in your *Miscellany* in the thirty-first of January, 1829, the article on

---

[29]*Catholic Miscellany,* October 20, 1927. See also "Bishop England's Works," Vol. I, p. 13. Sketch by George Reade.

the subject of the Church in Ohio. I feel unwilling to believe that it was written by a missionary of my diocese, replete as it is with gross errors and absurdities, and consequently I disapprove of it *in toto.*[30]

"That the Bishop of Cincinnati and his successors have been appointed, by a decree of the Pope, Superiors *ex officio* of the Dominican Order in this province is false and absurd, as will appear evident from the words of the decree itself. . . .

"Nor are seculars to be excluded from my diocese; on the contrary I am now preparing to open, on the first of April next, a seminary under the direction of secular clergy, and shall be glad to receive such candidates as may come recommended. . . . "

From the year 1830 until Bishop England's death, conventions of the clergy were held in different parts of the diocese. We are impressed with the frequency with which, he refers to the financial condition of the *Miscellany*. During that decade, hundreds of dollars were spent annually out of Bishop England's own money to defray its expenses. Priests from time to time contributed their little share to its support, but few could afford to give very much, because the Diocese of Charleston was regarded as the poorest in the whole United States. After twenty-two years of labor, the Bishop could count only eight thousand Catholics throughout the length and breadth of three large States, and many of them belonged to the almost penniless working-classes. In 1838, the liabilities of the journal mounted to the highest figure in its whole history. The debt that year was upwards of seven hundred dollars, the largest amount the publication lost in one year. Another attempt was made at this time to form an association to consist of fifty members, who should hold themselves responsible for the obligations of the *Miscellany*.

The editors, with these few rays of encouragement, groped their way along the dismal course of repeated failures. Father Baker for some years had the chief work of editing, but the journal[31] was never again clothed in the enchanting drapery of Bishop England's genius, and in 1846, four years after his death, it was found to be in a sinking condition.[32] Bishop Reynolds tasted the bitter cup of financial distress that had been the usual potion of

---

[30]*Catholic Miscellany,* 1829. See also *United States Catholic Magazine;* article, "Catholic Church in Ohio," Vol. VII, 1848.

[31]See "Bishop England's Works": Addresses to Conventions. There was not an assembly of the clergy where the affairs of the *Catholic Miscellany* were not discussed. Frequent editorial references are found in the paper itself.

[32]"Catholicity in the Carolinas and Georgia," cited above, p. 100.

his predecessor. During these years he did a great work for posterity by rescuing from the dusty volumes of the *Miscellany* Bishop England's life work which he collected in five large volumes. His labors were but ill repaid, for the publication of the work only piled up additional debts. His successor was to have as trying an ordeal as ever fell to the lot of any bishop. A mighty fire visited Charleston, and swallowed up the results of almost a half a century's labors. In a few short hours the cathedral, the Bishop's residence, and extensive diocesan library, and the office of the *Miscellany* were a mass of ruins.[33]

Swift upon the heels of this disaster followed the ravages of the Civil War. Not Charleston now, but the whole diocese became a prey to the devastating sword of General Sherman and his soldiers, "frightening her pale-faced villages with war." The repair of the injuries thus inflicted, left the courageous prelate little time to devote to the ill-fated *Miscellany,* so it perished as nearly all things perished in the South during the Civil War. The paper had its ups and downs as almost all pioneer efforts must have. We regret, however, that a journal that had weathered successfully the storms of forty years was cut off after a long period of usefulness.

---

[33]*Ibid.,* Chap. III, p. 125.

CHAPTER XIII

THE CATHOLIC PRESS

The *Catholic Press* was the second paper in this country to enjoy episcopal approbation. The *Connecticut Observer,* when it heard that a Catholic paper was about to be started in Hartford, published an article entitled "Romanism in Connecticut," in which the editor insinuated that perhaps the *Catholic Press* was established by the institution "Propaganda de Fide," and he wondered "what future times would think when they read in history that, in 1829, Hartford in the State of Connecticut, was made a Roman Catholic Mission."[1]

At a time when the storm of persecution against Catholics was gathering throughout New England, when their souls were racked by the rough winds of fear and tossed by the angry waves of prejudice and adversity, Bishop Fenwick with the keen eye of wisdom and a heart overflowing with zeal, poured out the oil of truth by establishing this journal inspired through his thoughtful love. For a while it was the only beacon light of Catholicism on the New England coast. From the character of its contributions, we are induced to believe that it was the product of more than one pen. Very likely the clergymen of Hartford were its chief editors. It was published every Saturday by A. M. Tally under the auspices of the Catholic Tract Society.[2]

The first issue appeared on July 11, 1829 printed on a page ten by fifteen inches. From time to time the *Catholic Press* undertook to answer some of the most narrow-minded of the countless Puritan journals. Of course, there was many an insult hurled defiantly at the Church and her doctrine which the *Catholic Press* was compelled to ignore, since the paper contained only four pages of three columns each. But the prompt challenge of its Presbyterian neighbor could not go unheeded. Bishop Fenwick arrived in Hartford on July 10 and immediately took up the gauntlet which had been thrown into the arena by the Rev. Mr. Hooker, the editor of the *Observer.*

"The *Catholic Press,*" said the Bishop, "had not yet issued its first number when the article 'Romanism in Connecticut' was read in the *Connecticut Observer* of this day (July 10, 1829). The editors take this early opportunity to thank the

---

[1]The *Catholic Miscellany,* Vol. IX, No. 4, p. 30.—Issue of July 25, 1829. See also "History of the Diocese of Hartford," by Rev. James H. O'Donnell, Boston, D. H. Hurd & Co., 1900, Chap. VI, p. 27.
[2]The *Catholic Press,* Vol. 1, 1829.

94

gentleman conducting that paper for the notice he has been pleased to take of the arrival of their *Press,* and at the same time beg leave to answer the question subjoined, viz.: 'How will it read in history that, in 1829, Hartford in the State of Connecticut, was made the center of a Roman Catholic Mission?' The editors of the *Press* assure him that it will read exceedingly well. They have it likewise in their power to state that the *Propaganda de Fide* at Rome are in no manner concerned in their *Press*—that the same was purchased with American money and will be under the control of American talent."

The Bishop then chided the *Observer* for using offensive epithets. "What does the gentleman mean by the word Romanism? Is it intended for a sneer? If so, we shall let the matter rest with the gentleman's own sense of propriety. Or did he really believe that the word truly designated our religious profession? If so he may with great propriety say to himself in the language of Sallust: *'Jam pridem amisimus vera vocabula rerum.'* "[3]

The Bishop's gentle reproof turned not away the wrath of his opponent, for the *Observer* had taken upon itself the task of eliminating for all time the Catholic Church in the State of Connecticut. In this unholy warfare that journal had the assistance of the greater number of sectarian papers in New England. In January, 1830, but six months after the *Catholic Press* was started, its editors were forced to make the following observation: "Few papers now come under our eye without affording a melancholy exhibition of the zeal for defamation."[4] As time went on, the spirit of misrepresentation and abuse of Catholics grew stronger and stronger. By January, 1831, just one year after the above statement was made, the Puritan press had so blinded its patrons with their own fanaticism, that in the city of Hartford every street was placarded with the following disgraceful notice.[5]

"To the Public:

"Be it known unto far and near that all Catholics and all persons in favor of the Catholic Church are a set of vile impostors, liars, villains and cowardly cut-throats.

"Beware of False Doctrine.

"I bid defiance to that villain—the Pope.

"(Signed) A True American."

This manifestation of anti-Catholic feeling is but another evidence of that religious intolerance which was soon to madden the

---

[3] *Catholic Press,* July 11, 1829, Vol. I, No. 1.
[4] *Catholic Press,* Vol. I.
[5] This notice appeared in the issue of January 22, 1831—The *Catholic Press,* Vol. II.

Nativist mobs to deeds of violence. "No quarter to Catholics" was the banner they flaunted in the eyes of the people whom they sought to annihilate. Imbued with the spirit which prompted the Hartford Convention just a score of years before to restrain the immigrant's freedom, they would now frame a law which would demand a residence of twenty-one years to foreign-born citizens before being invested with the privileges of citizenship. So bitter was the feeling against Irishmen in Connecticut, that all Irish militia companies were disbanded by special act of the Legislature. Oh strange irony that so mocks the deeds of men! Connecticut, which refused to support President Madison during the War of 1812, did supply soldiers in the Civil War. Of these, almost entire regiments were Irish. But wherever these facts are recorded, let it also be known that these Irish regiments refused to take up their muskets till the disgraceful and illiberal law against them was wiped from the statute books. Captain Thomas W. Cahill, their leader, on that occasion made this dignified reply to the Legislature:

"Six years ago, I was captain of a company of volunteer militia and a native of New England. I was with my comrades thought to be unfit to shoulder a musket in time of peace, and the company was disbanded by order of the then Governor of the State, under circumstances peculiarly aggravating to military pride. The law by which we were disbanded still stands on the statute book, and so long as it is there, my fellow-soldiers and myself feel it to be an insult to us and to all our fellow citizens of Irish birth and Catholic Faith. If we were not fit to bear arms in time of peace, we might be dangerous in time of war."[6]

It seems almost incredible as we view the excellent state of Catholicism in the Diocese of Hartford at the present time that, in 1829, there was not a single church in the whole State in which to hold services. On Sunday, July 12 of that year, the Right Rev. Bishop Fenwick offered the Holy Mass in the office of the *Catholic Press*.[7] On the evening of the same day he preached an eloquent sermon in the State House in the very apartment in which the Hartford Convention attempted to proscribe the liberties of Catholics. The happy effects of the Bishop's sojourn in the new Catholic mission were already beginning to bear fruit, for he writes in his diary: "The spirit of inquiry increases, people enter warmly into the subject of religion. They come to the printing office every night to confer with the Bishop. Spendid prospect for religion in Hartford."

----

[6]"History of the Diocese of Hartford," cited above, Chap. VI, p. 30.
[7]*Ibid.* See also the *Catholic Press*, Vol. I.

No doubt, the prelate won over the more liberal-minded people by his conciliatory attitude towards them. This is delightfully shown in a paragraph which he contributes to the *Catholic Press*,[8] when Catholics were attacked by a certain sectarian journal. "The editor of the *Episcopal Watchman* in last Saturday's paper seems to be greatly disposed to pick a quarrel with us; but on our part we do assure him that we are not inclined to any such business. Our views are altogether pacific. We wish, if possible, to live on good terms with all our neighbors and especially with those of his communion. They have generally treated us kindly and we shall endeavor to prove to them that their kindness has not been thrown away and that we too can be kind." Mrs. Nicholas Devereux, an old resident of Hartford and a Catholict convert, shows in a reminiscence that the favorable impression produced by Bishop Fenwick had the result of arousing a sympathy in the more broad-minded inhabitants of the Connecticut Valley. Speaking of the conditions of 1829, when the Connecticut Mission was started, she says:

> "After breakfast a slip of paper was pushed under our door, with 'Mass at such a number and street.' I was an Episcopalian and attended my own church. In the evening Mr. Imlay, a banker, called bringing with him a Mr. Ward, a Protestant gentleman of very liberal principles. After a while, the conversation turned upon religion and Mr. Devereux, whose first thought was always the Church, declared how much he regretted that the Catholics were not able to purchase a small Protestant church then for sale; but the Catholic priest, whose name I think was Father Fitton said, that it was impossible on account of funds. The conversation ended by Mr. Ward offering to buy the church in his own name and convey it to the Catholics, if Mr. Devereux would furnish the money. This was done and afterwards the money was repaid."[9]

The first resident priest of Hartford arrived in the city on August 26, 1829. Besides his priestly duties as pastor of a growing congregation and as misisonary for the entire State, the Rev. Bernard O'Cavanaugh found time to do editorial work for the *Catholic Press*. Many little notes found in the paper shed some light on the ecclesiastical history of the Connecticut Valley.

Daniel Barber, of Claremont, New Hampshire in a contribution to the *Catholic Press* of September 3, 1829, supplies this illustration:

---

[8] The *Catholic Press,* Vol. I, July 18, 1829. See also "History of the Diocese of Hartford," p. 185.

[9] "History of the Diocese of Hartford," cited above, p. 186.

"It is singular to reflect on the difference between the spirit of the former and the present time. The Episcopalian Church in Hartford was once destroyed by a mob at the head of which was a Col. T————. Now a Catholic chuch is shooting upwards, with but little noise or opposition. I have lived seventy-three years, in the course of which many changes have taken place. Everything, indeed, but the Catholic Faith is liable to change. The Protestant Episcopal Church of which I was minister thirty-two years has in that time so changed that what was truth thirty years ago according to their doctrine is now false. . . ."[10]

Father Fitton assisted Father O'Cavanaugh for some time and became his successor in 1831, taking also in hand the editorial labors of his predecessor, but after some time relinquished control when his clerical duties demanded his constant attention.

As regards historical data concerning missions outside Connecticut, an examination of the *Catholic Press* will reveal much that would please the historian. In its issue of December 18, 1830, a long account is given of the Rev. Dr. Reze's missionary visit among the Indian tribes of Michigan. Two other articles dealing with the establishment of the See of Baltimore and a description of the Diocese of St. Louis are full of interesting facts.

The *Catholic Press* indicated in its prospectus that it intended to give the earliest information of Catholic affairs, foreign as well as domestic. Yet, in spite of this promise, we find a dearth of news from abroad. The editors at the opening of the third volume attempt to explain this deficiency, alleging as an excuse that the conductors of the paper have been prudently cautious in clipping items from other religious journals, fearing lest they might be fabulous reports. It had frequently been suggested that the editor include an account of the political events of the day, but such a plan did not seem to coincide with the original purpose of the paper. As long as it was under clerical control, the *Catholic Press* did not deviate from its original purpose, that of presenting its readers with information on Catholic questions. But when the clergymen were compelled by force of circumstances and their priestly duties to relinquish their connection with the paper, Mr. Tally saw fit to satisfy the popular demand by devoting half of the paper to religious topics, leaving the other half to the discussion of current events. At this time it was enlarged to a full folio size - fifteen by eighteen inches. It now comprised four pages of four columns each and hardly an advertisement.

In the heyday of its existence, it had agencies in nineteen States

---

[10] "History of the Diocese of Hartford," cited above, p. 187.

and in parts of Canada; but in spite of its extensive circulation, the editors complained bitterly about delinquent subscribers. This fact is the more surprising, when we find that the subscription price was at no time more than two dollars a year in advance.

In December, 1832, the editor was considering the expediency of transferring the *Catholic Press* to Philadelphia, where the united efforts of several clergymen would increase its usefulness, and where the large Catholic population would afford it more permanent support. Mr. Tally expected to sell the entire equipment— paper, press, and patronage to the *Catholic Herald,* soon to be started in Philadelphia. The project, however, failed and the *Catholic Press* appeared again in January, 1833. Another attempt was made to transfer it to St. Louis, Missouri. This plan was hailed by the *Catholic Telegraph,* of Cincinnati, with great enthusiasm.[11] There were but a few Catholic newspapers in the West; hence this new journal was welcomed rather as a coadjutor than as a competitor. Had this design of the proprietor of the *Catholic Press* been realized, it would have appeared in the French and English languages. But unfortunately again, the project was unsuccessful. The satisfaction of Western Catholics was turned into regret, for the sectarians were assiduously directing their labors by insults and slanders in this very section of the United States.

The *Catholic Press* in 1833 became a paper of eight quarto pages. The day of publication was changed from Saturday to Thursday. Many of its former patrons expecting the removal of the paper from Hartford, withdrew their names from the subscription list. Under these difficulties, the editor toiled on for a short time, but after a few issues he was compelled to yield to the inevitable. The *Catholic Press,* the first paper to spread the light of Faith in many New England homes, was discontinued.

---

[11]The *Catholic Telegraph,* Vol. II, 1832.

CHAPTER XIV

The Jesuit or Catholic Sentinel and Its Successors

The summary of early New England journalism is but a panorama of the revivals of religious tolerance. Looking back upon the centuries of Puritan influence in America, the descendants of the Pilgrim Fathers have little to be proud of in their treatment of Catholics. One needs but to read Cotton Mather's "Magnalia" to discover the deep seated prejudice and bigotry that was the intellectual heritage of almost every Puritan family in New England. That divine, in a sermon entitled, "A Pillar of Gratitude," and delivered in 1700 in honor of Governor Bellomont's arrival in the colony, breathes the spirit of intolerance. The passage in which the Puritan bestows his "unnecessary praise" on this new protector is the following:

"There have been formidable Attempts of Satan and his Sons to Unsettle us: But what an overwhelming blast from Heaven has defeated all those Attempts. . . . At length it was proposed that a Colony of Irish might be sent over to check the growth of this Country: An *Happy Revolution* spoil'd *that Plot;* and many an one of more general Consequence than *That.*"[1]

Although the Irish had few inducements to attract them to New England, they did come in considerable numbers; and the grave countenances of the Puritans grew graver as they, with fear and trembling, beheld in their midst the face of the "mean-looking Irishman," as they were wont to call him. The Puritans sought exclusively their own good, or attempted to make it paramount. One of those goods, so they judged, was not to allow the Celtic blood to diffuse itself among them. They labored to maintain the traditional purity of their English ancestry. They attempted also to build up an exclusive theocracy similar to that of stubborn Israel, a theocracy in which temporal success and prosperity was a pledge of God's favor and a guarantee of eternal felicity. New England was the "promised land" and the Puritans were God's chosen people. The foreigner occupied a place in estimation that the Jews had of old assigned to the uncircumcised and unbelieving Gentile.[2] Like good Israelites they were taught to despise him.

---

[1] "Story of the Irish in Boston." Edited and compiled by James B. Cullen, Boston, 1890, p. 15.

[2] "The Puritan Commonwealth," by Oliver, p. 432. "History of New England," by J. G. Palfrey, Vol. I, ch. 9. "The Beginning of New England,"

Nothing shows this condition more clearly than the Boston Town Records:[3]

"Whereas great numbers of Persons have very lately been transported from Ireland into this Province, many of which by Reason of the Present Indian war and other Accedents befalling them, are now Resident in this town, whose Circumstances and Condition are not known, some of which if due care be not taken may become a Town Charge or be otherwise prejudicial to the welfare and prosperity of the Place.

"For Remedy whereof, be it Ordered That Every Person now Resident here, that hath within the space of three years last past been brought from Ireland, or for the future shall come from thence hither, Shall come and Enter his name and Occupation with the Town Clerk, and if married the number and Age of his Children and Servants, within the space of five days, on pain of forfeiting and paying the Sum of Twenty Shillings for each offence, And the Sum of ten Shillings for Every one that Shall continue in the Neglect or non-observance of this order, for and During the term of forty-eight hours after the expiration of the five days aforesaid, so often as the person offending Shall be complained of and Convict before any Justice of the Peace within the Said County, And be it further Ordered that whoever Shall Receive and Entertain and keep in his family any Person or Persons Transported from Ireland as aforesaid, Shall within the Space of forty-eight hours after Such Receipt and Entertainment Return the Names of all Such Persons with their Circumstances as far as they are able to the Town Clerk, On Penalty of Twenty Shillings fine for the first forty-eight hours, and Ten Shillings for Every Twenty-four hours he Shall be convict after the first forty-eight hours and so toties quoties."

As time went on, a little more toleration was practised, but Catholics were long regarded as the objects of Puritan distrust and their religion considered as "subversive of society." With the Revolution, the condition of Catholics began to improve, but in Boston the admonition of General Washington was required to calm the passions and the prejudices of its populace.

---

by J. Fiske, ch. 4. "Lowell Institute Lectures on Early History of Massachusetts," by G. E. Ellis, pp. 50-55. "The Emancipation of Massachusetts," by B. Adams, ch. I. "History of Massachusetts," by J. S. Barry, Vol. I, ch. 10. "The Puritan in Holland," "England and America," by D. Campbell, Vol. II, ch. 22.

[3]Boston Town Records of the Year 1723, p. 177.

On November 5, as he entered camp at Boston, he gave the following order:

> "As the Commander-in-chief has been apprised of a design for the observance of that ridiculous and childish custom of burning an effigy of the Pope, he can not help expressing his surprise, that there should be officers and soldiers in the army so void of common sense as not to see the impropriety of such a step at this juncture; at a time when we are soliciting, and have really obtained, the friendship of Canada, whom we ought to consider as brethren embarked in the same cause, —the defence of the liberty of America. At this juncture, and under such circumstances, to be insulting their religion, is so monstrous as not to be suffered or excused; indeed, instead of offering the most remote insult, it is our duty to address public thanks to these our brethren, as to them we are indebted for every late happy success over the common enemy in Canada."[4]

But in spite of admonitions, there still burned within the confines of the Puritan heart a mistrust and a misapprehension of the Catholic religion. After the framing of the Constitution they threw all their strength and prestige into the Federalist party and succeeded in electing John Adams. Hardly had he gained power than, listening to their promptings, the Congress passed the celebrated Alien and Sedition Laws. These imprudent measures caused the hordes of emigrants that flocked to America to seek refuge in the ranks of their opponents, the Jeffersonian or Republican party. To crown their perfidy as a political organization, the Federalists in 1814, through the Hartford Convention, called a protest against the War of 1812, and recommended that "naturalized foreigners should be debarred from membership in Congress and from all civil offices under the United States." Such, in brief, forms as it were, the historic background of Catholic journalism in New England.[5]

The *Jesuit or Catholic Sentinel* was begun on September 5, 1829, with the express purpose of defending the principles and doctrines of the Church.[6] In its prospectus the new periodical pictured the crying calumnies and misrepresentation that had so long and so unsparingly been heaped upon Catholics.

---

[4]"Washington's Writings," Vol. III, p. 144. Also *U. S. Catholic Magazine,* Vol. VIII, p. 85. See also, "Sketches of the Establishment of the Catholic Church in New England," by Rev. James Fitton, Boston, Patrick Donahoe, 1872, p. 76.

[5]For fuller details, see Chapter II—"Beginnings of Irish National Journalism."

[6]The *Jesuit or Catholic Sentinel,* Vol. I, No. 1, Sept. 5, 1829.

"A certain body of men," says the editor, "styling themselves the Teachers in Israel have shamefully abused the credulity and generous confidence of respectable congregations of the country at large. They went about not doing good, but disseminating falsehoods and working evil, and this they unblushingly accomplished under the mask of religion; in their tracts, at their meetings, and from their pulpits. The Catholic, however meritorious, was branded with infamy, was ridiculed as ignorant, was viewed with abhorrence, was considered as a moral monster, as abominable and idolatrous. Much as the times are altered for the better, we deeply regret that even at the present day the sectarian presses groan under the oppressive indecorous calumnies of virulence and abuse. . .

"The innate love of justice and discernment of the New Englander will not, cannot be much longer duped by a Pharisaical conspiracy, the object of which seems to be to impose on the minds of freemen fetters of the most galling and degrading character. Religious Truth has, thank Heaven, at last burst its way through the misty atmosphere of prejudice, is triumphantly scattering the dark and noxious clouds from the regions of the mind, and rolls on in all its vigor of successful enterprise in its congenial sphere of freedom. To impart fresh impetus to its prevailing power, it has been thought advisable to start a publication which may aid it in its course."

It was also stated that the net revenue would be applied to the founding of an Orphan Asylum in Boston. Little money, however, was realized for this praiseworthy object.

No sooner did the prospectus appear than several Catholics interviewed the editors of the paper, begging them to discard "so odious a title as the *Jesuit*."[7] Even an agent for the journal wrote to the office stating: "I regret the title which you have chosen for your paper." But why should the name Jesuit have been held in so great abhorrence? The fact was that the worthy and zealous disciples of St. Ignatius had been the most active in waging war against that species of tyranny and oppression which was trying to wrest from Catholics their civil and religious liberties. The Jesuits were always ready to break a lance when the majesty of truth was assailed. In their intellectual conflicts against insidious error and wearisome misrepresentation, they had been uniformly successful. The association which that name suggested to the prejudiced, made the members of the Society of Jesus the victims of the vile calumnies that were so persistently uttered against

---

[7]The *Jesuit,* Vol. I, 1829.

the Church. The opinions entertained by most Puritans was that the name Jesuit was synonymous with deep cunning, political craft, and subtle reasoning. Certain Catholics, by their timidity in the face of Puritan intolerance, preferred peace at almost any cost rather than encounter the fanatical fury of their assailants. They thought that the editors, by placing the name Jesuit at the head of their paper, were, so to speak, waving the red flag before the eyes of the angry bull.

The time had now come to shake off supineness and to assume an attitude of dignified boldness and independence. Moreover, Bishop Fenwick reverenced the name Jesuit, for he had been nourished in a Jesuit novitiate. We need not wonder than that the enemies of the *Jesuit,* as they view the apostolic efforts of the Society in propagating truth, felt their passions mounting higher and higher. Some of them sneered when the periodical bearing that name appeared in New England. The *Protestant,* of New York, then only a few weeks old, looked upon its Catholic contemporary as a "genuine Judas both towards God and man."[8]

The *Jesuit* differed materially from every Catholic periodical which had yet appeared. It had been a feature of some religious papers to devote as much space to news as to religious subjects, but the Boston paper made the propagation of doctrine its chief purpose. In the selection and arrangement of its matter it aimed at sustaining the interest of its readers by connecting this week's information with that which was to follow. All the numbers were so closely linked together that there existed a marked similarity of thought and reasoning throughout the whole year from the first issue to the last. A series of theological essays will be found in the files of the *Jesuit,* such as would attract the humblest seekers after truth. The style in which these were written was simple, strong and argumentative. They were adapted to instruct the mind by their clearness and brevity of expression than to please the ear by their harmonious cadences and the turn of their sentences.

The editor of the *Episcopal Watchman,* whom Bishop Fenwick on a former occasion had attempted to win over to a more peaceable attitude towards his Catholic brethren, was one of the first to clash with the *Jesuit.*[9] The Hartford paper had not profited by the gentle·rebuke given it in the *Catholic Press* of that city just a few weeks before. It continued its abuse with even greater animosity. The article to which the *Jesuit* took exception was a tirade on "Catholic Superstition." The *Jesuit* on this occasion, and also frequently during the stormy year which followed, battled

---

[8]The *Catholic Telegraph,* Vol. I. **1831.**
[9]The *Jesuit,* Vol. I, **1829.**

strongly against the calumnies of its most active opponents. So vigorous were its attacks on these sectarian papers that the criticism seems to have hurt the feelings of their editors. They contended that prior to the existence of the *Jesuit* the greatest peace, union, and harmony prevailed among the different dominations of Christians. Calvinists had never opposed the Unitarian nor Baptist the Episcopalian, nor Unitarian the Methodist, but now all were at variance with one another. There was a semblance of truth in this statement, but it was only a semblance. The reason for the apparent peace was that the various sectarian journals found no time to abuse one another; for they were busy attacking Catholics; there was not a pulpit but rang with the abuse of Popery, not a press but devoted columns to misrepresentation of Catholic tenets. Only when their assertions were challenged did they begin to dispute among themselves.[10]

During the course of the year 1831, Dr. Lyman Beecher, a Calvinist minister, came out boldly and invited the Catholic clergy to an intellectual and theological combat. The controversy was long and bitter; but, before it had ended, Bishop Fenwick and Dr. O'Flaherty had so humbled their adversary that, to cover his confusion, he was compelled to leave Boston. The surrender of Dr. Beecher, after a discussion lasting over a year, and the convincing arguments of the Catholic priests disarmed the honest prejudices of many a New Englander. Catholics in general began to feel more independent and walked abroad with the fearlessness of conscious superiority. These Catholic Lectures, as they came to be called, won for the members of that Church a confidence and a measure of public respect that had not been hitherto accorded them. Public sentiment had stamped the seal of reprobation on the unwarranted utterances of Dr. Beecher and his friends.[11]

The *Jesuit* found in these improved conditions great encouragement to continue its labors with renewed vigor. The editors now proposed to widen its scope. A greater variety of articles appeared in each issue. Foreign intelligence, and particularly Irish news received much attention. An effort was made to temper the tone of editorials, which during the controversy had become trenchant with sarcasm and often bristled with invective. The feeling existed that, if Catholics intended to follow up the advantage which their vigorous defense of Catholic doctrine had gained for them, they would have to proceed in a more dispassionate manner, for a period of calm is natural and expected after a storm.

During 1832, the Rev. Dr. D. O'Flaherty edited the paper alone.

---

[10] *Ibid.*, Vol. II, 1830-31.
[11] The *Jesuit*, Vol. II. See also the *Catholic Intelligencer*, its successor.

The name *Jesuit* which for two years had appeared as the title was thought to be inappropriate for a journal that was not exclusively religious. As it was now to have a regular sketch of European politics, the name *Catholic Intelligencer* was considered more suitable. Under the new arrangement and title, it lost much of its former prestige. It seemed as if the removal of the *Jesuit or Catholic Sentinel* from the title page meant also a withdrawal of the same from the bulwarks of Catholic truth. At any rate, the sectarian press, after a brief respite following the departure of Dr. Lyman Beecher, redoubled its energies and sought once more by every species of calumny and insult to fire the Puritan heart. How successful they were in this unholy warfare, later events will disclose. But it would be unjust to place all the troubles at the doors of the sectarian journals and the Puritans. The articles in the *Catholic Intelligencer,* in spite of so many resolutions to the contrary, were chiefly controversial, while their tone was violently polemic rather than apologetic. No doubt this policy found many converts and enlightened not a few, but on the other hand it aroused the fiercest antipathy and irritation of mind in as many more.

In the year 1833 Bishop Fenwick, seeing the course that events were taking, again lent his aid and direction to restore if possible the influence which his paper had formerly enjoyed. Experience had shown that the "fashionable" title, *Catholic Intelligencer,* had not improved conditions nor had it added any new subscribers. Bishop Fenwick expressed the conviction that perhaps the name "Jesuit" was not such an evil omen after all. "Notwithstanding the odiousness of our former title," he says, "we must confess we still feel something like attachment to it; and what is less pardonable in us, we feel every disposition to resume it and with the blessing of God, shall now resume it at all hazards."[12]

The paper was hardly well established again under its old management when events occurred in Boston, which, like the shock of a mighty earthquake, sent convulsions into every part of the United States and filled Europe with amazement. The night of the eleventh of August, 1834, will long be a memorable one to the Catholics and Protestants of America—the night of the burning of the Charlestown Convent. The peace of the just shone through the darkness on the tower and cross at Mount Benedict, and night's fair queen moved majestically through the skies, increasing in silvery brightness with each fleeting, silent hour. The good nuns of St. Ursula and the students had retired to rest. But hark, "what wicked dreams abuse this curtained sleep!" Ah, it is is no idle fancy that calls them from their

---

[12]The *Catholic Intelligencer,* Vol. I or (Vol. III of The *Jesuit*).

peaceful slumbers, but the howls of fiendish rage in men. The poor, defenceless inmates are at the cruel mercy of a mob of cowardly ruffians incited to deeds of violence by sensational rumors circulated by knavish newspapers. Hardly have the half-clad fugitives sought a temporary safety than the torch of the incendiary is applied, and the convent is soon reduced to a mass of smouldering ruins.

The *Jesuit,* in the issue of August 23, paints a most pitiful picture of these terrible outrages. The editor in his sketch appropriately chooses the expressive language of Byron as a most fitting introduction:

> "All that the devil would do if run stark mad,
> All that defies the worst which pen expresses,
> All by which hell is peopled or as sad
> As hell—mere mortals who their power abuse—
> Were here let loose."

"Evil tidings," he continues, "make the wind their post horse, and the inhabitants of every place in the country which rumor can reach, will have found reason to blush for the blot on the character of a portion of the Union." After relating the shameful depravity of that unhappy night, the editor makes the following comments:

"Before the occurrence of the events detailed above, we could not have believed it possible that in this age and in this country, fifty men could have been found base enough to be guilty of such enormity.

> 'Heaven's Sovereign saves all beings, but Himself
> That hideous sight—the naked human heart.'

"It must be degrading though the concession is admitted that the perpetrators were Americans—native Americans—Yankees. The ground rendered holy by the blood of the countrymen and contemporaries of Charles Carroll, has been polluted by the demoniacal act of those who inherit the blessings which he aided to purchase. At the last visit of Lafayette, Charlestown was the scene of a grand patriotic pageant. The friend of our country assisted in laying the cornerstone of a monument commemorative of one scene in the struggle in which he was a participator. That monument is still unfinished— and who is worthy to complete it? Under its very brow are the dark, the gloomy proofs, that there are those among the professional descendants of the heroes of '76 who are craven enough to war upon women; and sufficiently bigoted and ignorant to think they do God service by sacrilege, arson, and desecration of the grave.

"Look from Bunker Hill to Mount Benedict; on this

monument and then on that. On the one is an obelisk in memory of heroes; on the other a pile of blackened ruins; grounds trampled and desolate; a tomb broken open, rifled, desecrated; are the least enduring memorials of the respect of a part of the American people for that clause of the Constitution which warrants protection to the religious worship of every citizen. We say 'least enduring'; because the mischief to the buildings may be repaired. Mount Benedict may again smile as was its wont; but the facts are a matter of history."

For one whole generation, the crumbling and blackened ruins of that once noble edifice were suffered to stand as a monument of intolerance, of desecration and of disgrace, near a city that was regarded the home of freedom and the Athens of America. Another generation has passed, the monument of intolerance is levelled, and with it has perished also that spirit; but the monument to Liberty still stands on the neighboring hill. Freemen, as you mount the pinnacle of that massive granite tower, turn your eyes toward the setting sun, and looking towards Mount Benedict, thank God that Puritanism is dead. It has left nothing behind but its warnings.

"The synods, the confessions, the platforms, and the heresies which distinguished its reign in New England," says the author of the "Puritan Commonwealth," "are in marked contrast with the noble Church which it presumptuously hoped to displace and which, since the days of its Catholic defenders, has altered neither an article of its creed nor a principle of its government."[13]

The burning of the Ursuline Convent by a band of midnight incendiaries has long since passed into history, but there remains one feature of that unhappy event that claims our earnest attention. The most interesting circumstance is the illiberal attitude of the daily and the sectarian press. Few would believe that in a community long distinguished for its literary advantages, whose chief city assumes for herself the proud appellation of the American Athens, whose University boasts of priority of foundation and the richest endowment of any in the Union, there should have been such positive ignorance of Catholicism among its most prominent journalists. It was just because so many newspaper men were ignorant of the tenets of the Catholic Church that they were led to misrepresent her. When subjects of popular interest concerning Catholics arose, they hardly ever undertook to enlighten their readers. The editor generally took his tone from

---

[13]"The Puritan Commonwealth" by Oliver, p. 434.

the people. If the prejudices of the great mass of his subscribers were those which differed entirely from his own ideas, he was prudent enough to be silent. Occasionally, however, an editor could be found who had the courage of his convictions and acted on them, but such soon forfeited their claims for patronage and were made to suffer starvation—an editor's martyrdom. By their silence, when important questions regarding the rights of Catholics were at stake, they permitted opinions to grow up which their own consciences told them were false and injurious, and thus they became daily more and more the slaves of human caprice and miserable prejudice. No despotism could have been more successful in its abridgment of the liberty of the press, no absolutism could have exercised a more vigorous and tyrannical censorship than did the people of Boston.

In the *New England Magazine* of June, 1835, an unprejudiced writer, filled with indignation at this subserviency of the press, ventured to make the following remarks in regard to the Convent question, which at that date was still the chief topic of newspaper discussion:

"It will be recollected," says this writer, "that ever since the destruction of the Convent, this subject has been the most interesting topic of newspaper discussion. From the outset, various pieces have appeared in the newspapers intended to discredit the Ursulines and their friends; and if anyone will take the pains to revert to the files, he will find one piece after another in different newspapers, the object of which has been to throw discredit and mistrust upon the Ursuline Community and to prepare the public for the subsequent statement of Miss Reed. At length her book, 'Six Months in a Convent,' made its appearance—preceded, however, by notices of the work and remarks which should excite a strong curiosity to read the book. After it was published, several of the newspapers printed most laudatory notices of the work; while the rest—either editors unwilling to betray their consciences by an open approbation—were silent. Thus stood the newspaper press then, and thus it has stood ever since. No doubts or criticisms upon the genuineness of the book appeared; praise, overwhelming praise was in the columns of the same. One single newspaper, the *Catholic Sentinel,* appeared against the book and, by its intemperate zeal and harsh language added strength to the cause of the anti-Catholics —a fair offset, however, to some of the minor and more vulgar and abusive publications which especially espoused the cause of Miss Reed.

"In our remarks, then, we shall notice the conductors of the press as divided into two classes, those who were determined in the face of common sense and common reason and common justice to lead on the attack upon the character and reputation of the Ursulines, urged on by the bigotry of their opponents or the hope of gain; and those who believed the whole affair to be a humbug on the part of Miss Reed and her friends—a humbug actuated by bigotry, the determination to put down Catholicism by all means, fair or foul as they could, and the sordid hope of gain—those, we say who discredited her book but were cowed and afraid to speak out their opinion —that is, their subscribers—were prejudiced against truth and blind to conviction.

"If we are near the truth—and we mean to keep within its strictest bounds—we ask our readers how much reliance can be placed upon our independent press upon any subject. We ask them not to place confidence in absurd statements because they appear in print. We ask them to weigh well its character for firmness and incorruptibility.

"Bearing these points in mind, let us proceed to descant upon some of the leading journals that have prominently figured or that have been notoriously silent, upon the Convent question. And first of all, the Boston *Courier* claims our attention. When the Convent was first destroyed, this press came out with much indignation against the rioters, but for some cause or other was soon silent; a little time elapsed and it began to find fault with the institution, it quarrelled with the Boston investigating committee, it denied the right of the Ursulines to indemnity, it contained articles injurious to Catholics generally. The editor of the *Advocate* needs no introduction, he was the reputed author of the 'Preliminary Remarks' of Miss Reed's Book. He was 'General Grand High King' of the anti-Catholic Fraternity. The *American Traveller* was another sheet that made war unceasingly upon Catholics. The *Commercial Gazette,* although in many respects more respectable than the papers mentioned, made personal attacks upon highly respectable individuals. He permitted the publisher of Miss Reed's Book to make use of his columns as a vehicle for wantonly and shamefully attacking persons of great repute.

"There remains yet to be seen those that kept silent while the vituperative attacks of the rest were going one. Some of their conductors expressed themselves in private as fully and unconditionally as one could expect. Such papers were the *Daily Advertiser,* Boston *Morning Post,* and the *Atlas.* An honorable exception to this subservient press was afforded by a Baptist journal, in which one of the most respectable clergymen in this city has published a judicious article, powerfully written and containing opinions generally entertained by the most respectable portion of our community. The *Evening Transcript,* too, one of the silent journals, whose editor, we know, regards this question in its proper lights, deserves some praise for its boldness in one instance whereby it lost a batch of subscribers. This general review of the whole situation presents a fair illustration of the readiness with which the press may be made an engine of oppression and wrong."

There were plenty of stories afloat about the Ursuline Convent for months before the disgraceful night of August 11, 1834. Rebecca Reed, a convert and charity student at the nunnery in 1832, had left the institution and had relapsed into Episcopalianism, and afterward had endeavored by every species of calumny and insult to blacken the character of its inmates. Excitement rose high when, in 1834, a demented nun escaped from the school and sought shelter with relatives in Boston. Hardly had this unfortunate religious returned to her community, than the newspapers of Boston, fond of wild, sensational stories, caused false rumors and fanciful reports to be circulated among the people. On the Friday preceding the convent disaster the unscrupulous editor of the *Mercantile Journal* permitted the following account to be printed:[14]

"The young lady had been sent to the Nunnery to complete her education and became so pleased with the place and its inmates as to be induced to take the black veil. She subsequently became dissatisfied and made her escape from the institution, but was afterwards persuaded to return, being told that if she would continue but three weeks longer, she would be honorably discharged." It was further stated that "at the expiration of this renewed period her friends called for her but she was not to be found."

We can readily imagine the sensation this canard caused on the biased judgment of the average Puritan in Boston. The statement was greedily copied by the *Morning Post* on the following day with comments. The Boston *Commercial Gazette* accepted the story on August 9, but it was accompanied by a declaration on the authority of the Bishop that the rumor was false and that the prelate would make a statement on the following Monday. But in the meantime Edward Cutter, a Protestant layman, had taken upon himself the task of obtaining accurate information on the whole situation. A committee of five Selectmen made a

---

[14]"The Burning of the Charlestown Convent," pamphlet, compiled by Patrick Donahoe.

similar investigation; statements of both parties appeared in the Boston papers but, unfortunately, too late to avert the catastrophe.[15]

While hundreds of people were hastening to the scene of the conflagration, newspaper men were wrapped in deep sleep. No obtrusive reporter was there to gather in a rich harvest of *real* news for his journal. One paper, next morning, inserted about a half dozen lines. Perhaps the most satisfactory account of the outrage was printed in the *Jesuit* itself, whose editors, no doubt, were eye-witnesses of this mournful spectacle.

"It is our painful duty," says the *Jesuit,* "to record one of the most atrocious and disgraceful acts of violence ever perpetrated in any clime or civilized country. We allude to the destruction, by a lawless and fanatical mob, on last Monday night, of the magnificent Convent erected a few years since in Charlestown by Bishop Fenwick of this city. This splendid institution had for its object the education of young ladies in all the branches of polite learning, and at the time of the woeful disaster in question, had actually under the government of the Ursuline Nuns, between fifty or sixty young ladies, chiefly of the best families of Massachusetts.

"A report has been industriously circulated for several weeks previous, that a young lady was detained in the Convent against her will; that she was immured in a dungeon and there cruelly treated. However absurd the report, the fanatical preachers in Boston and the adjacent towns seemed glad of so favorable an opportunity to excite the public, and manifested every disposition to take all the advantage to decry its institutions. Inflammatory sermons were preached in neighboring towns, and in one or two churches in Boston, particularly in the Baptist Church in Hanover Street, as we have been given to understand, with a view to rouse the people against Catholicity. Even Dr. Beecher could not forbear assailing it last Sunday, in three sermons which he delivered in three different churches, availing himself of the opportunity which his return to the city afforded him of warning the public of the dangers of Popery, as evidenced by its general prosperity. Such violent fanatics are evidently the most dangerous of the enemies to good order and to the peace and harmony of society.

"However this may be, a small body of men were seen hovering about the convent between eight and nine o'clock on Monday night. Shortly after, a cart laden with tar barrels and combustibles passed on to the spot. These were soon

---

[15]*Ibid.*

set on fire as signals. The crowd began to increase; shouts were uttered, accompanied with blasphemous speeches, and the most horrid yells and vilest imprecations. The doors and windows of the convent were speedily broken in by stones and other missiles, when the mob rushed in, and in an instant began the work of destruction. The children were hastily taken out of bed and hurried out of the house; who all happily effected their escape, though half-naked, to the neighboring houses. The nuns and Superior were the last to leave the dwelling. In a moment after, the entire building was in a blaze; but not before the most valuable articles in it, which could be conveniently removed, were seized upon by the band of ruffians that had entered it. The nuns saved nothing, not even a change of clothes. The tabernacle itself, with the holy altar, was rifled, the sacrament taken out of the blessed ciborium and thrown into the fields. A few pieces only of it were afterwards picked up and restored. From the house they proceeded to the sanctuary of the dead. At the bottom of the garden, a beautiful tomb had been constructed which contained the dead bodies of five or six nuns. These were torn out of their coffins and exposed. We shall make no comment on these proceedings; they speak sufficiently for themselves.

"Early the following morning (the 12th inst.) the Bishop sent three carriages in quest of the nuns. They were found in different houses in the neighborhood. One of them was in a dying condition, being low with consumption at the time; another, in a state of mental derangement produced by the noise and tumult attending on the dreadful occasion; all of them, in short, in a state of great debility, in consequence of the continual watching for several days previous. It was surprising to see, after so gross an outrage and so much suffering, the calm, the tranquility which beamed upon their countenances, and their perfect resignation under the grievous calamity. Not a word of reproach, not a complaint was suffered to escape their lips. They undoubtedly felt sad (and who could not but feel!) for the act was base, cowardly and cruel. From the houses in which they had taken shelter during the night, they were conducted to the house of the Sisters of Charity in Hamilton Street, in Boston, where they now are in a state of absolute destitution, subsisting solely on alms and the charity of their friends.

"The amount of property lost by this execrable deed is exceedingly great. Twenty thousand dollars will scarcely restore even the building alone which they have lost; and we venture to assert, that the half of that sum will not replace the valuable furniture and costly instruments of music belonging to the convent, with which it was usefully adorned; for it is well known (and who knew it better than the intelligent and discerning citizens of Boston?) that no expense had been spared to render it one of the most splendid establishments of female education in this or any other country. The devotion of parents to it could not be excelled; their confidence in those to whom they had entrusted their children could nowhere be equalled. Notwithstanding all the alarms which fanaticism had excited during several weeks previous, and the menaces which had been continually uttered against the institution, not a single parent would withdraw his child from it. No; all of them, on the contrary, preferred to continue their children in it to the very last, at every hazard. They, too, have been great sufferers by this horrid act. Pianos of great value, belonging to several of the children, harps, guitars, gold watches, silver goblets and spoons, with all their clothing; these are among the losses which they have experienced. Some of them had been there for several years, and during this time had laid up a large provision of paintings, or ornamental needlework, and of other beautiful specimens of their industry, with which they had hoped to charm and delight the eyes of their beloved parents, on their return home in a few months more; these also have been destroyed, to the exceedingly great regret of these little ones, and to the no small disappointment of their friends.

"Too much praise can not be bestowed upon the excellent Mayor of Boston and upon the city authorities generally, for their prompt, manly judicious arrangements in protecting Catholic property in this city, when menaced by the same infernal mob of incarnate devils, as soon as they began to manifest a disposition to renew in Boston the scenes which they had perpetrated in Charlestown. For, while they were suffered by the authorities in Charlestown (who assuredly should have lost no time in protecting, at least, what remained of the property of the unfortunate Convent) to continue, during the entire of the following day and night, their depradations upon the fences, the fruit trees, the vines, even upon the dead of the tomb, and remaining walls of the once splendid building, without having taken a single precaution, or stationed a single municipal officer to interrupt such wanton destruction, the magistrates of Boston, to their honor be it spoken, were constantly upon the alert, and the wise, prudent, and judicious measures which they at once adopted and vigorously acted upon, have gained the esteem and confidence of all their fellow-men, and elicited the loud approbation of every good and virtuous citizen.

"We are happy to have it in our power to state, in conclusion that there is but one opinion pervading the community at large in relation to this atrocious diabolical deed, and in hurling upon it the detestation that it deserves."

In justice to the Protestant contemporaries of the *Jesuit,* who also expressed their indignation at this act of lawlessness, we produce now the combined accounts of the Boston *Evening Transcript,* and the *Atlas* :[16]

"The general excitement, occasioned by the proceedings of the night before last at Charlestown which yesterday, for the honor of the city be it stated, raged among us with an earnestness corresponding to the atrocious character of that affair, has to-day in a good degree, subsided. To the active exertions of the Mayor and other municipal authorities, the spirit and unanimity with which these were seconded by the whole community, and especially the great meeting called at Faneuil Hall, and finally to the very commendable course pursued, as will be seen, by the Rt. Rev. Bishop Fenwick must it be attributed, that after so stormy a day, the night passed off without disturbance in any direction. At Charlestown, also, the proceedings of the public meeting undoubtedly had a similar effect."

Among all the comment excited by this unprecedented enormity, we have noticed none which more justly describes the nature of the case than that of the *Atlas,* a portion of which is copied herewith.

"What a scene must this midnight conflagration have exhibited—lighting up the inflamed countenances of an infuriated mob of demons, attacking a Convent of women, a seminary for the instruction of young females, and turning them out of their beds, half-naked in the hurry of their flight, and half dead with confusion and terror. And this drama, too, to be enacted on the very soil that afforded one of the earliest places of refuge to the Puritan Fathers of New England, themselves flying from religious persecution in the Old World, that their descendants may wax strong and mighty, and in their turn be guilty of the same persecution in the New!

"We remember no parallel to this outrage in the whole course of history. Turn to the bloodiest incidents of the French Revolution, roll up the curtain that hangs before its sanguinary scenes, and point us to its equal in unprovoked

---

[16]"The Burning of the Charlestown Convent," by Patrick Donahoe, cited above.

violence, in brutal outrage, in unthwarted iniquity. It is in vain that we search for it. In times of civil commotion and general excitement, of confusion, and cruelty, and blood; when the edifice of civil society was shaken to its base, and crumbling to ruin; when the foundations of the great deeps were broken up, and rapine, and fire, and murder were sweeping like a torrent over the land; in times like these there was some palliation for violence and outrage, in the tremendously excited state of the public mind.

"But here there was no such palliation. The courts of justice were open to receive complaints of any improper confinement, or unauthorized coercion. The civil magistrates were, or ought to be, on the alert, to detect any illegal restraint and bring its authors to the punishment they deserve. But nothing of the kind was detected. The whole matter was a cool, deliberate, systematized piece of brutality, unprovoked under the most provoking circumstances, totally unjustifiable and visiting the citizens of the town, and most particularly its magistrates and civil officers, with indelible disgrace.

"The violation of the tomb in the garden alone would seem sufficient to justify these remarks severe as they are. The feeling with which yesterday morning, we witnessed the rude exposure of these remains to the glare of the day, and the gaze of an indiscriminate multitude are such as we hope may never be aroused again."

While there were many citizens of Boston and vicinity who felt keenly the disgrace that had been cast on the fair name of the Commonwealth of Massachusetts, the vast multitude, however, were still blinded by their prejudices and considered the outrages against Catholics as just punishment meted out to them by God. The *Jesuit* and its successor, the *Literary and Catholic Sentinel,* spent their energies in making angry protests against the continued restraints on Catholic freedom, notwithstanding the fact that Protestant citizens of Boston had pledged themselves at Faneuil Hall, "collectively and individually to unite with their Catholic brethren in protecting their persons, their property and their civil and religious rights."[17]　Much attention is paid by all the Catholic weeklies to the perplexing religious questions arising almost daily in Boston. Columns are devoted to lengthy reports on the awful travesties on justice in Massachusetts, on the riots caused by blockading an Irish funeral procession, on the mutiny and insubordination of the militia, excited by the presence of the

---

[17]Resolutions passed by Mass Meeting in Faneuil Hall, published in nearly all the Boston papers of that date.

Irish Montgomery Guards in the same camp with native Americans, on the "truth" or the calumnies contained in Miss Reed's book entitled "Six Months in a Convent," and on many other kindred subjects. The heart grows sick and the mind gets weary of recording those notices of religious strife that crowd into the few years during which the *Jesuit or Catholic Sentinel* ran its troubled career.

Published under the auspices of Bishop Fenwick, its managers were "The Roman Catholic Auxiliary Society," made up of Messrs. Thomas Murphy, then the leading layman in Boston; William Dyer, Roger Flinn, Christopher Peterson, John McNamara, Patrick Mooney, James King and William L. Cazneau. In the course of time internal bickerings and factional troubles so disgusted Bishop Fenwick, that on January 2, 1834, he sent Mr. Murphy a long letter to be delivered to the "members of the government of the Auxiliary Society" in which he said among other criticisms:

"The strife which has of late arisen among the friends of the *Jesuit,* and which I am sorry to hear, manifested itself to a very diversifying extent in the debate of last night, is of such weight with me that I can not hesitate a moment to throw myself in between the contending parties and insist upon peace.

"The *Jesuit* newspaper was originally instituted to promote the Catholic cause, so dear to us all, among a people not acquainted with its true principles, and to diffuse among them a correct knowledge thereof. But it . . . is now becoming an apple of discord and disunion among brethren of the same family . . . I beg you therefore, Gentlemen, to consider the first number of the fifth volume as the last which shall be issued with my sanction as a religious paper."[18]

Its standing as an official organ therefore being lost the *Jesuit* vanished and another publication, the *Literary and Catholic Sentinel* made its appearance with George Pepper as its editor and this motto:[19]

"Happy homes and altars free
With the mountain nymph, sweet Liberty."

The publishers and proprietors of the paper were Henry L. Devereux and Patrick Donahoe. The former was not a Catholic, although he did the printing for the *Jesuit* during the preceding year. The owners of the paper were unhappy in their choice of Pepper as the editor. He was not long at his post, when he

---

[18]Quoted in the *Sacred Heart Review,* Nov. 7, 1908.
[19]*Literary and Catholic Sentinel,* Vol. I.

made a personal attack on the Rev. Mr. Conwell, an Episcopalian minister, which nearly involved the proprietors of the *Catholic Sentinel* in a libel suit.[20]   Past sad experience with the *Truth Teller* taught the editor a lesson.   His retractation appeared in the following issue and the trouble ended.   Pepper wrote from a vocabulary of the most offensive epithets with which to bespatter his adversaries.   In his editorials he took almost every newspaper man in Boston to task in a series of articles called, "The Illiberal Portion of the Boston Press."[21]   Patrick Donahoe, giving his reminiscenses of Pepper fifty years afterwards, says: "Poor Pepper!   His temper corresponded with his name.   These were convent-burning times.   It required a great deal of patience to combat the convent burners and their supporters.   He used to pepper them to their heart's content."[22]   The *Literary and Catholic Sentinel* contrasted miserably in the religious tone of its editorials with that of its predecessor, the *Jesuit*.   Catholic papers generally began to denounce the editor with great vehemence. Perhaps Pepper's greatest failing was that he was hardly ever sober.

In September a disastrous fire swept the vicinity of the printing establishment of the *Catholic Sentinel*.   Its office building suffered considerable damage by water and the print material was hopelessly scattered.   On that account the periodical was obliged to skip one issue.[23]   As the year 1835 drew to a close, the management decided to stop it and another venture, styled, *"Boston Pilot"* was set afloat on Saturday morning, January 2, 1836, with this imprint: "Published Saturdays, at No. 11 Devonshire Street, by H. L. Devereux and P. Donahoe—George Pepper and Dr. J. S. Bartlett, editors."

In the last issue of the *Literary and Catholic Sentinel*, the unfortunate Pepper seems to have realized his shortcomings, for in this number he gives his reader his "Apologia," in which an attempt is made to show that there was some reason to his madness.   He states his case as follows:

> "When the *Literary and Catholic Sentinel* was established, prejudice and passion, fanned into a blaze of fanatic fury against Catholics and Irishmen by the illiberal portion of the Boston press, reached the very acme of violence, and its editor was consequently singled out for the most scurrilous abuse, and his literary and moral character was set up as a target at which every petty scribbler imagined he might aim

---

[20]*Literary and Catholic Sentinel,* Vol. I.
[21]*Ibid.*
[22]*American Cath. Hist. Researches,* Vol. XV, 1904.
[23]*Literary and Catholic Sentinel,* Vol. I.

with impunity the poisoned arrows of contumely and defamation. Thus exasperated and provoked by the rudeness of his maligners, it could not be expected that he, as an Irishman to whom the literary world has given credit for some talent, possessing the sensitiveness of feeling, ardor of passion, and susceptibility of insult which are our natural characteristics, could arm himself with the frigid philosophy of a stoic, or suffer· himself to be tortured by his assailants without indignantly turning upon them and repelling their reviling and provoking assaults. Every reflecting man of reason and intelligence will, he thinks, concede that he was absolutely constrained to resort to vituperative violence of retort and use gross epithets which were, he candidly admits, sometimes dictated by his petulant passion rather than by the prudential consideration of deliberating judgment."[24]

This would have been a suitable farewell for one who was folding the drapery of his editorial robes about him to lie down to pleasant dreams. Pepper's service with the *Boston Pilot* was of but a few months duration. After severing his connection with that paper, he started one of his own, but it had an ephemeral existence. Its editor lingered some time in Boston, depending on his friends for support. He finally took sick, died and was buried at Bunker Hill, where the monument erected to his memory is now mouldering away for want of care. His influence on Catholic journalism is best appreciated by Patrick Donahoe, who knew him well. "I was led to believe," he states, "that Pepper was an able writer, but was greatly disappointed. In his day, the poor Irish were glad to have anyone speak for them and they liked his harsh, violent ways. He did more harm than good."[25]

---

[24] *Literary and Catholic Sentinel,* Vol. I.
[25] *American Catholic Historical Researches* of Philadelphia, Vol. XV, 1904.

CHAPTER XV

New York Weekly Register and Catholic Diary

After the *Truth Teller* had fallen from grace by its activities in a purely political campaign and by its infection with the spirit of trusteeism, its usefullness as a Catholic weekly was much lessened. On that account some of its best contributors ceased to write for it. Naturally enough, at a time when the Catholic Church was troubled from within and without, an authoritative organ was indispensable in the great metropolis of New York.[1] As a reproof to its contemporary, the new paper was to bear the name of the New York *Catholic Press and Weekly Orthodox Journal.*[2] Such was the title that appeared over a prospectus in other Catholic weeklies a few months before this periodical was published. On second consideration, however, the name did not seem to satisfy the editors, for the appellation did not connote all that the prospectus suggested. Since the paper was to contain two distinct departments, religious and secular, the more appropriate name of the New York *Weekly Register and Catholic Diary* was substituted.[3]

No Catholic paper that had previously appeared, had its departments so well organized and so well defined as did this journal. The section on religion, under the special care of Father Joseph Schneller, comprised four divisions, each with a definite purpose of instructing, edifying and confirming Catholics or of informing and enlightening Protestants in the principles of Catholic belief and worship. On the first page were always found certain excellent proofs that Catholicism was in all its bearings perfectly compatible with civil and religious liberty. The second division presented a clear and lucid exposition of Catholic doctrine. Then followed a weekly review of those religious and controversial publications which tended to misrepresent the Catholic faith. Lastly some columns were devoted to giving a connected view of the state of the Church in various parts of the globe, also miscellaneous topics and interesting events in regard to Catholicism in general.

The latter half of the paper was taken up by the secular de-

---

[1] The data collected concerning this paper are the files of the New York *Weekly Register and Catholic Diary.*

[2] A prospectus with this title appeared in nearly every contemporary newspaper.

[3] The same prospectus appeared in the columns of the New York *Register and Catholic Diary* when that paper began publication.

partment and had as editor Patrick S. Casserly. This section comprehended everything designed for the amusement and instruction of the American citizen. It proved a valuable service to the immigrant, who at this time labored at a severe disadvantage on account of the bitter attacks by Nativists, who were making widespread and concerted efforts to maintain their political and industrial ascendency. The antipathy to foreigners had manifested itself at irregular intervals from the very establishment of the Constitution. During the period of early journalism, we have recorded the attempts of the Federalists to circumscribe and even to thwart the exercise of civil and religious liberties of Irishmen. The Alien Law was an endeavor to disfranchise the foreigner over a long period of years. The Hartford Convention would have debarred them forever from holding civil office. In so far as the exertions of the Nativists affected European immigrants in general, it was sporadic and accidental. It became apparent, as time went on, that the circumstance of birth was not the real objection. Their chief concern became an attack on the civil and religious liberty of Catholics.

Just as the Irish press in America had tempered the feelings and allayed the prejudices against the earlier Irish immigrants, so now a genuine Catholic press was ready to resume the combat against that party which had very lately ventured to come forth and attack them openly. In the New York *Weekly Register and Catholic Diary,* the opponents beheld a two-edged sword; the civil and religious liberties of Catholics were to be defended by both its clerical and lay editors, each in his proper sphere. In addition to this, Casserly gave a faithful synopsis of the great national questions and political events of the time. The complaint, so frequently expressed, that foreigners were too ignorant to exercise the franchise and knew but little concerning our republican institutions, was partly set at rest. In the second division of the secular department, ample place was given to the best selections in literature taken from the productions of the best writers in Europe and America. Thirdly, civic virtue was extolled. An occasional lesson in morals was contributed, tending to promote the brotherhood of man on the basis of Christian charity, one of the greatest influences for solidarity and one of the profoundest sources of human happiness. Finally, historical sketches were written giving a succinct view of the most eminent personages of ancient and modern times who have distinguished themselves in Church and State.

Here, then, was a paper where the theologian, the man of letters, and the patriot were enlisted in a noble cause. Here was a channel into which might be poured a portion of the fruits of their labors and talents. Here was a fort with its arsenal well stocked, which gave shot for shot at a time when the Catholic Church in New York most needed a champion. It was at this time that Samuel F. B. Morse, the inventor, writing from Europe, filled the sensational dailies of New York and the country with a series of fabrications known as the "Brutus Letters."[4] This correspondence pretended to acquaint the American people with the real object and activities of the Leopoldine Association[5] of Austria, which was an organization created to assist the propagation of the Catholic Faith in America. This was the time that newspapers could be found which applauded the lawless incendiaries gleefully exulting over the smouldering ruins of the Ursuline Convent at Mount Benedict. Rebecca Reed's book, "Six Months in a Convent," a sequel to the Convent disaster, found a ready sale everywhere. The New York *Weekly Register and Catholic* Diary states that "five thousand copies were disposed of on the first day of publication. Portions of the narrative had been copied by the daily journals."[6] Twenty-five thousand copies, we learn from the Boston *Recorder,* were sold as soon as the newspapers had begun to give publicity to the story, and the demands of the West had not yet received attention. The New York *Churchman* said that the book "found more readers than any other publication of the last half century."[7]

Father Varela attributed much of the advertising that this book received to the "Seventy-Three Calvinistic Ministers" of the paper called the *Protestant*. Writing to the *Catholic Diary* shortly after the story came from the press he says:

"Several ministers of the holy Presbyterian Church have spread many calumnies against the nunneries, and there is no kind of impunity that they could have attributed to the nuns as a fact to which they could testify. No sooner did they hear that such a book as the 'Six Months in a Convent' was to be published, than they began to call public attention and to prepare the mind of the people to receive a document which they thought would bear them out. But what a disappointment. The book contains none of these crimes with which the holy ministers charged the nuns. This has been a terrible blow to the *elects,* for the argument is unanswerable."[8]

Hardly had the sale of Miss Reed's book begun to decline,

---

[4] The New York *Register and Catholic Diary,* Vol. II.
[5] See "History of the Catholic Church in the United States," by John Gilmary Shea, Vol. III.
[6] The New York *Register and Catholic Diary,* 1835, Vol. V. See also "Bishop England's Works," Vol. V., p. 278.
[7] *Ibid.,* Vol. V., p. 291.
[8] *Ibid.,* Vol. V., p. 300.

when the "Awful Disclosures of Maria Monk" appeared. The *Protestant Vindicator,* formerly known as the *Protestant,* fond of gormandizing, when there were promised calumnies regarding Catholics, like the scriptural sow wallowed once more in the mire. The *Catholic Diary* of February 6, 1836, says of this cesspool of corruption and iniquity:

"Year after year, and week after week, it has been the fashion, nay, the chief occupation as well as the material source of profit to the malicious editor of the *Protestant Vindicator* to represent the Catholic ladies in nunneries as the worst set of wretches that ever disgraced human nature; and the Catholic clergy as the very personifications of rapacity, cruelty and vice.

"If indeed to be chaste, humane and charitable—if to instruct the ignorant, to relieve the distressed, to solace the afflicted—if to be adorned by every virtue—if to have renounced all the vanities of time be criminal in Catholic ladies—then, without doubt, are they the basest and most degraded among mankind. Who, it may be asked, is it that, disregarding the danger of infection, when poverty, pestilence and death have visited the miserable cabin, is always ready to minister the consolations of religion, to moisten the parched lips, and to pour the sweet consoling sound of pity in the ear of an expiring fellow-being? Who is it that, unmindful of his own necessities, willingly parts with his all, and becomes himself a suppliant, in order to procure a little sustenance for the forlorn and afflicted? Who is it that is continually doing all this and more than this? Oh, it is the despised and and slandered *Catholic Priest!* Who is it, on the other hand that is ever foremost in the ranks of revilers? Who is it that, professing to be a minister of peace—a follower of the meek and merciful Saviour,—marches at the head of a gang of the fiercest calumniators the world ever saw? Whose aim is it that his track should be marked with desolation and blood? Whose voice is the weekly signal for the indiscriminate slaughter of his fellow-men? The editor of the New York *Protestant Vindicator.*

"The editor of this vile print published on the 14th of October last the terrible tale of scandal which he now causes to repeat, under the assumed name of Maria Monk and in the form of a book. The incredible falsehoods were immediately noticed by the Protestant editors of the political journals in the Canadas. Extracts from the Montreal *Herald,* Montreal *Morning Courier,* Montreal *Evening Gazette,* Quebec *Mercury,* and *True Briton* are given in to-day's im-

pression. We have written for all the documents connected
with this infamous piece of slander, and, as soon as we shall
receive them, the public will be astounded."

It may be significant to remark that every one of the above
named papers made the *Protestant Vindicator* the subject of one
of the most scathing editorials, full of the bitterest denunciation
that ever fell upon the character of any journalist. The excerpts
found in the *Catholic Diary* had the influence of producing a reaction among secular journals against these calumniators.

It would be idle to attempt even to mention the various historical matters treated in the *Diary* regarding events that occurred
in the early history of Catholicism in America. American history
does not furnish any more interesting trait, nor one calling up
finer recollections or more generous disinterestedness than the
conduct of the Catholic founders of Maryland. The most reliable
sources were consulted in this series of excellent articles. In
addition, current events transpiring in America were always faithfully recorded, thus making that periodical a treasure house of historical data during that eventful period which ushers in the era
of the Church's notable growth in America.

American church building was becoming more and more a
matter of interest. People were settling in the Western terri-
tories, which a few years before were unexplored and uninhabited
wildernesses. Church extension was going on in States where
hitherto the name Catholic was but little known, or if known,
heard perhaps with feelings of horror and disgust.

As the immigration from Ireland was strong in the decade from
1830 to 1840, and as these settlers formed the bulk of the readers
of the *Diary,* special efforts were made to acquaint them with the
news of their native land and to defend them from the attacks
of the Nativist faction in politics. Some of the epithets employed by the press of that day clearly indicate the depths of
degradation to which prejudice and bigotry had reduced many a
journal. Anything that would arouse indignation in the heart of
the Irish population was employed. Their beau ideal of Irish
statesmanship, Daniel O'Connell, was subjected to every species
of insult and vituperation. He was called the "base brawling
demagogue," "a dishonest and self-interested man," "Ireland's
worst enemy," "foul incendiary," "the robber and grinder of the
poor," "a ferocious slanderer," "a deliberate utterer of calumnies," "a bully," "and intriguer," "A Catiline," "an Irish Machiavelli," "a pious, prying, preaching, fanatic," and many more libels
too offensive and too disgusting to be repeated here. Who would
think that all this opprobium and hatred could be crowded into
one article appearing in the New York *Courier and Inquirer.*
Such, however, is the case, and it illustrates the sort of contribu-

tions that could be found in many of the dailies of our large cities.

After the establishment of the New York *Weekly Register and Catholic Diary,* in October, 1832, it was encouraged by an ever increasing patronage, but yet it never was on a very substantial basis. The trials with which its beginnings were embarrassed were those incident to almost every initial effort in Catholic journalism. But it struggled on, gathering new strength by the bitter conflicts which it had to wage against the powers of darkness. The editor-in-chief, Father Joseph A. Schneller, though known to be brusque and eccentric in his dealings with men,[9] always maintained a spirit of dignity and moderation in his writings. This was his first effort at editing a Catholic paper. By dint of hard labor and experience, he soon became a practical journalist. The prospects for a permanent and progressive Catholic newspaper became daily brighter and brighter. Early in July, 1835, Father Thomas C. Levins, who had assisted Father Schneller in his editorial duties, withdrew, thus leaving the latter to his own resources.

Just one month elapsed, when a visitation by fire reduced the entire establishment to ruins. But with marvelous promptitude, the editor immediately proceeded to new quarters and the paper was presented to its readers after a short delay. On December 16, six months after the first fire, the most disastrous conflagration that had ever visited the American continent occurred in New York City. Events so distressing and so injurious to prosperity of this enterprising newspaper and to the exertions of its editors, greatly disheartened them. Father Schneller had even written a letter to the *Catholic Herald* of Philadelphia offering that paper the subscription list. But before negotiations were completed, he was again induced to take up the work of publication, being assured by his friends and subscribers that they would cooperate with him to make the paper a success.

The journal was revived on January 25 with James Kelly as publisher and Father Schneller still in the editor's chair. It was now known merely as the *Catholic Diary,* but retained as before its secular department. It continued to be printed on the usual eight quarto size pages, and as it again made its appearance, was hailed by its contemporaries, Catholic and Protestant, with great enthusiasm. The *Daily Southern Patriot,* of Charleston, informed its readers of calamities which had already twice befallen the *Diary* and recommended it highly as a "most useful and intelligent journal, an able and temperate advocate of civil and religious freedom—a friend of the institutions and the character of the

---

[9] "Records and Studies," Vol. II, p. 54.

people of the South—but more especially entitled to the friendship, countenance, and support of the children of the Emerald Isle."[10]

With these encouragements and promises of continued support, the *Diary* was again issued at a new office, No. 8 William Street. But misfortune once more knocked at the door of its editor. The troubles and anxieties of the past few months coupled with the burdens of the priestly office undermined the health of Father Schneller. As the third year was nearing completion, he announced that his paper would soon cease publication. On October 28, the date of the last issue, and the end of Volume Six, he writes his final editorial address:

"If the promises which were originally announced in the prospectus have been rigidly and scrupulously fulfilled for these three years under difficulties almost insuperable and losses almost ruinous, it was because I had sufficient means and well-grounded assurance as regarded these promises; hence to renew these promises would be foolish as well as imprudent, when the means are exhausted, when a precarious state of health may soon require a change of atmosphere and when no permanency of location is guaranteed. Past experience and reason have taught me not to enter upon any important undertaking except I possess the means and ability to execute it. If, during the period that has elapsed since the first number of this paper appeared, I have been in aught deficient or culpable, you will impute it to the unforeseen wants and difficulties against which it is impossible for the editor and proprietor of so large a paper always to provide, the more so when the duties of the sacred ministry require first care and constant attention."

In the short space of three years the *Catholic Diary* performed a great mission. Living at a time when illiberality and religious animosity took on in some measure the aspect of those wild orgies that figured at the enthronement of Reason in the French Capital, this paper, nevertheless, waged a crusade so calm and dignified as to cover screaming fanatics with confusion, and drew down upon them the contempt of all honest God-fearing Protestants. The secular and the sectarian press in 1832 was not so open to conviction as it was about a year and a half later. Rage and indignation for wrongs done or injuries inflicted, under these circumstances would have fanned the flames of prejudice. Facts and sound arguments compelled attention. To cite a case in point. —If the *Diary* had not republished the accounts of the Canadian

---

[10]This recommendation was published in the *Catholic Diary* when it reappeared in 1836.

newspapers, the sworn affidavits and other documents regarding the Maria Monk affair, William L. Stone of the *Commercial Advertiser* would never have set out for Montreal to begin an investigation. The result of this was soon to silence for all time those periodicals, whose iconoclastic fury was only commensurate with their greed for gain, that such sensations were sure to bring from a people, who had become so gullible and biased as never to reflect on the absurdities they were continually swallowing. The *Diary,* in the midst of all this bitter persecution, assumed an attitude of prudence, and clung with praiseworthy consistency to the Golden Rule which the paper made its motto: "All things whatsoever you would that men would do to you, do you also to them."

CHAPTER XVI

The Shepherd of the Valley

What more appropriate, what more romantic name could have been chosen for a paper that was to be the guardian of the Catholic faith in the great basin of the Mississippi River than *Shepherd of the Valley!*[1] A guardian was indeed necessary to tend the flock roaming feeble and defenceless in the vast and lonely wilderness. St. Louis, the chief centre of Catholic population in a newly created diocese, had become a prey to the spirited attacks of a number of religious adversaries in league, no doubt, with their brethren of the Eastern States. The strong tide of Catholic immigration that poured westward at this time aroused the suspicions of prejudiced minds, and the signs of this approaching agitation boded ill to the sheep of Christ's fold. These alarmists were already hovering near, when the *Shepherd of the Valley* was established in the year 1832. Then they "like quick kites with beak and talons prone circled the skies," to snatch, as it were, the weak and unwary lambs of the plain.

This periodical, so quaint and yet so apt in its designation, was edited and published during the first year of its existence by Francis H. Taylor on a medium sheet printed partly in English and partly in French. The *Catholic Telegraph* of Cincinnati, says that the paper would not have been started, "had not a certain class of bigots shouted from pulpits and sounded in the press the whole gamut of Calvinistic fanaticism." They looked upon Catholics as a danger to their freedom, forgetting all the while that the best parent and guardian of liberty among men is Truth.[2]

The principal task that confronted the *Shepherd of the Valley* was to clear away from the spiritual vision of non-Catholics the falsehoods and the calumnies which blinded this ill-informed people. But the editor of the journal had also in view the spiritual welfare of the Catholics. The rapid increase of piety and the practice of religious perfection were objects near and dear to his heart; hence he presented to his readers such matter as tended to give them a high moral and religious development. Though conducted on a small scale during the first year of its existence, the *Shepherd* considerably promoted the good of the cause which it had espoused. Much praise therefore must be given to the editor

---

[1] The files of this paper are rare and we are therefore compelled to seek for information regarding it in the contemporary Catholic journals: *Miscellany, Truth Teller, Herald, Telegraph, Jesuit,* etc.

[2] The *Catholic Telegraph*, Vol. I, No. 41, July 28, 1832, p. 327.

for his persevering industry, notwithstanding the difficulties under which he constantly labored. To this alone must be attributed those alterations in the journal that took place during the year 1832, when it was under his sole conduct.[3]

As Catholics redoubled their energies in the bold defence of Truth, the opposition became stronger and stronger. The New York *Register and Catholic Diary* in 1833 observed that a periodical like the *Shepherd* was even more necessary than in 1832, when it was first started.[4] The people of St. Louis and the surrounding country were not slow to recognize the benefits that had flowed from this publication after but one year's existence. They saw also that the paper would not long endure under its present difficulties. Consequently, influenced by these convictions and desirous of giving aid to so worthy an enterprise, a number of gentlemen formed themselves into a society bearing the title of the Western Catholic Association.[5] They were persuaded that by their united efforts the *Shepherd* would not only be improved, but that its regular publication would be rendered permanent and satisfactory. To give the patrons a specimen of the *Shepherd* as it would appear in the future in its improved and enlarged state, Mr. Taylor the former editor, through the kindly assistance of the office of the St. Louis *Times* published the last number of Volume One on an imperial folio page.[6]

A number of new features were introduced into the second volume and more space was given for foreign and domestic news. The Association hoped to raise the journal to a point not inferior to any of its kind in the Union. Lack of patronage had nearly imperilled the life of the *Shepherd* during the first year of its existence. In order to avoid this, the Association immediately aimed at introducing it as a family paper into every Catholic home in the Middle West. The subscription price in 1833 was three dollars a year in advance.

How long the *Shepherd of the Valley* continued under the auspices of the Western Catholic Association is not definitely known. At any rate, we know that in 1839 a new weekly journal, called the *Catholic Banner,* was brought out by Thomas Mullen. Even less information is recorded about this paper than of its predecessor. The *Shepherd of the Valley* was revived in 1851 by R. A. Bakewell and existed until 1854, when it became a wolf in sheep's clothing. For it is said then to have passed into the hands of Rev. Dr. High and Rev. Dr. Gilman who made it a Know-nothing organ under the title of the *True Shepherd of the Valley and St. Louis Know-nothing.*[7]

---

[3]*Ibid.,* Vol. 1, 1832.
[4]The *New York Register and Catholic Diary,* Vol. II, 1833, Nov. 23.
[5]*Catholic Miscellany,* Vol. XIII, No. 4, 1832, p. 31.
[6]*Catholic Telegraph,* Vol. II.
[7]The "History of the City of St. Louis," edited by Sharp.

CHAPTER XVII

The Catholic Herald

Perhaps in no place in the United States was the need of a Catholic newspaper more felt than in the City of Brotherly Love. For more than twenty years Catholicism in Philadelphia had passed through one of the most trying ordeals that it had as yet experienced anywhere in this country. The canker-worm of trusteeism had eaten its way into the very heart of religion and threatened the Church in Philadelphia with spiritual decay. Hardly had this heretical pest of Hoganism been exterminated than a storm of prejudice swept over the city, dashing with great fury upon the defenceless and enfeebled Church. The number of religious periodicals increased with such startling rapidity that very few denominations were without a weekly journal in which they could advance and defend their peculiar views of doctrine and church government. Had this been the be-all and end-all of their existence, the *Catholic Herald* would not likely have been started for some years to come. "If these sectarian publications," states the prospectus, "had been content with maintaining the system of doctrine which they have severally embraced, we would have continued as heretofore silent spectators of their controversies and confined ourselves to the publication of those works, which we are convinced present a satisfactory demonstration of the truth and purity of the Church. But when we observe in several of the religious journals false statements of fact, reflecting upon our religion and doctrines ascribed to us, which our Church condemns; when we know that our silence is assumed as an admission of the truth of these charges, and that thereby uncharitable feelings are created and prejudices confirmed, we deem it expedient to establish a religious periodical, through which we may be enabled from time to time, to lay before the public temperate vindications of our doctrines, according as the unprovoked attack of our adversaries may appear to be worthy of notice."[1]

The first number of the *Catholic Herald* appeared on Thursday, January 3, 1833, and at that time was in charge of three priests of the cathedral parish. Father John Hughes, who afterwards became Archbishop of New York, was chiefly concerned in the project, for he was soon to measure swords in a controversy with the Rev. John Breckinridge. It seems that in the autumn of 1832 the Presbyterian divine published in the *Christian Advocate*

---

[1] The *Catholic Herald,* Vol. I, No. 1.

certain desultory charges against the Catholic Church. Father Hughes commenting on this letter states: "I saw doctrines incorrectly stated, arraigned, tried and triumphantly condemned." He suggested to the Rev. Mr. Breckinridge that he begin at the first principles by discussing the "Rule of Faith." Much preliminary correspondence ensued and finally conditions for a real controversy between the two antagonists were decided upon.[2]

The first rule of this agreement shows that this religious combat was one of the motives which hastened the establishment of the *Catholic Herald*. The article says: "The parties shall write and publish alternately in the weekly religious paper called the *Presbyterian* and a Roman Catholic paper to be furnished by the first of January; it being understood that the communications shall be published after the following plan: One party opening the first week, the other party replying the next week, and every piece to be republished in the immediately succeeding number of the Roman Catholic paper. The communications not to exceed four columns of the *Presbyterian* nor to continue beyond six months without consent of the parties."[3]

Until the month of September, the *Catholic Herald* was filled with this polemical discussion. Father Hughes never doubted for a minute either the utility or the issue of the controversy. In a letter to Father John B. Purcell, afterwards Archbishop of Cincinnati, he says:

> "The opportunity of placing my letters under the eyes of certainly not fewer than thirty thousand Protestant readers is too precious to be allowed to escape unimproved. I do not pretend to say that it will make converts; but the perusal of them now may be the destruction of prejudice in some minds; and the first seed, reflection and still more affections of heart, may ripen into actual conversions when I and my letters shall have been forgotten."[4]

The outcome of the whole discussion is succinctly stated by Father Hughes in his review of a pamphlet written by the Rt. Rev. Bishop Onderdonk during the course of the year 1833:

> "For some months back," says Father Hughes, "there has been a considerable undertone of dissatisfaction among the better informed Protestants generally, not excepting Presbyterians themselves. They have never suspected the strength of the Catholic position on the Rule of Faith nor the weakness of their own. And in this mood of feeling they ascribed the

---

[2]"Life of the Most Reverend John Hughes, D.D.," by Hassard, p. 136.
[3]The *Catholic Herald*, Vol. I, No. 1.
[4]"Life of the Most Reverend John Hughes, D.D.," by Hassard, p. 140.

sufferings of the cause to the incompetence of the advocate. Even some of the Protestant clergy did not hesitate to say that Mr. Breckinridge was not 'the man' that should have been selected; that he had no business to engage in such a discussion without being authorized by those, whom he undertook to represent and in utter contempt of the poet's admonition:

> 'Sumite materiam vestris qui scribitis aequam
> Veribus; et versate diu quid ferre recusent
> Quid valeant humeri.'

"It is not for me to say," he adds, "whether it was these considerations that moved Bishop Onderdonk to take up the Rule of Faith and make it the subject of his charge to the assembled convention of the Protestant Episcopal Church of Pennsylvania.   The public attention was called to it in various newspapers, and not only the charge but also the *subject* of it, contrary to custom, was announced as something important and interesting at this time."[5]

Long after the antagonists had sheathed their swords, angry traces of the controversy may be found in both religious journals. When all trouble had subsided, the *Catholic Herald* pursued the even tenor of its way, furnishing its readers with essays on religion and literature, occasional reviews of religious publications and a statement of the principal events occurring in Ireland, France and America.   The activities of Daniel O'Connell were reported in this paper with the greatest detail, yet the Irish Catholics of Philadelphia failed to extend to the *Herald* that patronage which it merited.   In a city with a population of some twenty-five or thirty thousand Catholics, only four hundred regular subscribers could be found.

We may rightly wonder at this lack of appreciation by the children of Holy Church for its able defenders.   The same difficulties and discouragements that inflicted paralysis on Catholic journalism elsewhere were also at work in Philadelphia.   Pittsburg, the second city in Pennsylvania, stood in as much need of a religious press as did the City of Brotherly Love.   The *Herald* on June 4, 1835, took pains to count the number of anti-Catholic articles in one Pittsburgh paper and found no less than eighteen distinct attacks on the Church.   Yet that city furnished hardly any subscribers to the *Herald*.

Not by the press alone was the ancient religion assaulted. There was even a conspiracy led by the sectarian clergy to devise such means as would speedily eradicate Catholicity.   The same

---

[5]*Ibid.,* p. 144.

disgraceful outrages that humiliated Boston threatened to visit Pennsylvania. The *Catholic Herald* did not exaggerate the situation one iota, when it made the following observation: "We have never yet seen a Presbyterian paper in which there was not some low degraded insult, some foul charge, or some base misrepresentation regarding the Catholic Church. When Sterne wanted to arouse his congregations, he told them some wonderful story about the Pope. It is thus with the editors of most Protestant journals."[6]

But these sectarian papers discovered with extreme disappointment that they were endangering their very existence by continuing to abuse the credulity of conscientious Protestants; so the editors of these journals were compelled to curb their fanatical hatred of Catholics. This brief interval, however, was used for re-organization. In 1843, another outburst of wrath occurred in Philadelphia under the name of the American Protestant Association. The master-spirits had in the meantime prepared a pamphlet of some forty, or fifty pages, showing the intentions of the Association, its constitution, terms of membership, etc. The audacity of this measure was augmented by a call on Protestant laymen in all parts of the United States to join them in their ungodly warfare. Again, the public press assisted them in this anti-Catholic crusade. Newspapers, when they wished to start a sensation, printed the simple heading "Popery" in some conspicuous place and it was interpreted by certain readers as a signal of distress. "It is understood," remarks the *Herald*, "in its literal sense to mean by all who can pronounce Shibboleth—Help me Cassius or I sink."[7]

The critical period for Catholicism came in July, 1843, when the question of the Bible in the public schools brought Catholics and the members of the Association into bitter conflict. "For many years," says the editor of the *Herald*, "the paper labored in its humble way to convince the friends of public school systems in the country, that the question of admitting or excluding the Bible from them involved the whole Papal controversy. If these schools are a part of our political system, partaking so far of its spirit as to give equal toleration in all religions, and favor to none, it is very clear that the Bible can have no admission to them. And whatever argument can be used in favor of admitting that blessed book, may be urged with equal propriety, if not with equal force, in favor of admitting the catechisms or text books of any particular denomination."

With each succeeding month the battle grew more furious.

---

[6] The *Catholic Herald*, Vol. III.
[7] The *Catholic Herald*, Vol. XII.

By the beginning of November, when the Protestant league opened its winter campaign, we have no longer any reason to doubt what desperate measures that organization would take for the "extirpation of Popery." Dr. Tyng, who lectured before the Association on that occasion, gave utterance to an incendiary declamation with such frantic energy, that it sunk deep into the hearts of all bigots assembled. "The time has come, brethren," he said, "when we should no longer be content with a mere paper warfare."

Knowing the avowed intention of the organization, we shall not be surprised at the awful catastrophe that was so soon to follow. The dark deeds at Mount Benedict pale when contrasted with the terrible destruction that commenced on Monday, May 6, 1844. On that day began Philadelphia's "Reign of Terror." Fire, rapine, bloodshed, death—such are the records of the darkest age in America's religious history. Listen to the plaintive words of the editor as he views this scene of desolation:

"In the City of Penn, within a few rods of the spot where he concluded his treaty with the Indian tribes, and where he thought and the world said, that religious freedom had established her throne, another monument is raised to prove the existence and to mark the ravages of the glowing monster of religious intolerance. Every day it is acquiring force and strength amongst us: It seems anxious to raise its trophies along side those which commemorate the birth of American Liberty. As the blackened walls of Mount Benedict stand a scoffing commentary on the opposite monument of Bunker Hill, so will the smoldering ruins of St. Augustine's and St. Michael's tell a doleful tale to the traveller who passes from the hall, where 'liberty was proclaimed through the land,' to visit the spot where justice and liberty seemed to have chosen a dwelling place."

But alas! what a sight meets his gaze, what disappointment fills his heart as he views the desecrated altars!

While the excitement continued, the discreet editor made but few comments in the *Herald*. The still smouldering ruins of churches and schools told the story more powerfully than he could have written it. The paper, however, published comments of certain Philadelphia newspapers which shows the state of public opinion among self-respecting Protestants. The Philadelphia *Ledger* of May 11 had the following account:

"The scene of the riots presented a spectacle of perfect desolation. Ruin lifted its wan and haggard head through the blackened and yawning walls on every side, while the emblem of mourning and death hung from the muffled knocker and partly closed shutter. It was a heart-sickening sight, the like of which we hope we may never again look upon in this or any other city. And next to this, the humiliating display of the American bunting as a means of protecting the property of any class or sect of citizens from the prejudices or destructive propensities of another. Rows of houses for squares round the infected district, and in fact for some distance out in the suburbs have small tricolored flags protruding from the windows, a sight mortifying and humiliating to those who have been taught to believe that our laws afford equal and efficient protection to all."

On May 13, the *Spirit of the Times* dwelt with feelings of respectful sympathy upon the fact of the untenanted Catholic churches:

"All was quiet in our city yesterday," states this journal. "It was a strange thing, however, to see military promenading our streets on the Sabbath, but still stranger to feel that their presence was necessary to procure the enforcement of public peace! Into all the churches as the chiming bells pealed out their solemn tones, poured crowd after crowd of citizens to give thanks to the Deity for their safety. In all the churches we should have said, excepting the Roman Catholic. They stood desolate, silent, untenanted. In obedience to the order of the Bishop, they were not open for public worship. The solitary tread of the sentinel or the clank of the musket was the only sound that disturbed their solitary repose.

"And this was a Sabbath picture of the City of Brotherly Love. This was a picture of the Quaker City. Could William Penn have risen from his grave and looked at such a scene, could he have gazed on the bristling bayonets that offended the quiet eye in almost every direction, could he have been told that this pomp and panoply of war was necessary to secure the liberty of religious opinion, that here all this exhibition of military force was required simply to enable men to exercise one of the inalienable privileges of humanity, to worship God according to the dictates of their own consciences, what that great and good man would have said we leave to the reader to imagine. He could not have credited the evidence of his senses. He could not have believed his descendants so monstrously degenerated. He could not have dreamed for a moment that the people of his own Christian city would ever practise that bigoted intolerance, to escape from which he himself abandoned his country, his kindred, and his home and as an undying monument of his abhorrence of which he founded the community in which we live."

The *United States Gazette* gives us the following graphic description of the ruins of St. Augustine's Church:

"We saw on Saturday the ruins in Kensington, the blackened, crumbled walls of the Church, of the school house and of many, very many dwelling houses that the passions of men had doomed to destruction. The heart sickens at such exhibitions, and inquires for the justice of man; that allowed of such unlawful, unruly, violence; or of the justice of Heaven, which seemed to sleep amid the wrongdoings of the wicked, both when the murders were committed and the property wasted. We learned nothing there to answer that inquiry, but returning by way of Fourth Street we went up and stood amid the smouldering ruins of St. Augustine's, and when we renewed our inquiry, our eyes rested on the uppermost portion of the opposite wall, from which the fire peeled every particle of plaster and licked off the decorative paint, but, as if in defiance of the wrath of men and the fury of the flames, there stood in clear uninjured letters the inscription. 'THE LORD SEETH,' and we turned away satisfied in our heart, and exclaiming in quiet submission: 'Shall not the Judge of all earth do right?'"

While the Nativist mobs were still exulting in their deeds, many a Protestant was attempting to heal the painful wounds which malice had inflicted upon their Catholic neighbors. One sympathetic citizen, filled with indignation at the recent disgraceful outrages, circulated the following tender appeal to the Protestants of the city:

"Within twenty years, a fearful pestilential disease passed over Asia, sweeping before it into the bosom of death no less than sixty millions of human beings. The destroying angel then passed over Europe, consigning hundreds of thousands of men, women, and children to their silent graves. We, 'the people of the United States,' awaited his approach with humble resignation; yet with a 'firm reliance on Divine Providence,' making such preparations as prudence and experience pointed out. At that awful period, a minister of the Gospel in the City of Philadelphia, who had a large house and schoolhouse adjoining, caused to be removed out of them every article of furniture which could be dispensed with, and converted the whole building into a hospital. He had it admirably arranged, fitted up with all necessaries, and supplied with fearless and tender nurses; women religiously devoted to the faithful discharge of their duties. I was acquainted with the benevolent individual. Although we thought widely different on many religious subjects of much moment, yet we worshipped the same God and adored the same Redeemer. I was, by him invited, and walked all over this new establishment for cholera patients. 'The white-washed walls and nicely sanded floors,' exhibited its cleanliness and neatness. A plentiful supply of medicine and everything required was provided: there were sedan chairs with spring poles of the easiest possible construction, to convey patients to this asylum, wherever they might be found in want of care, skill, and medicine. It was so judiciously adapted to the purpose to which it was devoted; its doors were thrown so hospitably wide open, and its superintendent was so intent on doing good, that many patients were collected within its walls. I examined the records; the whole number of patients were three hundred and seventy of all ages and sexes. Of these, according to my best recollection and information, sixty-three were Catholics and three hundred and seven were Protestants.

"Having no faith myself in the infectious nature of disease, I went through the rooms and 'while memory holds her seat,' I never can forget the impression made upon me by the affectionate solicitude of all who were in attendance on the sick. There are hundreds now in this city who have more or less knowledge of the intense and anxious care and untiring solicitude with which the poor and the afflicted were watched over by night and day. Many a parent, husband, and wife was through the instrumentality of that hospital restored to their families.

"This could not be done without attracting public notice, however unobtrusive and retiring might be the being who dispensed his blessings; it not only commanded general attention, but the constituted authorities of the city, on the restoration of health, felt it their duty to tender amends for the expense incurred, and as far as possible for the eminent service rendered. All pecuniary remuneration was absolutely and at once declined. The thanks of our city councils were accepted.

"I would that I could end my narrative here, but I feel impelled to state what was the fate of the buildings, which had thus been devoted to charitable purposes.

"It had been a religious establishment, and near at hand was a church dedicated to Almighty God. In that church, the regular inmates of this establishment daily attended divine service. I had seen that church and the house—all that remains of them—within an hour of this time, they are in soul-saddening ruins! Nothing of them remains but smoked and blackened walls. Not a particle of wood or any combustible substance remains unconsumed. This was done not by a foreign foe, not by an invading army, not by a tribe of savage Indians. No! it was done by people who, in the days of their calamity—when pestilence walked abroad in their streets and carried away their relations and friends—were received and comforted and healed and made sound, under the shelter of the roofs they have destroyed. The altar, before which millions have bowed down and worshipped the living God, has been consumed by fire. It is reduced to ashes, which are momentarily scattered abroad by the winds. The noble organ, which so often warmed the heart of a Christian people with love to their Redeemer, the melody of which ascended to the throne of the Triune God—is destroyed—not an atom of it can be found. It has every morsel of it, been devoured by the fierceness of the flames. The surrounding churchyard, the resting place of the dead—is a sad confusion —the graves recklessly trampled underfoot—the tombstones broken and defaced, and the urn in which some pious Christian had enshrined the heart of their pastor is cast down.

" 'Father forgive them for they know not what they do' were among the last words of Him who, for a sinful world, perished on the Cross—of that Crucified Saviour for whose garments the soldiers cast lots. May no heavy visitation overtake our city for the sins of our people; but may their sins and ours be mercifully forgiven."[8]

The state of feeling, that brought disaster and disgrace to the City of Philadelphia, must in a large measure be attributed to the obnoxious sentiments contained in a certain portion of the religious and secular press. In addition to the attacks of public journals, much acrimony and prejudice were excited by the publications of the Philadelphia Tract Society, which stormed the State of Pennsylvania with its leaflets. In one year, the organization distributed nearly two million pages of printed matter. Besides this propaganda, there were the loud vociferations of bigoted preachers, who, instead of inculcating the word to their hearers as true ministers of the Gospel should have done, played rather the part of demagogues, and harangued their congregations on the menace of "Popery" to our free institutions.

Shortly after these troublous times, the *Catholic Herald* changed editors. In January, 1847, Henry Major was given control. This gentleman was formerly an Episcopalian minister. After his conversion, he became a professor at the Catholic Theological Seminary in Philadelphia, but as his new position did not provide sufficient sustenance to himself and family, other means of liveli-

---

[8]This hand bill was circulated througout the entire City of Philadelphia. It also appeared in the *Catholic Herald*.

hood had to be found. The suggestion was made that, perhaps, under his good management the *Herald* would be able to furnish him with a more remunerative income. Major took upon himself the duties of editor, and for ten years the wavering destinies of this Catholic journal were in his hands. During this decade, the paper passed through the stormiest period of its existence. The pen of Henry Major was trenchant in its attacks upon Orestes A. Brownson, in hopes, perhaps, that such controversies would attract readers to his paper. At last, disheartened by repeated failure and disappointed in his cherished ambition of making the *Herald* a success, he relapsed into Episcopalianism; but it was said that he repented his action during his last illness and died a Catholic.

When Major severed his connection with the *Herald* at the end of 1856, it was consolidated with another Catholic journal called the *Visitor*. Under this double title, it was conducted with varying success for about ten years, when it was discontinued. Many a change of editors occurred during that decade. At the beginning of this period the *Catholic Herald and Visitor* could boast of three editors—James McDonnell, Charles S. Greene and Charles A. Repplier.[9] This arrangement did not prove satisfactory, however, and Mr. Repplier became the sole conductor of the journal until 1863, when James Spellissey, who had for four years previous to this date been the anonymous editor of the Boston *Pilot,* took charge of the enterprise. During the eventful times of the Civil War, the temptation of Catholic journals to meddle with the politics of the day was almost irresistible, but the Philadelphia paper, profiting by the experience of certain contemporaries, adhered loyally to the Union cause.

Like some hideous nightmare, financial failure continually menaced the editor. Printing material nearly doubled in price, and the currency was depreciating rapidly. Very likely, embarrassments such as these were the unhappy cause of the *Catholic Herald's* sudden dissolution.

---

[9] The *Catholic Herald and Visitor,* Vol. I.

CHAPTER XVIII

The Catholic Journal

In the year 1833, an effort was made to establish a periodical called the *Catholic Journal*[1] in the District of Columbia. The editor and publisher, A. F. Cunningham, chose Washington as the field of his endeavor on account of its peculiar importance as the Capital of the nation. Another reason, which prompted him in selecting the District of Columbia, was the status of its citizens, debarred as they are from the privileges of legislating in the councils of the nation. Under such conditions, the editor felt that a strict neutrality could more easily be maintained with regard to political parties. By avoiding such issues, attention could be exclusively given to his main purpose, namely, a calm yet energetic defense of truth and a clear and lucid exposition of Catholic doctrine.

The religious department was conducted under the advice of Catholic clergymen, and the editor invited on all occasions their coöperation by contributions. For the promotion of literature and science, he availed himself of such articles as the friends of the *Journal* were pleased to write. He also selected from various sources such other matter as he deemed of sufficient importance and usefulness to merit republication.

The news department comprised a faithful history of events as they occurred in the District, and had the paper continued, it would have been a fruitful source of information for the historian of our day. There was also a judicious selection of foreign and domestic intelligence interspersed at intervals with interesting anecdotes and lively incidents. Special attention was given to Irish affairs. The editor was a native of the Green Isle, and hence felt a keen sympathy in the struggle for liberty, which was engaging the attention of her ardent and devoted leaders. Special essays, some original, others selected from the zealous advocates of the rights of the unhappy and shackled citizens of Ireland, tended to arouse a public opinion in favor of Erin's Sons at a time, when the Native American Party was springing into being.

The *Catholic Journal* should have shone as a sun, spreading its rays and permeating every portion of the country by its warmth and light. Such was not the case, however, for chilled and obscured by the wintry clouds of non-support, it was discontinued August 1, 1833, within the very first year of its issue. The subscription price of this weekly folio newspaper of four pages was three dollars a year in advance.

---

[1] The only reference we have concerning this ephemeral journal is a prospectus found in the contemporary newspapers. A few brief notices of it also appear from time to time in the editorial columns of these papers.

CHAPTER XIX

The Minerva and the Catholic Advocate

The immediate precursor of the *Catholic Advocate* of Bardstown, Kentucky, was the *Minerva,* a monthly magazine published by the faculty of St. Joseph's College. Here was formed that galaxy of brilliant editors, who were to illumine the pages of the *Advocate* for many years. The *Minerva* was literary in character rather than religious, but, as its contributions were the writings of an exclusively Catholic body, we may regard it as coming within the scope of Catholic journalism.[1]

This monthly consisted principally of essays and reviews, thoughtful, interesting and ever learned in their treatment and expression. There was a pleasing variety in its articles, such as would give a stimulus to the culture of the mind. One of the chief contributors to this entertaining and instructive magazine was the Rev. Dr. Martin J. Spalding, who afterwards became Archbishop of Baltimore. He wrote for the *Minerva* a series of papers, and showed himself an excellent literary critic. The articles that best exhibit his style are "Journal of Travels in Southern Europe," an essay on the "Study of History" and a paper entitled "Thoughts on Man."

The lack of a religious paper in the diocese developed year by year into a sore necessity. Kentucky, during the thirties, had, like every other part of the United States, its share in the persecution of Catholics. All that they asked for was truth without alloy and a fair display of justice. The following manly appeal served as a prospectus:

"The fact that Catholics are a vigorous and energetic body can not be denied. Their continued action, like that of their fathers in the faith, derives a new stimulus from misfortune and oppression. It must ultimately be productive of much good or of much evil. The spirit which animates them is powerful and it would seem, from the history of eighteen centuries, unconquerable. Its tendency is highly useful or dangerous in the extreme. If they are what they are said to be, let them be doomed to disgrace and ruin; their fate will be just. If they are honest and slandered men, it is the duty of the liberal and intelligent portion of their fellow-citizens to support and shield them against sectarian bigotry.

---

[1] "The Life of Archbishop Spalding," by Rt. Rev. John Lancaster Spalding, Chapter VI, p. 71.

"The verdict of public opinion should never be given but after a patient and dignified hearing of the accused. Hence, on the part of the public, the duty of listening to their vindication, and examining into the merits of their cause; and on the part of Catholics, the still sacred obligation of appearing at the bar of their country, and stating their principles, their belief, their practice as Christians and as citizens. In some cases, not to confute is to confess the charges. Silence would be in these circumstances treachery to themselves, a virtual and cowardly abandonment of their rights as free-born Americans and even a sort of apostacy from the religion which they profess.

"The language of their actions has hitherto been, it is true, clear and strong. Upon all occasions they have proved themselves peaceful, patriotic, and brave; prodigal alike of their blood and of their intellectual resources for the benefit of all. In the hour of danger they have fought under the banner of their country. In the time of peace, they have devoted energies to the education of her youth, that vital part of the republican system. But the religious excitement or hypocrisy of designing men heeds not or misconstrues that language so intelligible, we hope, to the majority of our fellow-citizens. It is lost upon those men in whose breast a holy zeal, as they call it, for the cause of Christianity and the welfare of their country has not left even a faint vestige of the true American spirit. The love of God and mankind is, in these men, incompatible with the sense and exercise of toleration and justice. They form, we know, a minority, but if they are comparatively few, they are vigilant, active, untiring. They penetrate and act everywhere. In the legislative hall and in the humblest cabin, in the pulpit and during the convivial hour, or in the domestic circle, the voice of slander is heard, and solemnly proclaims or insidiously whispers dark things of the Catholics. Their institutions are slandered, their tenets perverted, their attachment and fidelity to the country denied, the public indignation and proscriptive measures openly invoked against them; and, did we not know that we live in the nineteenth century —that we tread the American soil—that we breathe the free air of a republic—that the march of religious tolerance is onward—we might fear a return of those dark and bloody times, when the fiend of persecution reared his horrid head and appalled the world. The press wafts on her mighty wings, and spreads, in every place, from Maine to Florida, a contempt and distrust for Catholic principles, Catholic practices, Catholic institutions, and, what is more alarming, the persons of Catholics. The journalist, the novel writer, the essayist, and the divine unite to bring about the same end, and to crush the devoted Catholic.

"In several parts of the Union, our religious papers have done much to counteract the evil. But, as the attack is, so the defence should be, commensurate with our soil. Upon every point stands an enemy, therefore from every point should spring a friend and protector.

"With these views, and with due acknowledgment of the merits of our already established periodicals, we offer the *Catholic Advocate* to the West, to Kentucky and principally to our brethren in the faith."[2]

The idea of a religious paper for Kentucky was first suggested by B. J. Webb, who became publisher and proprietor. As early as 1830, he had the project already in mind and confided his plans to the Rev. Dr. Reynolds who afterwards was made second Bishop of Charleston. The priest gave him the highest encouragement and assured him that the clergy of the diocese would coöperate with his noble endeavor. To make the work a success, practical experience, however, was necessary and this could only be obtained in a printing office. As foreman in the job department of the Louisville *Journal,* Webb soon became master of the typographical art and was admirably fitted to undertake the task of publishing a Catholic journal. When the time came to embark on this new venture, he once more consulted Dr. Reynolds, who decided to use his influence with the faculty of St. Joseph's College to whom Webb had suggested giving the editorial control. With diocesan priests as its chief contributors, the publisher found no difficulty in obtaining the concurrence of the Ordinary in so laudable an undertaking. The Bishop assigned the task of editing to the Rev. Martin J. Spalding, the Rev. G. A. Elder, the Rev. C. H. de Luynes and the Rev. William Clarke. In the early volumes, the discriminating reader will find many articles marked by that elegance of style and diction that always graced the writings of the Rev. Martin J. Spalding.[3]

Father de Luynes also gave his rare talents to help along the cause of Catholicism in the West. He was of Celtic origin and hence possessed that vivacity of temperament so characteristic of Irishmen. His priestly education was obtained in the Seminary of St. Sulpice, Paris, where he was the classmate of the renowned Lacordaire. With him he had so close a friendship that the two young priests decided to unite their efforts in behalf of the Church of Christ. God had decreed otherwise: Father de Luynes was

---

[2]The Prospectus may be found in the first numbers of the *Advocate.* See also the "Life of Archbishop Spalding," cited above.

[3]"Centenary of Catholicity in Kentucky," by Hon. Benjamin J. Webb, p. 319, Louisville, Charles A. Rogers, 1884.

persuaded by Bishop Flaget to exercise his missionary zeal in the Diocese of Bardstown. In 1838, two years after the *Catholic Advocate* was established, he became its sole editor and kept that post amid the multiplicity of his priestly duties until the *Advocate* was removed from Bardstown to Louisville.[4] Father Elder's contributions were considerable. His principal themes were on matters relative to parental obligations. He was convinced that children were susceptible of moral guidance at a very early age and hence he tried to impress upon their parents the necessity as well as the advantage of an early religious training for the young.[5] Father de Luynes joined the Society of Jesus in 1841. His last years were spent at St. Francis Xavier's College, New York where he died, January 20, 1878.

Shortly after the *Advocate* office was opened in Louisville, the Rev. John McGill became chief editor. He was bound by ties of closest friendship with the publisher. This union of sentiments was further cemented by relationship, since the priest was Webb's brother-in-law. During Father McGill's editorship, the *Advocate* entered upon the best year of its existence. His well-known literary habits, pure taste, and exquisite critical judgment rendered him eminently well suited for the position. This champion of the Faith lived in an era of controversy and strife, when the whole of America was fomented even to deeds of violence against Catholics. He used the powers of his rare and gifted mind to beat back the surging waves of intolerance as they dashed with tempestuous fury against the Church.[6] Certainly one of his most successful efforts was directed against Dr. Craig, a minister of the Episcopal Church. This controversy appeared in the weekly numbers of the *Advocate*. Two works were published about the same time and abound in weighty and earnest thought. One was timely exposition of the doctrine of "The True Church," in which he showed the keen reasoning of a vigorous brain. He had a power of vitalizing argument by appeals to heart, to intellect, and to conscience, which always carried conviction to the souls of his readers. The other work, a translation of Audin's "Life of Calvin," appeared as a serial in the *Advocate*. Here he displayed

---

[4] *Ibid.*, p. 397.

[5] *Ibid.*, p. 278.

[6] About a decade afterwards, there was perpetrated in the city of Louisville, one of the most cruel persecutions of Catholics that this country has ever known. It almost rivals that destruction of life and property that took place during the Philadelphia riots. Bishop Spalding writing to Archbishop Kenrick a few days after the outbreak said: "We have just passed through a reign of terror, surpassed only by the Philadelphia riots. Nearly a hundred poor Irish or Germans have been butchered or burned and some twenty houses have been fired and burnt to the ground. The city authorities, all Know-nothings, looked calmly on and they are now endeavoring to lay the blame on the Catholics."

the purest taste as to words and to idiom, while his style possessed a grace and elegance that was admired by all.

The *Catholic Advocate* was conducted much after the fashion of other religious periodicals of that day. Considerable space was given to the defence and exposition of Catholic doctrine. As might naturally be expected, the idea of the former publication exercised an influence on the *Advocate*. Essays on literary and philosophical subjects were regularly treated. An effort was made to furnish a summary of the most interesting foreign and domestic news, and it mattered not whether such intelligence was religious or political, as long as it was desired by the Catholic reader. Consequently, in the files of the *Advocate,* the Church historian will find helpful information concerning the growth and progress of Catholicity in the West. At Louisville and Cincinnati, the proto-priest, Father Badin, passed his declining years. A letter which he wrote to the *Advocate* shows that he was beginning to lose his memory. The brief notice runs as follows:

"STEPHEN THEODORE BADIN: To his friends, greeting: As old age renders me forgetful and as I frequently leave at places where I may happen to be, books and various articles of clothing, and as my books which I have loaned have not yet been returned, I do hereby give such friends an invitation to forward such articles, especially my cloak, to the nearest residing clergyman, requesting him to have them delivered to me as soon as will be convenient. 'Reader, be not surprised at the request, the Apostle made a similar one.' "[7]

Another happy feature of the *Catholic Advocate* was a page of the choicest spiritual reading. Let us remember that the periodical was published at a time when books were not so numerous as now. What a joy and solace such reading must have been to the Catholic settler living alone in some wilderness in Kentucky. How pleasant to be able to employ the quiet hours of the Lord's Day with "Sunday Readings." Only the best masters were printed in the *Advocate*. Thus "True Devotion," by the renowned Abbé Grou, was presented to the readers of the paper during the course of the year 1839.

The *Advocate* chose as its lodestar the *United States Catholic Miscellany*. Like the great Bishop of Charleston, whose "powerful strokes presiding Truth impressed," the editors of the *Advocate* labored to inculcate the same lessons in style equally powerful. The Bardstown paper soon came to be regarded with special favor by all its contemporaries, and articles appearing in it were reprinted by other Catholic periodicals. If the *Advocate* imitated

---

[7]The *Catholic Advocate,* Vol. VIII, October 15, 1842.

the good taste of the pioneer *Miscellany,* it was destined also to sip like its chosen ideal the cup of wormwood. The history of the *Catholic Advocate* presents the same succession of distressing financial failures during the fifteen years of its troubled existence. We admire the courage and tenacity of purpose that characterized the propietor, Ben Webb, who shouldered all these burdens, and became, as it were a philanthropist in order that the Catholic religion might be propagated in the West. The *Advocate,* it is true, circulated in nine States, but the proceeds from such subscriptions barely sufficed during an existence of three years to cover the expenses of publication. When the See of Bardstown was moved to the more prosperous City of Louisville, the journal was established in the latter place and prospects seemed brighter for the publisher, but he was destined to be disappointed. In 1843, the total number of subscribers was but seven hundred and fifty. Yet at this very time, there were over twenty thousand Catholics in Kentucky alone.[8] How few indeed were the patrons in comparison with the population.

Seeing that support of the *Advocate* was so meagre, the Bishop addressed to his flock a pastoral letter in which he made a strong plea for subscribers. But episcopal approval woke no responsive chord in the hearts of the Catholics of Kentucky. In 1846 came the crisis. The publisher had borne his reverses with heroic fortitude, but during this year the losses sustained were so disheartening that he was compelled to register a complaint, though he disliked to do so. In his paper, he inserted a communication containing the following earnest appeal:

"In this issue the publisher of this paper appears in his own columns to ask of his subscribers in particular and the Catholic community in general an earnest and attentive hearing. There is much danger that the publication of this paper will be discontinued. Were it a mere individual enterprise, the publisher might gladly cease the struggle against accumulating difficulties and turn his attention to the pursuits in which he should be no longer harassed by doubts and embarrassed by failure. But he feels that such is not the character of this paper. To himself it has long ceased to be profitable, and he has come to look upon it as a Catholic enterprise, the failure or success of which is the concern of every Catholic within reach of its circulation. Viewing it in this light, he has been willing to contribute to its prosperity by unremitted attention and continued use of capital which, while it might have been profitably employed, has sunk with the sinking prosperity of the paper. Thus far has he labored.

---

[8]The *Catholic Advocate,* Vol. VIII.

He finds that his loss for the current year falls but little short of two hundred and fifty dollars. Add to this the interest of the amount of capital bestowed, and the labor and material employed upon the paper and you have a sum too large for a single individual to bear. From his capital, the publisher does not insist upon a return, but he does insist that he is no more bound to so heavy a loss than other Catholics in the diocese. He must be just to himself and to others, and he therefore is compelled to declare that if the subscriptions to the paper do not meet its expense at the close of this volume he must discontinue it. In that case the Catholics in Kentucky will be without an organ. They will have no adequate medium of defence and exposition. An outpost of strength will have been prostrated, a light darkened in their midst. Its place cannot be supplied by the pulpit. The preacher can not descend to the same minuteness of' detail, and many things in which the press is most valuable, are entirely beyond his province. He can not and does not speak the current history of the great Catholic world which, when means of communication are preserved, is moved with a common sympathy by the slightest cause as the ocean by the gentlest wind.

"Error speaks through the press and traduces our holy religion. Let the press answer and its refutation will go to ears on which the words of a Catholic priest would never have fallen. It will speak also to Catholics and convey edifying and interesting information which the limited means of some, and the local situation of others would have prevented from attaining. These things this diocese casts from herself.

"In Louisville, where this paper is published there are nearly five thousand Catholics—a number of itself handsomely competent to the support of this paper. But the fact is, in spite of this competency of numbers, that the paper is most wretchedly supported here. Nearly one-half of the subscribers residing in the city, have discontinued and the subscription list here is already too paltry in value to deserve a thought. Some take Catholic papers at a distance; this is highly praiseworthy, but they ought not allow their home paper, which is fighting all their battles to go without assistance. The conduct of the opponents of our faith contrasts but too favorably with ours. Their different organs in this city have a circulation of between two and three thousand persons. The publisher is willing to waive all profit provided he suffers no loss.

"The only time that the proceeds of this paper were at all adequate to the reasonable expectations of the publisher was in 1842, when the Rev. Ignatius Reynolds assisted the publisher in booming it.

"At the last Diocesan Convention, the assembled clergy made up a sum of one hundred and fifty dollars to meet any deficit in the income and to insure the publication of this paper for another year. The sum of itself is entirely insufficient for the end proposed. Nor could the publishers in any case accept it from them. He feels that he would be taking from the necessities of the poor and narrowing the slight income of gentlemen who do not now receive a sufficiency.

"Outstanding debts due to this paper to the extent of over three thousand dollars warn the publisher against the continuance of a system of credit. These people are resisting one of the engines of Catholic progress; they are doing an injury to the cause of religion."[9]

There was a note of sincerity in this letter which indicated that the publisher was in earnest and consequently subscribers took the warning. A meeting was called and measures taken to sustain the publication. This action by its friends did much to increase its patronage, but the appeal after a year or so was forgotten and the editor prepared to meet his fate. In 1850 the *Catholic Advocate* was consolidated with the *Catholic Telegraph,* of Cincinnati.

---

[9] The *Catholic Advocate* (1846).

CHAPTER XX

THE NEW YORK CATHOLIC REGISTER

When the New York *Catholic Register*[1] was established in September, 1839, its only competitor in New York City was the *Truth Teller*. Sufficient reliance could not be placed in this latter journal, since it had already soiled itself with trusteeism and could therefore no longer be looked upon as the authoritative mouthpiece of Catholics. A journal was needed that would meet the approbation of the Bishop. Consequently, in the prospectus the publishers of the *Catholic Register* asserted that it would be distinctly religious and contain only such intelligence as related to Catholicism.

The exigencies of the times demanded a journal that was not the organ of a political faction. Such indeed has been the position of the *Truth Teller,* ever since it leaped into the political arena in order to campaign for General Jackson. Party allegiance biased the judgment of its editor.

In an article which appeared in the first issue of the *Catholic Register,* the editor suggests the reasons why a new Catholic weekly has been rendered necessary. He says:

"For the long period of fifteen years, the Catholics of New York have been served with a paper, the utility of which is evidently proved by so long and uninterrupted patronage, but a vacancy has always been left, which the lovers of religion constantly desired to see properly filled. We need not say that we speak of the *Truth Teller,* which has always and actually is rendering very important services to the Catholic community, but being more of a political than a religious nature, it cannot present our doctrines on an extensive plan, though its columns have always been open to explain and defend them. Consequently, a paper exclusively religious is called for, and such is the *Catholic Register,* by which together with other Catholic contemporaries, we hope to accomplish the great object of defending our doctrines against errors and our community against calumnies."

Patrons of this new Catholic weekly acted wisely in giving their early aid and encouragement to the project. For when Governor Seward informed Catholics that part of the school fund might be

---

[1]The facts related concerning this paper are gathered from the pages of the periodical itself. As the journal had but one year of separate existence, further reference has been thought unnecessary.

theirs, if only they petitioned the legislature, the *Truth Teller* at once raised the hue and cry of a political plot. The sectarian press was not slow in picking up the slogan which the suspicious editor of the *Truth Teller,* blinded by self-interest, had suggested. During the year 1840, much interest was at all times manifested by the press in this situation so full of concern to Catholics.

The New York *Catholic Register* was owned by the firm of Gallagher and Smith. The editor, the Very Rev. Dr. Felix Varela, had had a long experience in Catholic journalism and was an author of many learned works. His activities in periodical literature we have recorded elsewhere. He edited the *Register* during the short span of its existence—a little more than a twelve-month. He avoided personal controversies of every nature, for he felt that the best defense of Catholic doctrine was a simple logical explanation of the Church's teaching. He aimed at offering the public the means of successfully counteracting the erroneous impressions almost daily derived from a hostile press, and more particularly from the religious newspapers of the country. He devoted part of the paper to disseminating useful knowledge of the arts and sciences. For this work his methodical mind was peculiarly adapted, since he had written several treatises on scientific and philosophical subjects. He likewise presented weekly an epitomé of the events occurring in Europe and America, that were most likely to interest a Catholic community. At the end of six months the *Catholic Register* counted over two thousand subscribers.

Encouraged by this patronage, Bishop Dubois placed a notice in the new periodical calling a meeting of the Catholics of New York to discuss the expediency of enlarging the *Register,* which at that time contained only eight pages of three columns each. Many Catholics attended, and resolutions were passed favoring a more extended sphere of action for this enterprising journal. Money was given by many present to help carry out the scheme. This money, however, was given only as a sort of loan, for it was to be returned, according to the provisions of a written agreement. The meeting then adjourned until a later date when a committee reported that sufficient money was on hand to warrant the publication of an enlarged newspaper, more dignified in tone and appearance and adorned with the choicest literary gems.

The necessity for this step was, perhaps, suggested by the appearance of a friendly rival for patronage. Another weekly newspaper, the *Freeman's Journal,* made its appearance on July 4, 1840. In its improved dress, the New York *Catholic Register* gave promise of long life, but rumors were soon afloat that it was about to be merged into the *Freeman's Journal.* As late as December 10, 1840, the *Catholic Register* denied these reports.

"In order to satisfy the minds of all concerned," it is stated, "we beg leave to give notice that such an union is not to take place, but it is the intention of the proprietors to struggle on independently with the firm hope that, overcoming the difficulties which press upon them, they will be able to continue and become established on a strong and lasting basis. It is necessary, however, to remind all our delinquent subscribers of their duties."

Between the above date and the first of January, 1841, negotiations were completed, and the *Catholic Register* did actually become merged in its contemporary and the name was retained with the double title, the *Freeman's Journal and Catholic Register.*

CHAPTER XXI

THE FIRST CATHOLIC MAGAZINE

At a time when religious tenets were becoming secondary considerations, when the sectarian mind was infatuated with idle nothings, when the pen and the scissors were constantly employed to rehash numberless old calumnies against the Catholic Church, there appeared in Baltimore, then the "Rome of America," the first magazine devoted exclusively to the defence of Catholic doctrine. The *Metropolitan*,[1] as it was appropriately called, was the product, not of one, but of many minds. Started in the beginning of 1830, when Catholicism had already obtained a firm foothold on American soil, its editor[2] and contributors were in a more favorable position to place the resources of their cultured minds on the shrine of holy Truth. And indeed some such review was necessary, where the doctrines of the Church might be seriously expounded to an educated yet a deeply prejudiced people.

In this magazine, the editor hoped to furnish a convenient vehicle of thought for the spread of Catholic teaching to people of inquiring mind in the United States. In his address to the public, found in the January number of the year 1830, the editor states:

"It has long been a subject of astonishment to many why, in the present important condition to which the Catholic religion has attained in this country, considering the number of clergymen scattered over the union, or living in the literary otium of our colleges, men who have, most of them been regularly trained in letters as well as to theology, and whose education, it is granted on all sides, fits them for any undertaking of this kind, it is astonishing, we repeat it, why so long a time has been suffered to pass without anything like a review or a magazine through which interesting and useful instruction might be conveyed to the inquiring mind and a medium afforded of defending ourselves against the attacks and misrepresentations of the malevolent and the ignorant."

This periodical, graced as it was with the approbation of the only Metropolitan of the Catholic Church in this country, gave the discussions an authority in the eyes of all, equal almost to the language of Rome itself. "It is our design," says its editor, "to

---

[1] The *Metropolitan Magazine* of 1830 and the prospectus of that periodical as found in contemporary Catholic journals are the chief sources of information for this narrative.

[2] The editor was the Rev. Dr. Charles Constantine Pise, who afterwards became affiliated with the New York Diocese.

strengthen the belief of those who appertain to the Church, to remove the prejudices of those who have been misinformed on these subjects, to induce all to read and instruct themselves and then to leave them to their consciences and their God."

Each number of the magazine contained forty pages on subjects chiefly theological. In January there were essays on "Reason and Faith," "St. Peter at Rome," "The Divinity of Christ," "'Ecclesiastical Researches" on the pontificate of St. Peter. Some of these subjects were continued in subsequent numbers. Information of value to the ecclesiastical historian may also be found in the pages of this magazine. In the January issue, for example, data may be obtained regarding the churches, and pious and charitable institutions of the City of Baltimore. The March number contains an article entitled "Notice of the Establishment of the Catholic Religion in the United States." The particulars of this sketch are taken from an old French manuscript preserved in the library of the Archbishop of Baltimore. The writing bears evidence that it was originally in English. Probably it was translated by Bishop Carroll. The facts contained in this document date back to 1625. This article is concluded in the April number. Another document of value to American Catholics is an "Extract from the Discourse on George Washington" delivered by the Right Rev. Dr. Carroll in the year 1800.

A number of journals such as the *Protestant,* the *Southern Religious Telegraph,* the *Christian Watchman,* and the *Christian Register* claimed the constant attention of the editor of the *Metropolitan.* The prejudiced newspapers attempted to metamorphose the evidences of Catholic truth into mere shadows, but the editors of the *Metropolitan,* skilled in the use of dialectics, made pygmies of these philistines. Against this power of verity and sound logic, these offenders were like stormy petrels far out on a raging sea, winging their flight to no determined point, tossed hither and thither on a tempest of the wildest chimeras, which the brain of man had ever invented. Thus, when men are unacquainted with the topics which they attempt to discus, they must necessarily lose themselves in a cloud of Cimmerian darkness and absurdities. The most benighted of these journals was perhaps the *Protestant,* which like a bat, shunned the light of truth. This, however, did not dismay the editor of the *Metropolitan.* "We will cleave to our cause," he says, "and with a courage not moved by threats or calumnies or assaults, we will propagate our religion, we will extend our conquests, and, since the God of truth is with us, we must rout the spirits confederated against us."

A severe criticism is also directed against the "Encyclopedia Americana," published at that time. The writer thus begins his appeal against this injustice:

"In the name of candor and honesty are we to witness, in silence, the palpable falsehoods, and sarcasms, with which this work abounds! Are we to sit down with folded arms and behold without emotion the American public imposed upon so grossly? No, we owe it to our honor, our fellow-citizens, our religion, to raise our voices—and that we may not appear mere angry declaimers, to point out in several articles the greatest absurdities."

The author of this article laments the facts that the tenets of the Catholic Church were systematically misrepresented in almost every publication of the day from the "Encyclopedia Americana" down to the smallest tract.

The defense of Catholicism in this magazine shows a scholarly knowledge of the writings of the Fathers. We find the authority of tradition on almost every page. For instance, one convincing writer, after a dip into patristic literature for proofs of divine doctrine exclaims: "If we are dupes, we err in company with Cyprian, Gregory, Basil, Chrysostom, Ambrose, Augustine, Leo, and the other champions of Christianity that won the admiration and the homage of the ancient Christian world."

That this magazine, filled with the brightest gems of Catholic truth, was allowed to perish after the brief existence of one year, presents but another sad example of the irony of fate. This periodical had all the claims to immortality but one,—patronage.

CHAPTER XXII

Catholic Juvenile Journals

The first Catholic juvenile paper,[1] published in the United States, appeared in Boston on March 31, 1830 under the same auspices as that of the *Jesuit, or Catholic Sentinel*. The object of this journal was to explain to children in simple language the principles of the Church's doctrine. The motive which stimulated the editor to supply our Catholic youth with such wholesome reading was the necessity of forming early in their young minds a correct knowledge of their holy religion.

During impressionable years, the seeds of faith are most easily implanted in the souls of children. The editors, in thus preparing the younger generation to meet the problems of life, were laying the foundations on which they expected to rear the edifice of a firm and lasting Catholicism in New England.

The *Expostulator, or Young Catholic's Guide* sought to teach its youthful readers those truths, which would enable them to answer everyone who should ask them for a reason of the faith that was in them. Here indeed was verified those words of the Royal Prophet: "Out of the mouth of infants and of sucklings thou has perfected praise because of thy enemies, that thou mayst destroy the enemy and the avenger."[2]

The *Espostulator* was a weekly newspaper printed by John Smith and edited chiefly by the priests in charge of the Cathedral parish in Boston. It contained four large octavo pages full of such matter as would cause children, aye even grown people, to yearn for more. Each week an essay on some moral subject was presented to the reader in a way that would especially appeal to his youthful fancy. The examples were generally drawn from Scripture and told after the manner of a story.

In the first number, a well written article on virtue gives in a pleasing and attractive style the main characteristics in the lives of Suzanna, Eleazar, Job and Tobias. In subsequent issues, the principal virtues are treated in a most fascinating way. Occasionally in the pages of the *Expostulator,* we find a short story or an exciting episode such as youth delights to read. Another feature was the exposition of Catholic doctrine in the plain and easy language of children. The editors were not slow to realize that these simple lessons would be read by many who, although

---

[1] The facts regarding this paper have been obtained by an examination of its files preserved in the University of Georgetown.

[2] Psalm VIII, 3.

kindly disposed towards Catholics, were nevertheless ignorant of her fundamental doctrines. Thus, while the paper was intended chiefly for children, it was read also with profit by adults.

Unfortunately, the *Expostulator* lasted but one year. The subscription price which was reasonable enough was one dollar and a half a year in advance. Very likely the difficulty of conducting and managing two papers under the same auspices soon became apparent to the editors. It was found more prudent therefore, during the stormy decade beginning with 1830, to concentrate all their efforts on the more important work of stemming the tide of calumny and persecution of the aggressive and illiberal Puritans.

The *Expostulator* was the first Catholic children's weekly paper. A few years afterwards, in 1838, there appeared in New York City, the first Catholic juvenile magazine.[3] In establishing this periodical, the editor was but following the example of the sectarian press. It was observed that their religious juvenile journals had increased almost ten-fold in a decade, and that these periodicals were being liberally patronized and most extensively circulated. Even the most mediocre could claim five thousand patrons, while some of the better class of children's magazines had more than thirty thousand subscribers.[4] These periodicals were but another means resorted to by the enemies of Catholicism to perpetuate among the rising generations the prejudices and hatred of their forefathers. They disseminated among the young, notions and rhapsodies entirely inconsistent with the spirit of Catholic truth. The faith of the Catholic child was also placed in imminent peril by the insidious attempts of the infatuated sectarians to fill the text books of the schools with the most pernicious falsifications of things Catholic. They endeavored to annihilate everything that Catholics hold dear and sacred in their holy religion.

With this avalanche of misrepresentation, which threatened to bury all vestiges of truth in its mad plunge, Catholics were compelled to struggle with might and main. But, as that icy mass of calumny, suspicion, ignorance, and contempt dashed against the Rock of Peter, it was shattered under its own impulse. In this defense, the *Children's Catholic Magazine* contributed its little share, for at one time it had something like thirteen thousand subscribers.

Soon after the magazine was started, the editor aroused the enthusiasm of his youthful patrons, by offering a handsome gold

---

[3] This juvenile magazine received favorable comment from the *Truth Teller,* the *Herald,* the *Advocate,* the Boston *Pilot,* and even such secular journals as the New York *Gazette* praised its efforts.

[4] The *Catholic Advocate,* Vol. III, 1838.

medal for the best literary article in prose or verse contributed by anyone under the age of eighteen. In the November issue, the result of this contest was made known. The prize was won by Matthew Horan, of Albany, who wrote a prose article entitled "A Walk or A Juvenile Defense of the Catholic Religion."[5]

A blunder of the editor in the first number of the magazine almost imperilled its existence. He printed a versified form of the Ten Commandments, but unfortunately the poet had employed the Protestant version. This led to a severe criticism of the little magazine and its editor. To prevent a similar occurrence, the Bishop deemed it prudent to place the paper under the supervision of the Very Rev. Dr. Felix Varela and it remained under his guidance until it ceased publication.[6]

The first number, appearing in March, 1838, contained a short but interesting sketch of the "Life and Character of Alfred the Great." In the November issue, there appeared a death notice of Daniel F. X. Perry. This young man snatched away in the prime of life, gave promise of a very brilliant career. From the age of two, he had been an inmate of the New York Orphan Asylum, and during his stay at that institution had won the esteem of all Catholics by his virtuous life and rare talents. Two of Ferry's compositions appeared in the first volume of the *Children's Magazine.*[7] These were written when he was only thirteen years old, and were specimens of a mind endowed with rare gifts.

These excellent qualities did not pass unnoticed by the Very Rev. Dr. Power, who in 1832 sent him to Rome to study for the priesthood. Ferry was not long in the Eternal City, when he was taken with a fever which compelled him to return to New York. Hardly had he arrived at his old Asylum home, when he died. The account of the funeral services are given in detail in the *Children's Catholic Magazine.* The obsequies took place in the presence of Bishop Dubois and many clergy. Dr. Power eulogized the life of the noble youth. No doubt Daniel Ferry was much loved by this excellent priest, for he says in the course of his sermon: "Little did I think, when I sent my bird to bask in the rays of an Italian sun that when he returned, it would be in the storm and with the arrow of death sunk deep into his bosom."[8]

In the fifth issue of the *Magazine,* the editor makes some observations and comments on the school books used at that time. Woodridge and Willard's texts attacked Irish Catholics with great

---

[5] The *Catholic Advocate,* Vol. III, 1838. See also "Records and Studies," Vol. XV, p. 160.

[6] *Records* of the American Catholic Historical Society, Vol. XV, p. 160.

[7] *Ibid.,* p. 161.

[8] *Ibid.,* Vol. XV, pp. 165 et seq.

vehemence, and this made the editor, George Gottsberger, somewhat indignant.   He declared his sympathy in behalf of oppressed
Irishmen with almost the passion of a Celt.

This magazine of not more than sixteen pages and not larger
than an ordinary prayer book was a source of annoyance to the
Protestant Vindicator (formerly the *Protestant*) and to the
Churchman, two of the strongest sectarian organs in New York
City.   A correspondent of the *Vindicator* unwillingly portrays
how "the wrathful skies gallowed these wanderers in the dark."
He states:

> "The Romanists are doing all in their power to disseminate
> their despotic and heathenish doctrines among us freemen,
> but they will find that enlightened America is not ignorant,
> superstitious, priest-ridden Ireland.   They are now employed
> in publishing popish works and establishing popish papers, a
> fund for which I know is made up here every year.   The
> Pope's senior head man here has lately laid by a special sum
> to publish a magazine to disseminate their dangerous doc-
> trines in disguise among our children and families.   This
> work is called the *Children's Catholic Magazine.*   It is the
> duty of every true friend of the religion of Christ to cry out
> against such base iniquity.   They dare not meet us openly,
> but take such Jesuit ends to endeavor to sow the seeds of
> anti-Christ in the bosom of our children.   May God bless
> our efforts to frustrate their design."

In the *Churchman* we find a subscriber writing that "the
Children's Magazine contained bigotry and superstition and was
a work which no Christian mother should give her child, unless
she wishes him to imbibe popish sentiments."[9]

The *Children's Catholic Magazine* lasted about two years and
then suspended publication.   A new prospectus stated that it
would appear again in April much enlarged and that the subscription rate then would be a dollar a year in advance.   The periodical,
however, did not resume publication until November.   The reason
for the delay was that sufficient patronage was not assured until
near the close of the year 1840.   The subscription price for the
first two years of its existence was fifty cents, but even at this
low rate it had many delinquents.   With all its improvements it
did not long survive, in spite of the fact that it received most
favorable comment from such leading papers as the *Truth Teller,*
the *Catholic Herald,* the *Advocate* of Louisville, the Boston *Pilot*
and the New York *Gazette.*   Under its old name it lasted only
another year.   There was a slight change in the title in 1840,
when it became known as the *Young Catholics' Magazine.*

---

[9] *Ibid.,* pp. 166 et seq.

CHAPTER XXIII

The Catholic Telegraph

The early efforts of the *Catholic Telegraph,* the oldest surviving newspaper of our Faith in America, is inseparably connected with the growth of the Church in Ohio. The founder of this journal was also the pioneer priest and missionary of that State, and became in the course of time the first Bishop of the Diocese of Cincinnati. The *Telegraph,* in one of its first issues, states that in 1810 Father Fenwick began to penetrate the forests of Ohio, whence he merited the title of "the Apostle of Ohio."[1]

To secure for him the benefits of a solid Christian education his widowed mother underwent many sacrifices. He was confided to the charge of the English Dominicans, who conducted a college at Bornhem near Antwerp, in Flanders. When his studies were completed, he became a member of the Order. He served his community faithfully for many years, first in the capacity of professor and afterwards as procurator. Shortly after he had assumed the latter charge, the French revolutionary army broke into Flanders, and the college at Bornhem became a prey to their devastating hands. The priests and religious of this convent were treated with the utmost cruelty, the college was seized, the properties of the Order were confiscated, and Father Fenwick himself was thrown into prison, where he was placed in imminent peril of death, but from which he was delivered, as he afterwards acknowledged with pious gratitude, by the special intervention of the Blessed Virgin.[2]

Once liberated, he set sail for the United States, the land of his birth, after succeeding in persuading his superiors that much good could be accomplished by the establishment of a colony of Dominicans on American soil. Shortly after his arrival, Bishop Carroll, whose diocese at that time was co-extensive with the Union, pointed out to his zeal and to that of his pious assistants the destitute missions of the West. In 1805 Father Fenwick made his first visit to the great Valley of the Mississippi. The stupendous task of gaining converts to the Faith and of tending to the spiritual needs of Catholics scattered over a territory extending from the Ohio River to the Great Lakes, required rare courage and self-sacrifice.[3]

---

[1] The *Catholic Telegraph,* Vol. I, No. 2, 1831.

[2] *United States Catholic Magazine,* Vol. VI, 1847, article, "Catholic Church in Ohio," No. 1, p. 25 et seq.

[3] *Ibid.,* p. 25 et seq.

In the twenty or more years that preceded the establishment of the *Catholic Telegraph,* as many churches were reared in different parts of Ohio, which fact shows that the zealous labors of Father Fenwick were beginning to bear fruit.[4] During that period, his missionary efforts were recognized and rewarded, for he was made the first Bishop of Cincinnati. But while we are recording the marvellous growth of the Church in Ohio, we must also mention that Catholics, there as elsewhere in America, were compelled to endure the bitter attacks of religious adversaries. Catholics saw themselves maligned and insulted and had no means of vindication. Their enemies conducted the secular and sectarian press, which endeavored to scatter broadcast the seeds of bigotry.

Among the gifts which Bishop Fenwick received while on a visit to Europe to collect funds for his new diocese, was a printing press which, immediately on his return, he set up in the Atheneum,[5] a college near the cathedral. On October 22, 1831, the first issue of the *Catholic Telegraph* appeared.[6] It was an eight page paper, twelve by nine inches in size, closely printed and without advertisements.

The first editor of the new journal was Father John Mullin, one of the priests of the cathedral, who, before he became a soldier of Jesus Christ, had spent his early life as a sailor on board a man-of-war. He wielded his pen as a spiritual sword in defense of the truth.[7] Hitherto the bigoted press had attacked the Church and her doctrines without fear of retaliation, but soon after the *Telegraph* appeared, these journals realized that a champion had arisen to defend the claims of Catholics against all who dared oppose them. Perhaps nowhere is the purpose of the paper more clearly stated than in the first number.

"The primary object in issuing the *Catholic Telegraph,*" says the editor, "is to aid the diffusing of a correct knowledge of the Roman Catholic Faith. By doing this, we are conscious of discharging a two-fold duty, namely, of contending earnestly for the faith once delivered to the saints, and of removing some of the difficulties, which prevent our dissenting brethren from rendering that justice to the ancient faith which a correct knowledge of its tenets would generally lead them to accede. Strict attention shall be paid to state the truth fully and fairly in the columns of the *Catholic Telegraph.* Truth has nothing to fear, while it must acquire new lustre from impartial scrutiny."[8]

---

[4]The *Catholic Telegraph,* Vol. I, No. 2, 1831.
[5]*United States Catholic Magazine,* Vol. VI, p. 25, et seq.
[6]The *Catholic Telegraph,* Vol. I, No. 1, 1831.
[7]The *Catholic Telegraph,* Vol. 75, No. 35, Aug. 30, 1906.
[8]The *Catholic Telegraph,* Vol. I, No. 1.

Father Mullin had an able associate in the person of Josue M. Young, who, besides being well-informed on many subjects possessed an excellent knowledge of the printer's art. It is related of him that frequently he stood at the case and without copy "set up a good editorial on almost any subject." He was a convert to the Catholic religion, and as he was on terms of the closest friendship with the priests of the cathedral whose companionship he chose, there daily grew in his soul a yearning to become associated with them in the ministry of the gospel. His success and ability in this higher vocation far exceeded his own expectations, for in the course of time he was consecrated Bishop of Erie.[9]

Under his management, the *Telegraph* grew in popularity and strength. The editor, in the second issue, contrasts the kindly reception that was accorded this Catholic paper with the blind intolerance that prohibited the erection of churches a few years before. The presence of a few unoffending priests at an earlier date was a signal to beware that "the wolf was upon his walk, that the ark was in danger; that a prompt and simultaneous effort was necessary on the part of the community to avert their civil and religious liberty." Sectarian zealots with glowing eyes and faces flushed, ascended the pulpits to spread the alarm. The Dark Ages were recalled. The terrors of the Inquisition were exhibited with all the grotesqueness that one would expect to find in a dime museum. With his distorted imagination, the religious devotee beheld the headless trunk and mangled bodies of innumerable Protestant martyrs. The *Telegraph*, however, was not deceived by this apparent sudden change of front. Other Catholic journals had experienced similar phenomena at their inception. The outbursts of wrath and hatred, that succeeded these words of welcome, showed that the suspicions of the Catholic editors were not at all ill-founded. Scarcely an issue of the early *Telegraph* can be found in which there are not evidences of a revival of the old prejudices uttered by many of the catch-penny journals of the day.

The Cincinnati *Journal*, a Presbyterian paper conducted by the Rev. Mr. Blanchard, especially came under the observation of its Catholic contemporary. Speaking of the *Telegraph*, the *Journal* referred to it as "the Papal Newspaper that had recently appeared in the city."[10] In the course of an editorial, Mr. Blanchard ventured to remark that "the right of every denomination in the country to publish magazines, pamphlets, books and newspapers in defense of their own peculiar tenets, is a beneficial result of Protestant principles."[11] What ingenuity! Yet this and similar

---

[9]The *Catholic Telegraph*, Vol. 75, No. 35, Aug. 30, 1906.
[10]The *Catholic Telegraph*, Vol. I, Nov. 5, 1831.
[11]*Ibid.*

expressions were frequently found in Protestant religious journals.

With each succeeding issue, the *Telegraph* waged a relentless war on the Cincinnati *Journal,* whose editor attempted to cover up his confusion by abusing Catholics with every species of insult. Finally he was beside himself with rage and in the words of the Catholic editor:

> "He gnawed his pen, then dashed it to the ground
> Sinking from thought to thought a vast profound.
> Plunged for his sense but found not bottom there,
> Yet wrote and floundered on in mere despair."[12]

We need make no apology for poetical exaggeration here, for later events confirm the impression that the Rev. Mr. Blanchard was a fanatic. Nothing gives us a better insight into his character than an occurrence which took place on Christmas Day, 1833. In the issue of the *Telegraph* of January 10, 1834, there appears the sensational heading "Editor of the Cincinnati *Journal* in Petticoats."[13] That the episode, so pitiful yet so ludicrous, may lose none of its force and flavor, the editorial is here reproduced as it appeared in the *Telegraph*:

> "Oh had the editor of the Cincinnati *Journal* the hundredth part of the consuming zeal of Dr. Poundtext, McBriar Mucklewrath or even Old Mortality he never would have stooped to assume the armorial of a woman for all the advantages which such a metamorphosis could procure for him. Yet the act bespeaks him a harmless pattern of a man, who could with so much apparent ease shrink into the dimensions of a girl to get a view *incog.,* of the doings of the Papists on Christmas day. No wonder the little 'Protestant Creature' was so astounded, when it beheld the splendid ritual opened, that contrasted so strikingly with the impoverished nudity of the new-fashioned worship. We trust, however, that he escaped unhurt and that the relacing of his corset strings has restored his breathing. We disclaim all intention to discompose even the gravity of his muscles, and in self-defense protest that his panic was the effect of his imprudence. We were wholly unconscious of his presence, a circumstance that prevented us from removing the misty medium which so woefully distorted his vision. For this apparent want of due courtesy, we beg leave to file a plea which cannot fail to hold us perfectly excusable, to wit: the waggish theologue was so encased in silks and shawls and ribbons; for mind, that it would have required the spear of Ithuriel to place him before us in his *propria persona.* We are not quixotic

---

[12] The *Catholic Telegraph,* Vol. II.
[13] The *Catholic Telegraph,* Vol. III, No. 2, Jan. 10, 1834.

enough to mistake a wind-mill for a giant, but if the chivalrous knight of the *Journal* desire to break a lance with the defenders of the ancient faith, he will easily find an opportunity, if he but leave his *feminine* coverings at home."

The reasons, why the prejudices of some of these settlers were so pronounced, must be traced to their ancestral training. The early pioneers of Ohio migrated thither from New England.[14] They formed the larger and more influential portion of the people. Moreover, they brought with them the time-honored Puritan sentiments regarding the Catholic Church. It became necessary for Catholics to dissipate the clouds of prejudice and misrepresentation which obscured the vision of their traditional enemies. The time was ripe for some one to speak authoritatively on the leading tenets of the Catholic Church, so that people might hear and know the truth.

The opportunity presented itself when the Rev. Alexander Campbelle challenged any Catholic clergyman to meet him and on an equal footing to discuss religious differences. Mr. Campbelle was a masterful orator and a strong debater. He generally swayed the multitudes who came to listen to him. The *Telegraph* was but fairly established, when some persons invited him to give a course of lectures in Cincinnati. The enthusiastic ovation which he received on that occasion indicated that a religious strife would be engendered, if steps were not taken to avert it. His attacks on the Catholic Church were so flagrant and insulting, that they aroused the indignation of Bishop Purcell. In a communication sent to one of the daily papers, the prelate took the Rev. Mr. Campbelle severely to task for attempting to stir up religious animosity among the peaceful citizens of Cincinnati. Then came the challenge. People looked anxiously about to see who would pick up the gauntlet. It was generally believed that Catholics would choose their ablest theologian. What was their surprise, then, when Bishop Purcell, at that time in the prime of life, offered to meet Campbelle. History has already recorded what the result of the controversy was. The learned bishop's persuasive language gained for him a complete victory. An account of the discussion may be found in the *Telegraph* for the year 1837.[15]

In the ninety-nine years of the *Telegraph's* career, there was but one short suspension due to the prevalence of cholera in the city. As early as August, 1832, the dread disease was beginning to claim its victims in the West. During the month of September,

---

[14]*Uunited States Catholic Magazine*, Vol. VI, pp. 26 et seq. See also *Telegraph*, Vol. 75, No. 35, etc.

[15]See files of *Telegraph* for the year 1837. Also *Telegraph*, Vol. 75, No. 35, etc.

the first pioneer Catholic journalist succumbed after a hard fight against the scourge. A few weeks later, Bishop Fenwick, while making visitations in his diocese, was taken sick. Father Martin J. Henni was sent for, but before he reached his destination the distinguished prelate died. He writes: "I witnessed only the mound which contained his remains."[16]

The second Bishop of Cincinnati was the Right. Rev. John B. Purcell, whose debate with the Rev. Alexander Campbelle we have just noted. Like his predecessor, he realized the usefulness of a Catholic journal as a means of propagating and defending the doctrines of the church. After the paper had proved itself worthy of his confidence, he gave it his official approbation. "Next to the administration and reception of the sacraments," he says, "we desire nothing more earnestly than the circulation and reading of the *Telegraph.*" Other bishops also made it the organ of their dioceses. Thus in 1850, the Sees of Cincinnati, Louisville, Cleveland, Vincennes, and Detroit gave it episcopal approval.

At no time was the *Telegraph* ever a money-making scheme. The revenue derived from it as years went on, was indeed small, but the receipts were turned to good account. The proceeds were used for publishing books and tracts to be distributed among non-Catholics. The works reached persons to whom the newspaper itself was but little known. Thus an inestimable amount of missionary labor was performed, and the prejudices against the ancient Faith were gradually uprooted.[17]

Under the editorship of the Very Reverend Edward Purcell, the paper was much enlarged and its usefulness was extended. He was assisted by the Rev. Sylvester A. Rosecrans, who afterwards was elevated to the new See of Columbus. The patronage of the paper would have been greatly increased, had not Father Edward Purcell shown himself at all times a proud, defiant, disagreeable autocrat towards the priests of the diocese. Archbishop Purcell owed much of the financial troubles of his later life to the mismanagement of his brother.

Doctor Rosecrans, his associate, was undoubtedly a man of singular attainments, who labored zealously for ten years at his appointed task. "His journalistic work," writes a later editor, "could never be mistaken. It bore always the stamp of a mind rich in thought and of crystal clearness. The Faith never had in this country a more able defender."[18]

When Doctor Rosecrans departed for his new See in Columbus, his place as associate editor was filled by Captain R. E. Farrell,

---

[16] *Telegraph,* Vol. 75, No. 35.
[17] See files of *Telegraph* for the year 1839.
[18] The *Catholic Telegraph,* Vol. 75, No. 35, etc.

who had lately served in the Army of the Tennessee. He remained with the paper for only three years. In 1865 William Foos, formerly of Wilmington, Ohio, was appointed to that position. This new editor soon left the *Telegraph* and T. A. Corcoran was next chosen.[19] In May, 1869, another change occurred, and the assistant editorship was given to the Rev. J. F. Callaghan, who later on in the same year became proprietor of the journal. He chose as his assistant Thomas F. Galwey, who gave excellent service to the *Telegraph* for many years, and afterwards accepted a similar position on the editorial staff of the *Catholic World*.[20] In 1880, Doctor Callaghan made a visit to Rome and at that time placed the paper in the hands of H. W. I. Garland. In this layman the *Telegraph* possessed a person of rare talent. He was exceptionally well-read in literature and other subjects, and possessed great versatility in applying knowledge which he had acquired. Mr. Garland in his day had travelled much and could speak several languages. In 1878, a few years after his conversion to the Catholic faith, he drifted from England to America. Shortly after his arrival here, he attached himself to the staff of Father Cronin's Buffalo, New York, *Catholic Union*. Here his rich fund of information and easy style were very much appreciated. When he assumed charge of the editorial department of the *Telegraph*, he made many notable changes which greatly improved its condition. But the aged Archbishop Purcell was sinking under the burden of the disastrous failure brought about by those under his charge.[22] These were trying times for the young editor, because it was hard for him to adapt himself and his style to the clientele of the *Telegraph*. Some supported the Archbishop, others attacked him bitterly. Mr. Garland, "a stranger in a strange land," felt the difficulties of his position and longed to escape from them. He was weary of the petty bickerings round about him, and heartily "sick of Catholic journalism" as he saw it, until his death came, in 1882.[23] The words of the *Telegraph* on this sad occasion are true and full of meaning. They write his epitaph: "He died among strangers, a stranger in a strange land, by strangers tended, by strangers mourned. By strangers' hands his eyes were closed, whose last light would gladly have rested on the scenes and the faces which gladdened them in childhood. But now he is at peace."[24]

The ownership of the *Telegraph* soon after the death of Mr.

---

[19]*Ibid.*

[20]*Ibid.* See also *Freeman's Journal*, Nov. 11, 1882.

[22]*Catholic Telegraph*, Vol. 75, No. 35. See also *Freeman's Journal*, Nov. 11, 1882.

[23]*Catholic Telegraph*, Vol. 75, No. 35.

[24]*Ibid.*

Garland passed to Owen Smith,[25] but ill-health in 1890 compelled him to seek other fields of duty, and the paper was next purchased by Joseph Schoenenburger, who at one time was editor of *Der Wahrheitsfreund*.[26] In 1892, the Right Rev. Rector of St. Mary's Seminary, Father Mackey, became editor, until the following year, when in place of his name in that capacity there is printed a list of the leading contributors to the journal.[27] About this time grave fears were expressed that the oldest surviving Catholic newspaper was soon to perish. To the credit of Cincinnati's leading Catholic laymen it was saved from the fate of so many of its contemporaries of other days. Undoubtedly the one who at that period underwent the greatest and most heroic sacrifices was the genial Doctor Thomas P. Hart.[28] Here was a man high up in his profession, hazarding his time, his means and his chosen avocation, that the *Catholic Telegraph* might live and grow. Except for one year, when Charles J. O'Malley was associate editor, Doctor Hart has continued alone in his editorial work.[29]

But the *Catholic Telegraph* was yet to be tried in the crucible of tribulation. A notice in heavy black type in the issue of February 26, 1903, tells the sad story: "The office of the *Catholic Telegraph* with all its appointments, is at present writing a mass of raging flames."[30] Everything but the contents of the safe were destroyed. Not a file of the paper escaped the ravages of the fire. This loss, however, was repaired by the generosity of two of its patrons who furnished the office with their own greatly treasured volumes of the *Telegraph*. After this adversity, the pioneer journal arose once more from the ashes that seemed to spell its ruin and to-day, three decades since its unlucky experience, it still labors in behalf of God and truth. One whose name must not be omitted from the long list of those who have given valuable service to the *Catholic Telegraph* is Miss Anna C. Minogue. Her brilliant talents, good taste and rare executive ability have in late years done much to give to it an elegant literary finish.[31]

As we look back upon the century of the *Telegraph's* existence, there is one note more striking than all else. It is the persistent effort made by its various editors to sustain the *Catholic Telegraph* in the face of almost insurmountable difficulties. Other papers had passed through similar experiences, but had succumbed to the stroke of fate. This, as already stated, had at no time a pecu-

----

[25]*Ibid.*
[26]*Ibid.*
[27]*Ibid.*
[28]*Ibid.*
[29]*Ibid.*
[30]*Ibid.*
[31]See current issues of the *Telegraph*.

niary interest to subserve and here we may say was the secret of its strength. Like its contemporaries, it realized the apathy of a large part of the Catholic population towards sustaining religious journals which were fighting their battles. But it was not disheartened by this indifference. Its policy at all times was to educate the Catholic mind to recognize and appreciate the value of the services that Catholic journals were rendering. Thus in March, 1833, the *Telegraph* makes the following plea:

> "While every sect and shred of a sect throughout the land sustains each of their numerous periodicals devoted to their interests, and almost all of them are more or less engaged in distorting our doctrines and misrepresenting our practices, it is a consideration addressed to the duty, the zeal, the charity for his neighbor, the pride, the ambition, the interest of every intelligent and virtuous Catholic to aid in sustaining the few which are engaged in their defense."[32]

When once Catholics saw the necessity of supporting a religious journal, which would defend them from the attacks of their enemies, efforts were made for the founding of a sort of lay apostolate, making the *Telegraph* an organ through which they were to propagate the word of God. In the issue of December 14, 1839, such a society was proposed. It was known as the Catholic Society for the Diffusion of Knowledge. It had two chief objects: the sustaining of the *Catholic Telegraph,* and the diffusing correct information on Catholic tenets by the publication of standard Catholic works. An initiation fee of twenty-five cents was charged. A standing committee of five persons, elected quarterly, was empowered to take charge of the paper in all matters, except its editorial department, which was to remain wholly under the control of whomsoever the bishop might appoint. We have no record how long this lay apostolate was kept up. No doubt a great deal of good was accomplished by distributing Catholic books and tracts among non-Catholics. This brought many to examine and embrace the true Faith.

The most trying ordeal that the paper had to face was at the time of the Civil War. Before the opening of hostilities, it repeatedly stated that the "Southern people had cause for complaint."[33] At the election of Lincoln, the paper boldly asserted, "no Catholic hands have done this deed of treason—no Catholic votes pursued the Southern citizen to injury and oppression."[34] When war broke out the *Telegraph* ceased its criticism. Personal views were smothered and loyalty's banner was unfurled. In fact

---

[32] The *Catholic Telegraph,* Vol. II, 1833.
[33] The *Catholic Telegraph and Advocate,* 1859.
[34] *Ibid.,* 1860.

the editor states his views in emphatic terms: "We thought that the South was imposed on by the North," he says, "but now individual opinion must yield to the obligation we owe to the Union."[35]

The course pursued by the *Telegraph* during this crisis saved it from an ignominious death. It is true that it lost many Southern subscribers by casting its lot with the North. In fact, the war policy embarrassed J. P. Walsh, who had been the publisher for eleven years. He was compelled to withdraw on account of loss of patronage. John Hermann, proprietor of *Der Wahrheitsfreund,* rather than see the paper perish, undertook to publish both papers, until such a time as the *Telegraph* might find itself on a good financial basis.[36] The trials and vicissitudes borne by the editors during these stirring times had their reward. The cause of Catholicism was benefited in the West by the praiseworthy attitude of the *Telegraph.* To the loyal conduct of its editors throughout the whole course of the war, must be attributed that sustained vigor which has supported it in all subsequent troubles.

No more appropriate conclusion can be given to this history of a remarkable journal, than the words of him who added such lustre to its pages.

"The *Telegraph,*" wrote Editor Garland, "has done some service to God and country. In the long past it has encountered some of the trials which St. Paul has recorded in the history of his own life. But like him it survived them. It has seen the birth and death of scores of Catholic journals in this country. It has enjoyed the constant generous attachment of thousands of friends and the implacable hatred of enemies. In defending the Catholic truth, it never spoke with uncertain voice. It never faltered and played poltroon and coward in the thick of any battle, when the rights and interests of Catholics were at stake. It has defended Catholic altars and Catholic firesides with costly loyalty, that only the tongue of falsehood can question. If, during its long life, it has had trials, it has won enduring honors—and will most probably reap the same harvest in the future. Its past record marked deep with the true lines of Catholic journalism points out the course it will pursue."[37]

---

[35]*Ibid.,* 1861.
[36]The *Catholic Telegraph,* Vol. 75, No. 35.
[37]The *Catholic Telegraph,* Vol. 75, No. 35.

CHAPTER XXIV

The Pilot

In the *Boston Pilot,* the immediate successor in Jaunary, 1836, of the *Literary and Catholic Sentinel,* the inception of which has already been noted, one decided improvement over the method of conducting the *Literary and Catholic Sentinel* was made. Pepper's activities were confined to the literary and the news departments of the *Pilot,*[1] and Doctor Bartlett was given charge of the religious department. Bartlett, a convert, was a practising physician, who recently had moved to Boston, where he opened an office at the home of Thomas Murphy, 22 Atkinson Street.[2] The bombastic language of Pepper was in marked contrast with Bartlett's well written paragraphs, and must have amused the more intelligent of the *Pilot's* readers.

The journal had been running only about two months, when an accident to Dr. Bartlett incapacitated him for writing. His professional duties also kept him so occupied, that for some time he could give no attention to journalism.[3] Ill-health finally forced him to resign his position as religious editor and in a few weeks he died.

In the brief period that Dr. Bartlett was editor of the *Pilot,* he had been assidious in promoting the Catholic cause. His studies had been extensive and his learning profound. Although beset by enemies, who did not fail to persecute him by every means in their power, he freely forgave his assailants. He had many amiable qualities which must have endeared him to a large circle of the *Pilot's* readers. His father was a Unitarian minister of Marblehead who left his son unimpeded in his investigations of the proofs of the Catholic Faith. Dr. Bartlett became a Catholic and never hesitated in his acknowledgment of the Truth, though some of his old time Puritan friends bitterly chided him for his course.

Soon after Bartlett's death, Pepper severed his connection with the *Pilot,* and not many weeks afterwards followed his associate to the grave. After Pepper died, the paper struggled on for a few months and then Devereux withdrew. This left Patrick Donahoe alone as the conductor of the journal, and handicapped by lack of patronage, it suspended publication on January 7, 1837.

After a brief interval, Mr. Donahoe again summoned up

---

[1]The *Boston Pilot,* Vol. I, No. 1.
[2]The *Boston Pilot,* Vol. I, No. 1.
[3]*Ibid.,* Vol. 1.

sufficient courage to give Catholic journalism in New England another trial and he revived the *Pilot*. His efforts were praiseworthy and wonderful, when we consider the limitations of his early education. While yet a youth he entered the office of the *Columbian Sentinel,* where he learned the art of printing. We can imagine how difficult the task was for this pioneer, when he states that, during the early years of the *Pilot,* his only aid he had in printing, editing and circulating the paper was that of two girls and a boy. The number of subscribers to the *Pilot* at the end of nine years was but five hundred.[4]

The *Pilot* of that day was a national rather than a religious newspaper. The Irish of New England read it, because it contained news from Ireland. Every issue was filled with long discussions on the Repeal Movement, which helped to build up the paper's circulation, and Donahoe was able to place the conducting of it once more in the hands of an editor, and to give his personal attention to the business side.

About 1842, there came to New England a precocious youth of about the age of seventeen. Shortly after his arrival, he delivered a speech on the Repeal of the Union, which so captivated his hearers, and Donahoe was himself so impressed with the youth's ability, the subject and treatment of his oration, that an offer of employment on the *Pilot* was made and accepted by him.[5]

This youth was Thomas D'Arcy McGee. In less than two years, he became editor of the paper. McGee lacked that solidity of judgment age and experience bring. He was full of the bubbling enthusiasm of the youth, who does not weigh well the consequences of his actions. Some of his radical editorials in the *Pilot* made Patrick Donahoe daily more and more uneasy, as the revolutionary agitation of the Young Ireland Party progressed, fearing that McGee would compromise the orthodoxy of his paper.[7] One of his contemporaries, Orestes A. Brownson, later speaks of this portion of McGee's life in tones of sharpest criticism. "If our friend McGee," he remarked, "who is now doing such noble service in a good cause, had not been brought up a Gallican and taught to believe that his religion had no concern with his politics, he had never occasioned the scandals which nobody deplores more than he does."[8]

The situation was relieved by an invitation from the Dublin *Freeman's Journal* for McGee to return to Ireland and join its staff. He did so but soon left that paper to become one of the

---

[4]*Records* of the American Catholic Historical Society of Philadelphia, Vol. XV, p. 315.

[5]"The Story of the Irish in Boston," J. B. Cullen, 1889.

[7]Contemporary journals criticized the *Pilot* severely, especially the *Catholic Telegraph* and *Freeman's Journal*.

[8]"Brownson's Works," Vol. II, p. 113.

brilliant corps of Young Irelanders who aided Davis and Duffy in getting out the historic *Nation*. When the government began to suppress the movement and arrest its leaders, McGee, who was one of the most active and efficient of them, escaped disguised as a priest to the United States. In New York he published a paper called the *Nation,* but got into trouble with Archbishop Hughes on account of his revolutionary ideas and violent diatribes against the priesthood in their relation to Irish politics. He moved to Boston, changing the name of the paper to the *American Celt,* and somewhat modified his radicalism. Then he moved it to Buffalo, New York, and back again to New York City, where in 1857, he sold it to D. & J. Sadlier & Co., who on its relics established the *Tablet*. McGee then went to live in Canada, where, at Montreal, he published another paper the *New Era,* and became a prominent figure in Canadian political life, changing his political view and advocating British supremacy. The Confederation of the British Colonies of North America, as the Dominion of Canada was due largely to his initiative. His new political course made him very obnoxious to his former patriotic associates and his attacks on them so embittered their feelings that he was assassinated, at Ottawa, on April 7, 1888, by an overwrought fanatic. Sir Charles Gavan Duffy, his old associate of Young Ireland and the Dublin *Nation,* draws this portrait of him after he came to the United States:

"His life was wasted in barren controversy . . . He found his true work later. In Canada he became the leader of the Irish immigrants, a great parliamentary orator and one of the founders of the New Dominion. As the minister of a free state he developed unexpected powers and was universally recognized as a gifted and original statesman.

"No man ever had distinguished services more grudgingly admitted. He had gifts which placed him on a level with the best of his associates, and for years he applied them exclusively to the service of Ireland. As a poet he was not second to Davis, as an orator he possessed powers rarer and higher than Meagher's—persuasion, imagination, humor and spontaneity. There is only one act in his life for which I offer no defence. He came back to Ireland and pampered the pride of her enemies by repudiating his early career."[9]

Following McGee as editor, the Rev. John T. Roddan, a very able man who had been educated at the Propaganda College, Rome, carefully directed the *Pilot* and won it national circulation. Prominent among his contributors aiding in this were the Rev. Dr. D. Moriarty, the Rev. John Boyce, New England's

---

[9] Duffy, "Four Years of Irish History," p. 775.

first Catholic novelist; Dr. J. V. Huntington; Charles Bullard Fairbanks, the classic "Aguecheek," and Michael Hennessy, whose papers on Irish-American history and genealogy over the pen name "Laffan," were a most popular and widely read feature for more than a generation.

In 1852, Father Joseph M. Finotti, compiler of the important "Bibliographia Catholica Americana," formerly a member of the Society of Jesus, became the literary editor of the *Pilot*. Besides his duties on the weekly journal, he was pastor in Brookline. A diary, some five volumes in all, which he wrote during these years, shows that the publisher and the editor were frequently at odds as to the best method of conducting their paper. Very likely the eccentricity of character was mostly on the side of Father Finotti.[10]

With the *Pilot* Patrick Donahoe also conducted a most successful book publishing concern which had a long list of Catholic and Irish books, valuable and useful additions to current literature. An agency for passage tickets and remittances to and from Ireland developed into a profitable private banking concern and he became one of the most prosperous Catholics in New England.

In striking contrast to the conduct of many other Catholic weeklies, the Boston *Pilot's* attitude before and during the War of Secession was highly commendable. In an attempt to explain the attitude of Catholic journals, Dr. Brownson bestowed great praise on the *Pilot*:[11]

"Up to the actual levying of war against the government," he said, "the great body of our Catholic population undoubtedly sympathized with the South. They were attached to the Democratic Party, whose strength had always been in the slave-holding States; they were, many of them like ourselves, strongly attached to the doctrine of State rights, which was made the basis of the right of secession; and the metropolis of the Catholic colony was in Baltimore, a city of strong Southern sympathies. They had been taught to regard the abolitionists as Puritan fanatics and dangerous to the peace and safety of the Union; and the Democratic journals had assured them that the Republicans were only disguised or undisguised abolitionists. But when the rebellion broke out and its real character and purposes became manifest, Catholics very generally in the loyal states, especially Catholics of foreign birth, and their children born here, refused to support it. To their shame be it said, the old American Catholics in the struggle of the nation for life, have proved

---

[10] A manuscript copy of Father Finotti's diary is preserved in the Georgetown University archives.

[11] *Brownson's Works*, Vol. 20, p. 247.

themselves far less American, far less loyal than the foreign-born Catholics settled amongst us. Boston Catholics, nearly all belonging to a recent migration, have been far more American than Baltimore Catholics claiming to be descendants of the Maryland pilgrims. The Boston *Pilot* has been far less un-American than the Baltimore *Catholic Mirror;* and the Pittsburgh *Catholic,* edited by both foreign-born and foreign-educated Catholics, has shown a far more patriotic spirit than the *Telegraph* and *Advocate,* whose senior editor is an American and a convert."

But Patrick Donahoe did more than advocate a strong Union sentiment among his readers. When the war broke out, he took an active part in the organization of the volunteers for the defense of the Union. When the Ninth Regiment of Massachusetts, composed entirely of Irishmen, was formed, he was made treasurer of the fund for its equipment and preparation. On the day of its departure for the front, he gave ten bags of coin, each containing one hundred gold dollars, which he requested Colonel Cass to distribute among his soldiers. The Twentieth Regiment, called the *Faugh-a-Ballaghs,* also received his valuable assistance, and he aided the soldiers at Camp Cameron near Cambridge during the first years of the War.[12] No doubt, the *Pilot* suffered severely during the progress of the rebellion, but when hostilities were over, it gained more than it had lost by its unswerving loyalty to the Union. In the thirty or more years that Patrick Donahoe had conducted the *Pilot,* he had built up a comfortable fortune.

The *Pilot,* however, was not to escape unscathed. In November of the year 1872, a great fire swept the City of Boston, and the fine granite block, in which was the home of the *Pilot* and the publishing concern which cost about one hundred and fifty thousand dollars, was completely destroyed. Over one hundred thousand dollars worth of stock, machinery and fixtures were consumed. New quarters were selected on Washington Street, when another conflagration, eleven days after the first, visited this new office and once more the whole establishment was reduced to ashes. With the little resources still remaining, a third attempt was made to restore the paper; this time on Boylston Street, but before six months it was again destroyed by fire. Nothing daunted Mr. Donahoe, and for the fourth time he revived the journal.[13] When this announcement appeared the following paragraph was printed in the *Pilot*:

"When a fire comes to Boston nowadays, it comes looking round all the corners for its old friend the *Pilot.* It is evident

---

[12]"The Story of the Irish in Boston," by J. B. Cullen, p. 227.
[13]"John Boyle O'Reilly, His Life, Poems and Speeches," by James Jeffrey Roche, p. 135.

that the fire has a rare appreciation of a good newspaper and a good companion to pass a brilliant hour. Nevertheless we do not want to appear too light-hearted on this occasion; it might lead people to think that a fire was not of much account anyway. Of course, we are used to being burnt out and it does not affect us much after the first mouthful of smoke and cinders. But when it comes to us three times in seven months, we protest. We are not salamanders; the oldest phoenix of them all would get sick of such a gaudy dissipation. For the remainder of our lives in Boston we want the fire to let us severely alone."

But the spectre of misfortune still haunted the *Pilot*. This time disaster, more serious, was to overtake Patrick Donahoe. The private bank, which he had conducted for many years, failed in 1876, leaving him with liabilities amounting to nearly seventy-five thousand dollars. The cause of these financial troubles mainly was Mr. Donahoe's kindness, benevolence, and charity. People in trouble came to him for assistance, and his purse strings were always loosed. He was in the habit of endorsing their notes, and in this way he lost almost two hundred and fifty thousand dollars. These reverses could have been borne, had they occurred over a period of years, but coming as they did at the same time as the losses occasioned by three successive fires, his fortune dwindled almost to nothing.[14]

Archbishop Williams came to his rescue and purchased the *Pilot* retaining a three fourths interest in it with the object of repaying the bank's indebtedness, the other fourth going to John Boyle O'Reilly, who had been editing the paper since 1870. The Archbishop also made O'Reilly the business manager of the paper and arranged to have the bank's depositors paid their claims in yearly instalments. Mr. Donahoe resumed his foreign exchange and passenger agency, and in 1878 established a monthly periodical called *Donahoe's Magazine,* which soon attained substantial success. In 1891 his heroic efforts to rebuild his fortunes were crowned by the repurchase of the *Pilot* and he resumed its control with all his old time ardor. Notre Dame University conferred the Laetare Medal on him in 1893. Despite his years of toil he carried on the business of his publication until March 18, 1901, when he died at his home in Boston in his ninetieth year.

John Boyle O'Reilly, who remained as editor of the *Pilot,* began his career as a printer in Ireland in the office of the Drogheda *Argus.* After he had obtained a fair knowledge of the typesetters art, and shorthand-reporting he worked for newspapers in various English cities. When the Fenian Brotherhood

---

[14]*Ibid.,* p. 135. *Records* of the American Cath. Hist. Soc. of Phila., p. 331.

was organized, he became one of its more ardent enthusiasts. In 1866 he was arrested on the charge of treason, tried by a special military commission and sentenced to twenty years penal servitude. After he had been an inmate of the six English prisons of Pentonville, Millbank, Chatham, Portsmouth, Dartmoor and Portland, he was transferred in October, 1867, to a convict settlement in Western Australia, where having endured its privations and hardships for some time, he made up his mind to escape. The preparations for his departure, as well as his actual embarking, were arranged by the Rev. Patrick McCabe, a Catholic priest, who attended to the spiritual needs of the political prisoners in the settlement. The many trials, the lack of food and even of drink, and the exposure to inclement weather which he experienced during his week of anxious expectation for a vessel, rival anything that can be found in romances of the sea. Finally he could wait no longer and set out in an ordinary row boat, exposing himself to the perils of the deep and almost despairing of reaching a ship that would take him aboard. At last an American whaler signalled to him. In utter exhaustion he sank on the deck of the Gazelle, and when he had sufficiently recovered, told the crew of his marvellous escape. At the Cape of Good Hope, he boarded the Sapphire of Boston, then bound for Liverpool. There he disguised himself as an American sailor, and again took ship, this time on the Bombay, which carried him to the United States.[15]

All the events which we have here related, occurred in 1869, when John Boyle O'Reilly was but twenty-five years of age. The following year he received editorial employment on the *Pilot*. Almost the first task given him by Patrick Donahoe was to accompany the Fenian expedition into Canada, and to report the activities of the organization for whose cause he had undergone the greatest sufferings and trials. As correspondent for the *Pilot* he criticized this ill-organized expedition, with frankness. After 1870, when the Fenian Movement languished, perhaps no one regretted it less than O'Reilly himself.[16]

Hardly had he returned to Boston, than the Orange riots in New York became the talk of the hour. O'Reilly did not defend the Catholics on this occasion, but on the contrary severely rebuked them for their unruly party spirit.[17]

In addition to his editorial work O'Reilly contributed many of his poems to the *Pilot*. The musical rhythms of his verse were but the pulsations of a heart ever noble, ever patriotic, ever brave.

---

[15]"John Boyle O'Reilly, His Life, Poems and Speeches." See also Cullen, "The Story of the Irish in Boston," pp. 207, et seq.

[16]"John Boyle O'Reilly, His Life, Poems," etc.

[17]*Ibid.*

James Whitcomb Riley once paid the following tribute to the poet of the *Pilot*:[18]

> Singers there are of courtly themes
> Drapers in verse—who would dress their rhymes
> In robes of ermine; and singers of dreams
> Of gods high-throned in the classic times.
> Singers of nymphs, in their dim retreat,
> Satyrs, with scepter and diadem,
> But the singer who sings as a man's heart beats
> Well may blush for the rest of them.
> I like the thrill of such poems as these—
> All spirit and fervor of splendid fact—
> Pulse and muscle and arteries
> Of living heroic thought and act,
> Where every line is a vein of red
> And rapturous blood all unconfined
> As it leaps from a heart that has joyed and bled
> With the rights and wrongs of all mankind.

The "Amber Whale" and the "Dukite Snake" were among the first of his efforts at narrative verse. The former appeared also in the New York *Tribune* whose editor, Horcae Greeley, gave O'Reilly a tempting offer to join the staff of that paper. But this was met by a counter-offer from the publisher of the *Pilot*. In 1874, O'Reilly was receiving a salary of three thousand dollars a year and the next year he was offered four thousand.[19] This, however, did not represent his net income, for he was being handsomely paid by magazines and newspapers for his splendid contributions. He was regarded at that time as a poet and a journalist of national reputation. In the issue of July 11, 1874, O'Reilly contributed a poem to the *Pilot* in which he rose to sublime heights of thought. His writings always had a purpose. Their intention was to elevate the soul to nobler and higher ideals, or to teach some lesson. In this excellent production, he inveighs strongly against what in our day would be called "race suicide." We shall quote one passage, full of bold and strikingly original figures:

> Ho, white-maned waves of the Western Sea
>   That ride and roll to the strand.
> Ho, strong-winged birds, never blow a-lee
>   By the gales that sweep toward land.
> Ye are symbols both of a hope that saves
>   As ye swoop in your strength and grace,
> As ye roll to the land like the billowed graves
>   Of a suicidal race.

---

[18] "O'Reilly, His, Life, Poems," etc., p. 300.
[19] *Ibid.*, p. 126.

> Ye have hoarded your strength in equal parts,
>   For the men of the future reign
> Must have faithful souls and kindly hearts,
>   And bone, and sinew, and brain.

No journalist crossed words with his Catholic contemporaries oftener than did Dr. Orestes A. Brownson. Perhaps, in his whole career, this master of dialectics never found a man more worthy of his steel than was John Boyle O'Reilly. The occasion for a vigorous combat came, when the editor of the *Pilot* wrote something which aroused the indignation of the philosopher. The *Pilot's* policy, since O'Reilly had been editor, was one long energetic struggle to unite the struggling factions of the Irish race into a strong and powerful nation. Religious differences which had always been the obstacle of such union, were ever regarded by the editor as a matter to be set aside. Nothing provoked O'Reilly more than to meet intelligent men clinging to the notion, that a Catholic Irish party was the only means of saving Ireland. Dr. Brownson took exception to the *Pilot's* repeated appeals on behalf of Irish Protestants, and as the philosopher thought such an advocacy unbecoming in one professing to be a Catholic, a lively conflict ensued. Dr. Brownson, while reviewing a book written by a clever Irishman, R. Shelton McKenzie,[20] singled out the *Pilot* for stern rebuke.

To the broad-minded editor of the *Pilot,* this attack was more bitter than the most energetic misrepresentations of the Nativists and Know-nothings. He let loose his pent up indignation and assailed Brownson with sharp censure.

Stiff as were these battles between the two editors, no hard feelings were created thereby. When *Brownson's Review* ceased publication in the following October, O'Reilly wrote words full of generosity and kindness for his old time foeman:[21] "Farewell, staunch and fearless old man! You have done a large labor and have done it in full manhood and good faith. Those who objected shall be the first to praise. Your life has been a success as every life must be that follows principles through light and darkness."

As O'Reilly appreciated Brownson, so Brownson appreciated O'Reilly. He was glad when he found a person who showed himself a thinking man, ready to grapple with any question. He felt that the great need of the Catholic people in America was the creation of solid Catholic literature. No one came so near filling the high ideal set by Brownson than did the editor of the

---

[20] McKenzie was literary editor of the Philadelphia *Press* and among other works wrote a life of Charles Dickens. He also edited Shiel's "Sketches of the Irish Bar."

[21] "O'Reilly, His Life, Poems," etc., p. 149.

Pilot. "He struck his harp and nations heard entranced." O'Reilly's whole work, even his prose productions, thrill us with the lofty sentiments that he breathed into them. Being a man of intellectual prowess and courtly demeanor, he dignified Catholic journalism by everything he wrote.

But not merely as a poet and journalist did John Boyle O'Reilly captivate his readers. He achieved eminent success as a story-writer and a novelist. In the *Pilot* of November, 1878, he began a serial story entitled "Moondyne," which afterwards appeared as a book and passed through twelve editions. If it was extensively read, it nevertheless received some severe criticism. James Alphonsus McMaster, editor of *Freeman's Journal*, frowned on this novel as being pagan and un-Christian. To this censor, the editor of the *Pilot* replied with his usual dignity.[22]

"Hasty and harsh and unjust judgment," he said, "are no proof of good will; yet we are willing to believe that Mr. McMaster means every friendly word he has written. That 'Moondyne' should be mistaken for a pagan does not seem possible, but, from the testimony of friendly critics, we are willing to conclude that his silence on the matter of creed may be misconstrued. It was not the author's intention that 'Moondyne' should be thus mistaken; it was directly opposite to his intention. To demand of a Catholic author that his chief character shall be a Catholic is absurd. A novelist must study types as they exist. The author of 'Moondyne' made a study of a man who might be typical of the penal colony, evolved by the pressure of unjust laws on erring but human lives. To have put a Catholic or Protestant *preacher* in the position might have pleased some; but he saw fit to put the man there who actually belonged to the place. The leading traits of 'Moondyne' were mainly studied from life. The author had before him a strong, virtuous, silent man, cognizant of all the wrongs of the law, sympathetic with all the suffering, saying nothing, but *doing,* so far as his power enabled him, the full duty of a wise, honest and Christian man. He saw the injustice of existing laws, and he foretold the day when all human codes should be tested, not by the needs of a government, but by the expressed and immutable law of God.

"There is not, could not be an anti-Christian word in 'Moondyne.' If there were, it should not stand one moment. The words put up and knocked down by Mr. McMaster were not in 'Moondyne.' They are his own.

"Mr. McMaster calls on the author of 'Moondyne' to sub-

---

[22]O'Reilly, His Life, Poems," etc., p. 186.

mit to authority. It is impertinent to speak so to one who has not rebelled against authority, who respects the law and the author as profoundly as the editor of the *Freeman*. We must remind Mr. McMaster in a friendly but firm way that *he* is not 'authority,' nor must all who dare to write a book submit to him for approval."

To give an exact appreciation of John Boyle O'Reilly's work belongs rather to literary criticism than to the realm of history. Hence we have contented ourselves with recording but a few of the most remarkable events that characterized his career as a journalist. His sudden death by accidental poisoning, October 10, 1890, startled the whole country. Being troubled with insomnia, he had taken some medicine which proved a fatal sleeping potion.[23] For his untimely death heartfelt sympathies were expressed on all sides, and the City of Boston honored his memory by a great citizens' meeting in Tremont Temple. On that solemn occasion the Hon. Patrick A. Collins, his companion of twenty years, gave expression to the sadness that filled his soul. With these tender words we shall close the career of one of the most talented Catholic journalists that America has ever known:

"Even in this solemn hour of public mourning," said his old time friend, "it seems hard to realize that we shall see him no more. Men who knew us both will expect from me no eulogy of Boyle O'Reilly. You mourn the journalist, the orator, the patriot of two peoples—the strong, tender, true, and knightly character. I mourn with you and I also mourn alone. But after all, the dead speak for themselves. No friend in prose or verse can add a cubit to his stature. No foe, however mendacious, can lessen his fame or the love humanity bears him. Yet we owe not to him but to the living and to the future, these manifold expressions of regard—these estimates of his worth. The feverish age needs always teaching. Here was a branded outcast some twenty years ago, stranded in a strange land, friendless and penniless; to-day wept for all over the world, where men are free or seeking to be free, for his large heart went out to all in trouble, and his soul was the soul of a free man; all he had he gave to humanity and asked no return. Take the lesson of his life to your hearts, young men, you who are scrambling and wrangling for petty dignities and small honors. This man held no office and had no title. The man was larger than any office, and no title could ennoble him. He was born without an atom of prejudice and he died without an evil or ungenerous thought.

---

[23]"O'Reilly, His Life, Poems," etc., pp. 363 et seq.

"He was Irish and American; intensely both, but more than both. The world was his country and mankind was his kin. Often he struck, but he always struck power, never the helpless. He seemed to feel with the dying regicide in 'Les Miserables': 'I weep with you for the son of a king murdered in the temple, but weep with me for the children of the people—they have suffered longest.'

"Numbered and marked and branded; officially called rebel, traitor, convict, and felon wherever the red flag floats; denied the sad privilege of kneeling at the grave of his mother— thus died this superb citizen of the Republic. But his soul was always free—vain are all mortal interdicts. By the banks of that lowly river, where the blood of four nations once commingled, in sight of the monument to the alien victor, hard by the great mysterious Rath, over one sanctified spot dearer than all others to him, where the dew glistened on the softest green, the spirit of O'Reilly hovered, and shook the stillness of the Irish dawn on its journey to the stars."

After the death of O'Reilly, the *Pilot* was placed under the editorial direction of James Jeffrey Roche, who conducted it until he was honored by President Roosevelt in 1904 with an important appointment in the American Consular Service at Genoa.

He was followed by one who had been for years on the editorial staff of the *Pilot,* Miss Katherine Eleanor Conway and whose experience in Catholic journalism admirably fitted her for this responsible position. For many years, she had been a reporter for the Rochester *Daily Union,* and a correspondent and contributor for several of the New York newspapers. Bishop McQuaid, of Rochester, saw in Miss Conway qualities that were soon to make her a successful journalist. He opened his library and gave her great encouragement by his personal direction. In 1873, she began a little Catholic magazine called the *West End Journal.* This periodical she conducted until 1878, and at the same time was a contributor to the Philadelphia *Catholic Record* and certain New York story papers. After that date, she accepted a position as assistant on the *Catholic Union and Times,* which she held until 1883, when she went to Boston and became an editorial writer on the *Pilot.*[24] Like James Jeffrey Roche she was continually in the literary atmosphere of John Boyle O'Reilly and, as time went on, acquired a share of the great journalist's literary taste. She occupied the editorial chair of the *Pilot* until 1908. The older generation that supported the *Pilot* had died out, and with the changes of years and customs, the growth of other diocesan weeklies the *Pilot* lost its national circulation and prestige so the Donahoe family sold the paper to the Archbishop of Boston who made it a local diocesan organ.

---

[24]Cullen, "The Story of the Irish in Boston."

CHAPTER XXV

Der Wahrheitsfreund

The greatest benefit which the Very Rev. John Martin Henni, afterwards Archbishop of Milwaukee, rendered to the German Catholics of the Middle West was the establishment of *Der Wahrheitsfreund,* a German Catholic newspaper.[1] He saw clearly that the newly arrived Catholic immigrants from Germany stood in need of some enlightened instruction both in matters touching their religion and their citizenship in the republic. He realized that the best results could only be obtained by a periodical capable of reaching the Germans scattered, as they were, on farms in the forest regions of Ohio and Kentucky. He knew that the best means of uniting his people in the work of building up the Church in those States, was to furnish them with a newspaper that would acquaint them with the activities of their neighbors. In addition to this, he recognized the difficulties that foreigners must encounter in a strange land among strange people. To lessen as far as possible the obstacles to their progress, he intended to procure for them suitable means to promote their civil welfare. The institutions of democracy were to be examined, American customs and laws studied, and the great political questions of the day treated with sufficient detail to give Germans in America a knowledge of political affairs, that would make them intelligent and desirable citizens.

The spirit of the times called for a journal, which would protect the civil and religious liberties of Catholics against their stern and stubborn adversaries. The whole doctrine of the Catholic Church, her faith, her morals, her discipline, and her history were as much misrepresented to the German settler as to the English-speaking citizens on the coasts of New England. The same intolerance, which had occasioned the scenes later witnessed in Boston, Philadelphia, and Louisville, was present everywhere; for at that period, Catholicism was but poorly understood by those whose prejudices had existed for generations. Truth pent up within the four walls of a church could not hold in check the monstrous lies that were poured out from thousands of presses. America was deluged with books, pamphlets, and reviews; and foreigners were not immune from their influence.

The newspaper that was destined to do effective work in re-

---

[1] The facts regarding *Der Wahrheitsfreund* are taken principally from a book entitled "Dr. Johann Martin Henni, ein Lebensbild aus der Pionier-Zeit von Ohio und Wisconsin," von Martin Marty, O. S. B.

pelling the enemies of the Catholic Faith among the German people was appropriately named *Der Wahrheitsfreund* (*The Friend of Truth.*) At the top of the first page of the journal, directly over its title, the princely Archangel Michael was pictured, as treading under foot and piercing with a spear the infernal dragon. This ensign was happily chosen, for it represents the successful struggle of the power of light over that of darkness.

The prospectus represented all the disadvantages under which the German settlers labored, namely deprivation of the means of beneficial reading in their mother-tongue, the lonesomeness because of separation from the happy associations of their native land; ignorance of the laws, customs, and the idiom of the American people, the lack of Catholic churches. The editor then showed how a German paper would help to minimize all these inconveniences.

The paper was to consist of two departments, one religious and the other secular. In the religious section, it promised to give its readers an exposition and defense of the dogmas of the Catholic Church; there were to be essays on its history in all ages; and finally the latest information regarding the Catholic Faith in Germany and America. The purpose of the secular department was to give an account of the more important political events occurring in Europe and America; a special review of affairs in Germany was to be made for each weekly issue. The surplus receipts derived from subscriptions were to be applied to the support and welfare of German orphans.

Before drawing up this prospectus, Father Henni sought the advice of wise counsellors as to the best plan of conducting a good German paper. Among others he wrote to Father Demetrius Gallitzin, the Prince priest of Loretto, Pennsylvania, who sent him a letter, part of which reads:

"I must take the liberty to remark that the most, yes, I must say all the Germans who come to America are uneducated persons, who read their prayer books and their catechisms and perhaps can write a little, but whose intellectual faculties have never been developed. He who writes for such people should write in a well-measured style so that he may be understood. But perhaps I am in error, for I speak only about those Germans that live in this county. They belong without exception to the working classes, who must earn their bread by the sweat of their brow, and they therefore cannot spare much time for intellectual training. What regards the Germanizing of these simple Christians; I will leave to your judgment, whether or not you can accomplish any good among the German people."

The letter was gratefully received, but it is certain that Father

Henni was not much influenced by its sentiments. It merely shows that he systematically sought the opinions of men of experience, far and near, before he embarked on a venture, much of the success of which depended upon getting a proper start.

A brief survey of the first number, dated July 20, 1837, will give us the spirit in which the paper was conducted in after years. The following features are found in that issue: A translation of certain decrees of the Third Provincial Council of Baltimore held in April; an essay on the subject of unbelief; an editorial entitled "Religion," which contained an address to the readers of the paper; an article on the Presbyterian Church, giving particular attention to the lack of unity between the old and new school; an attack on the Cincinnati *Evening Courier* for publishing misrepresentations about Catholics. Then followed the secular department in which the news of the day was briefly told.

While Father Henni was editor, Mr. Lehmann, the publisher, states that he was strict in observing his sacerdotal duties. He was always ready to visit the sick and administer the Sacraments to them. He was a zealous friend of the poor, a father to the widow and the orphan, a shepherd who sought the lost sheep and brought them again into the fold. In the printing office, too, he was loved by all, and none was ever known to murmur when obliged to work over-time, especially when, as was sometimes the case, copy was delayed. Everyone in the office instinctively knew that it was not the editor's fault, but that the duties of his office had hindered him. His good nature attracted people of all conditions to seek his aid and advice, so that those who knew him intimately often wondered how he found time to edit a newspaper.

Father Henni was eminently successful in his attacks upon the hostile sectarian press. The *Protestant,* a religious journal conducted by George Walker at Germantown, Ohio, was anxious to battle with him, but was soon forced to retreat. Dr. Nast, who edited the *Apologist,* was the next opponent to face the editor of *Der Wahrheitsfreund.* He retired from the encounter with even greater confusion than did the editor of the *Protestant.* Dr. Nast, raised a Lutheran, had in quick succession professed Deism and Pietism, and finally ended by declaring himself in favor of Methodism. For one of such fickle temperament, Father Henni easily found arguments that quickly silenced his adversary.

Controversies of this nature were unprofitable to the readers of *Der Wahrheitsfreund,* because the trend of such discussions was difficult to follow. Polemics were therefore avoided as much as possible, and, in their place, lighter and more useful expositions of Catholic doctrine were substituted. As time went on, laymen became interested in the work Father Henni had previously carried on almost single-handed. Clement Hammer, then residing in Detroit, whose writings were attracting considerable notice, went to Cincinnati and became a regular contributor to *Der Wahr-heitsfreund*. Father Franz Ludwig Huber also aided the progress of German Catholic journalism by placing his excellent and well selected library at the service of the editor, and of such as felt disposed to contribute articles to that periodical. Frequent sketches on the activities and the condition of the Catholic Church in various parts of the West were written by Joseph Kundeck and Mr. Kundig. An active propaganda was waged by the paper against the Nativist Party. "Every unprejudiced American will admit," remarks the editor in one of these articles, "that without the labor of the Irish, very few railways and canals would be built, and that the best and finest colonization in the land is due to the presence of the Germans and the Dutch." In 1842, an article on "Secret Societies" contributed to the Cincinnati *Volks-bühne* attracted the attention of *Der Wahrheitsfreund,* whose good-natured editor replied by composing a dialogue, the object of which was to stop the criticism of Catholic doctrine on this question by the opposing journal. In this article, the Pastoral of Archbishop Hughes on secret societies formed part of the dis-cussion, and explained the attitude of the Catholic Church to-wards such associations. The treatment had the effect of silencing all further prejudicial remarks on this question.

In those stormy times *Der Wahrheitsfreund* was truly a beacon light whereby the faithful were guided to the haven of safety. Many a German Catholic family was encouraged and strengthened in its faith by the fine spiritual tone of the paper. The circula-tion might have been larger, and the amount which the Orphan Association received was always very slight. Money was very scarce, especially in the years of the journal's infancy. The sub-scription of two dollars and a half was not much, when considered by itself but in those days there were a hundred other needs for money. Homes, schools, and churches had to be built and sup-ported. After the first year, advance payments were demanded, and thus *Der Wahrheitsfreund* was preserved from the fate of so many other papers of that epoch. Doctor Herman Lehmann was publisher for the first six year of its existence, after which time he purchased it from the German Orphan Union and for many years conducted it at his own expense. In 1843, Doctor Max Oertel the famous Lutheran convert, became the editor and he held that position until April 2, when he went to New York to start a new German paper called *Die Kirchenzeitung*. From 1846 to 1850, it was under a man of great ability, Anton Böckling. With the increase of German Catholics and an improvement in their condition, the periodical became yearly more and more prosperous. In 1847, a daily edition, the first American Catholic daily in any language appeared, but the project not proving a success, it was soon discontinued.

When the Revolution of 1848 broke out in Europe, many refugees came to the United States. At that time there drifted to America one George Fein, who, soon after his arrival, went to Cincinnati with the express purpose of causing as much trouble to the German Catholic population as an unlimited vocabulary and a good pair of lungs would permit. The daily papers, at that time nearly all hostile to Catholics, gave him notoriety and he attracted many listeners to his lectures. His attacks grew more and more furious, so that Catholics feared a repetition of the disgraceful Philadelphia riots in Cincinnati. Recognizing that fire, murder and bloodshed might follow in the tide of prejudice that was rising in the city, Mr. Lehmann, though advised not to notice the calumnies of this incendiary was thoroughly aroused. "We cannot keep silence in this matter," he said, "without conceding thereby that right and truth are not on our side. By continuing in this course, Catholics will become discouraged, will grow lax in their convictions, apostasy from the Faith will be the effect, and that is just what the enemy wants. The material harm will not hurt as much. Let them destroy my printing establishment. Let them level our churches, schools, and parish houses; these we can build up again—but the churches and schools that shall be made empty by apostasy can be of little use to us or our posterity."

Catholics had accepted the challenge malignantly hurled at them, and *Der Wahrheitsfreund* set to work to neutralize the influence of this slanderer. Fein knew that a newspaper battle would be prejudicial to him. Recent experiences had suggested caution. If he was to be forced out of Cincinnati, he was anxious to leave with the appearances of victory, so he hit upon the plan of addressing the people from a public platform. He invited his opponents to attend the lecture and to respond after he had finished his speech. If they did not present themselves, it would be understood that fear of their opponent had kept them away. The invitation was accepted, however. The publisher and the editor of *Der Wahrheitsfreund* were given a conspicuous place in the front row directly under the eye of the speaker. The plan was to occupy most of the evening in heaping ridicule on these Catholic champions, and to make things so disagreeable that they would seek relief in flight. If they fled, of course the report would be circulated that they were unable to defend themselves against so able an opponent, and before a prejudiced public they would be scoffed at the more. Should this scheme fail, Fein was to consume the whole time with his discussion and thus leave no time for a rejoinder.

He began his speech by relating the great ovations he had received in Wein, Berlin, Frankfurt, and London; but he said that he never found anywhere such infamous Jesuits as he beheld in

Cincinnati. He then paused to await the effect of that utterance, and voices resounded in different parts of the hall: "Where are they? Where are they?" He pointed the finger of contempt at the two silent spectators in the front seat and said: "There they sit." At this hundreds of voices thundered: "Hang them. Hang them." These shouts were partly drowned by whistling, hissing, and stamping, which lasted many minutes. These demonstrations were repeated many times during the evening. Mr. Böckling, the editor was not at all disconcerted by this treatment, but took a pinch of German snuff and handed the box to Mr. Lehmann with an air of satisfaction. The speaker kept up the discussion on Jesuitism until one o'clock in the morning, when his tired audience showed signs of unrest. When the crowd dispersed, the publisher and editor went directly to the printing office to prepare their reply. This appeared next morning in the daily edition of *Der Wahrheitsfreund*.

Fein, seeing that his plot did not work successfully, and knowing that his adversaries were not practiced debaters, challenged them to an oral discussion. This strategy placed the editor in a somewhat embarrassing situation which became still more complicated, when a volunteer appeared in the person of Doctor Ciolini, an eccentric old physician, who was at one time a Catholic. He offered himself as champion against the German Goliath. The editor was on the point of refusing the offer of this suspicious interloper, when Archbishop Henni of Milwaukee advised the acceptance of the challenge but to sign only "Doctor." This step outwitted the arch-conspirator, who immediately guessed that his opponent was none other than Dr. Henni, a skillful debater. Fein declined to meet his adversary because he had not declared his name. The people of Cincinnati began to see that Fein was nothing but an adventurer, and his once ardent admirers forsook him. After the downfall of this intriguer, there came an era of peace. The clouds of intolerance were vanishing and the sunshine of better days for Catholicism was in sight.

During its ninth and tenth years *Der Wahrheitsfreund* abandoned the quarto size and adopted a small folio page. This form was found inconvenient for binding, so it reassumed a quarto size, but the number of pages was doubled. In its twenty-first year, a new and handsomely illustrated title was adopted. Herman Lehmann remained as publisher until August 31, 1850, at which date he sold the journal to Joseph Hemann. After fifteen years of excellent service this German Catholic journalist, disposed of *Der Wahrheitsfreund* to Benziger Brothers, who retained it until it ceased publication in 1910.

The editors of this journal had brief tenures of the position: J. N. Probst conducted it for a month; Peter Kroeger took up the work in January, 1851, and continued it until December, 1854. Then Anton Böckling, who had once occupied the editorial chair with such success, again took that position; but served only two years. The next incumbent was Francis J. Brandecker, who was editor from March, 1857, till September, 1862. At that time there was formed an association of contributors consisting of Messrs. Miettenger, Fasse, and Riedal; but this plan was discontinued when the Benzigers became its owners. The following editors also conducted it for short periods, some of them not extending their services over a year: Franz Furger, A. Schwenniger, H. Baumstark, J. M. Blum, Joseph Bürgler, Alvis Jeuttner, and Benno Ritter.

CHAPTER XXVI

The Freeman's Journal and Catholic Register

The early years of the *Freeman's Journal,* like those of all pioneer newspapers, were filled with disappointments and financial embarrassments. Its first editors, James W. and John E. White, nephews of the Irish novelist, Gerald Griffin, commenced its publication about the middle of the year 1840 with the brightest hopes of future success,[1] but after more than a year's experience, they realized that Catholic journalism was a losing investment, and disposed of the paper to Messrs. Eude and Walsh. James White, when retiring, spoke of the excellent results obtained in the face of many difficulties. Ever since the first day of issue, it had been the constant, untiring, and on more than one occasion, the sole advocate among the press of New York for a modification in our system of public instruction. Mr. White, while editor, did not relinquish his practice of law. The embarrassments as well as the excessive labor of his joint pursuits resulted in serious injury to his personal affairs, and he was soon compelled to withdraw from newspaper work.[2]

After Mr. White's departure, Eugene Casserly, son of Patrick S. Casserly, whose name we have already met in connection with the New York *Register and Catholic Diary,* became its editor, much against the wishes of his more experienced father. The *Truth-Teller,* which had long since fallen from grace, attempted by its antipathy to the new editor to regain lost popularity. William Denman, whose combative and explosive temperament had forced George Pepper, editor of the *Irish Shield,* from New York City in 1829, now exerted himself to blast the character of Casserly. In the issue of March 2, 1844, the editor of the *Freeman's Journal* warned his enemies that he would bear in silence the reproaches of his father, but as to the newspapers and the persons who wished to place a stigma upon him he would not endure, and he admonished them that should necessity require it, he would seek the protection of the law.[3] John T. Devereux also had an interest in the paper for some time, but retired when Bishop Hughes became the proprietor in 1842.[4] In the space of two years, the journal had changed hands four times. The Bishop placed its management in the hands of his secretary Father James Roosevelt

---

[1]The *Catholic News,* April 11, 1908; *Freeman's Journal,* Vol. 50, Feb. 23, 1889; *Freeman's Journal,* Vol. 1, No. 1.

[2]The *Catholic News* and *Freeman's Journal,* as cited above.

[3]*Freeman's Journal,* Vol. IV, May 2, 1844.

[4]The *Catholic News,* April 11, 1908.

Bayley, but in spite of this zealous priest's efforts, it sank to so feeble a state that it became a serious burden on the Bishop's hands. Indeed the trouble and worry of conducting the *Freeman's Journal* was so great, that in 1848 he decided to dispose of it outright. On March 27 of that year, he instructed Father Bayley, to write the following letter to Orestes A. Brownson, then in Boston:[5]

"The Right Reverend Bishop, having resusciated the *Freeman's Journal* from the state of debility into which it had fallen, is desirous to turning it over into some good safe hands. He has authorized me to write to you, to inquire if you would be willing to take it out and out. Its affairs are in a very sound state, no debt, and a good clean list of subscribers. It would afford you at present a clear income of twelve or fifteen hundred dollars, which might be doubled without difficulty."

The proposition, however, did not seem to attract Brownson.

About this time, James Alphonsus McMaster made his appearance as a journalist. Early in this year he contemplated starting a semi-monthly magazine in New York. "You will smile at the name I have chosen for it," he wrote to Brownson, "Possibly you may not like it—it is to be called simply *Ave Maria.*" Later on in the year, during the month of June, it seems that McMaster abandoned the idea of starting a review, and instead he planned a semi-weekly, independent, Catholic newspaper. No doubt the fears of the Bishop were by this time aroused, when he heard of the whole scheme, for he was certain that two papers could not thrive, where one was merely obtaining an existence. McMaster in the meantime had sought advice from several priests, who seem to have given him great encouragement. At any rate on June 12, 1848, he wrote:

"The clergy, many of whom have been spoken to, approve of it, and as regards the Bishop, I shall tell him before I begin, but I neither ask nor expect his consent. I may shock you awfully. I do not consider that it appertains any more to his jurisdiction, than to arrange the colors of the coats I shall wear during the summer. I hope for a wide circulation, as it is to have no diocesan trammels, no responsibilities; and it is to give the news oftener, fuller and more correctly than the lumbering things that they call 'Irish papers'. Our friend, George Hecker, is interested and volunteers to advance, or, if need be, lose the money necessary in the undertaking."[6]

Again this project of McMaster came to naught. Not long

---

[5] *Ibid.* See also Brownson's "Middle Life," also "Later Life."
[6] The *Catholic News,* April 11, 1908.

afterwards, however, he entered into an agreement by which he obtained the control of the *Freeman's Journal,* the money for financing the enterprise having been obtained from the Hecker family. During the years that preceded McMaster's long règime, in Catholic journalism, many important events had transpired in New York.[7]

The *Freeman's Journal* providentially began its existence at a time, when a well managed periodical was of the greatest value. The School Question was the grand issue among the Catholics of New York. Their object was to obtain from the Legislature a portion of the fund for educational purposes, to which they had contributed as citizens of the state. Petitions had already been forwarded to Albany, when an unfortunate editorial appeared in the *Truth Teller,* which stupidly endeavored to convert what was purely a question of Catholic principle into a political one. The *Truth Teller,* with characteristic bitterness, questioned the motives of the great body of Catholics, who were trying to secure only that which was theirs in justice. The warfare started by this discredited journal was eagerly seized upon by the Church's enemies as a pretext for beginning the same hostility on a larger scale and with greater vehemence.[8]

We can best appreciate the turn of events by an article which appeared in the *Freeman's Journal*[9] on November 20, 1841:

"The public mind for the two weeks past," says the editor, "has been plied on the subject of Bishop Hughes and the School Question with every description of newspaper rhetoric, from the dull calumnies of the hypocritical *Sun,* and the worthless outpourings of a still lower and more maligant vehicle, to the frantic falsehoods of the *New Era,* the *Journal of Commerce,* the *Commercial Advertiser,* and other similar organs of bigoted cliques and interested politicians. No vengeance seemed too heavy to be invoked by those pure and moral censors upon the head of him who warned a people whom he was bound to protect, to beware of political leaders, who had become the partisans of an intolerant monopoly, notorious as the irreconcilable foe of their and their children's rights. A clamorous outcry of proscription and denunciation was raised, such as had never before, perhaps, been witnessed in this city. 'The State was in danger', 'the Bishop was aiming at the subversion of the constitution and effecting a union between the State Goverment and the Catholic Church'. These and many other allegations were daily and hourly sent abroad upon the wings of the press; and

---

[7]*Ibid.*
[8]The *Freeman's Journal,* Vol. 1.
[9]*Ibid.* Vol. II.

the affrighted public had many grave homilies and prophetic warnings read them on the subject of the dread feuds and murderous outbreaks that would inevitably ensue, if the Catholics would not submit to let their children be taught either Protestantism or infidelity, as it should please the Public School Society in the plenitude of its wisdom and benevolence to decree. Another string was harped upon too—the Catholics were addressed by several organs of the Holy Alliance, who seemed to have made the discovery that there was a great body of intelligent and liberal-minded Catholics in the city, and all these the monopolists declared, in a most self-satisfied manner, would not, they were sure, sustain the Bishop—he was utterly alone, if the veracious soothsayers were to be believed. But an early check was given to the delusion. Twenty-two hundred free and independent voters, breaking loose from the trammels of party attachment and giving their suffrages to the independent ticket, that was only nominated four days previous to the election, startled the calumniators and exposed to the world, how baseless were all their accusations, and how impotent were all their attacks. But the Catholic citizens of New York were determined to go still farther. On November 16, 1841, a great mass-meeting was held, and they here went on record, by giving a still more emphatic denial to the extravagant absurdities that were being so wildly propagated by the press of New York."

A brief excerpt from the Bishop's address on this memorable occasion will give further evidences of the spirit of the press in these trying times:[10]

"During all this time of multiplied, various, and undisguised aggression on the Roman Catholics in their religious character, the secular or political press looks on in silence. When several strong denominations attack one that is weaker, in a manner which turns religion into politics and politics into religion, the sentinels of our liberties at the press are asleep. But when that one assailed denomination meets the assault and repels the assailants with the same weapons which the latter had selected, then the danger of mixing religion is for the first time trumpeted in the public ear! If Protestants mingle religion with politics to abridge the Catholics of a common right, it is all well enough; but if Catholics do the same for the purpose of protecting common rights, then it is all wrong. Now I agree with the public press in the *principle,* that one of the greatest evils which could happen to society, is the

---

[10]*Freeman's Journal,* Vol. II. See also the "Works of Archbishop Hughes", by Lawrence Kehoe.

mixture of religion and politics. But in the application I
hold that it is those who *first* introduce the evil, who employ
it in assailing the common rights of others, and not those who
employ it in their own defense, who are entitled to blame.
There is not an editor in New York who can deny the facts
stated in the last paragraph; and yet during all this time we
hear not a murmur of complaint from one of them. The
Post came and proclaimed no tidings. The *Sun* was eclipsed;
the *Commercial Advertiser* gave no warning; the *American*
forgot its name and embodied all the anti-Catholic toryism
without the talent of the London *Times;* whilst the *Journal
of Commerce* was what I suppose it ever will be in morals as
well as merchandise the *Journal of Commerce.*

"Nay, whilst the religious papers such as the New York *Observer* became political, the political papers especially the *Commercial Advertiser,* the *American* and the *Journal of Commerce* became profoundly religious. Their politico-religious
appeals were daily addressed to this 'Protestant country,' to
this 'Protestant Community' against the unfortunate 'Romanists.' This is known to all their readers. They cannot and
will not deny it. And yet these are journals among the
loudest to preach of the degradation which must accrue to
religion by any contact with politics. But their preaching condemns their own practice first of all, and inconsistency in
blaming the 'Romanists' for employing in their own defense,
the tactics which *they* had employed in aggression stares them
in the face."[11]

Many of the newspapers of the great metropolis became hostile
to Catholicism when they beheld its growth. The New York *Sun*
in 1842 had the largest circulation of any journal in the United
States. From time to time, it entered into a wholesale and indiscriminate abuse of foreigners, but principally of Irish Catholics. What made these attacks all the more severe was the fact
that it claimed to be strictly non-partisan, whereas there was
nothing but knavery and double dealing, when politics was in
question. It was particularly on questions of the Catholic Faith
and the Catholic clergy that it most frequently offended. Sometimes its language betrayed the infidel's ready sneer; sometimes
it spoke of the mortal dread of a union of Church and State;
sometimes it warned its readers of the dangerous designs of scheming ecclesiatics, or the menaces of the Catholic Church to society.
Dr. Brownlee's "Lectures on Popery" formed part of the reading
matter of its subscribers.[12] It is not difficult for us to imagine the

---

[11]*Ibid.,* Vol. I, p. 290.
[12]*Freeman's Journal,* Vol. III, Oct. 15, 1842.

injury inflicted on the character and standing of a large and respectable portion of the community by such vicious attacks. Had its scurrilities only circulated among the most educated and enlightened classes, their vulgarity and recklessness would no doubt have received a proper condemnation. But the *Sun* was read by people of all classes. It fell into the hands of the most credulous, it flattered the prejudices of the ignorant, and it implanted violent national antipathies, where they had not previously existed. Finally it assisted in producing that morbid and excited state of public feeling, which in the short space of two years developed into the Nativist riots.[13] Besides the journals we have just enumerated, the one newspaper in particular that Bishop Hughes regarded as the "fountain of all the vituperation, calumny, and slander which was poured out upon him for many years"[14] the New York *Herald,* edited by James Gordon Bennett, who had himself been raised in the Catholic Faith, which he did not then practice.[15]

It is indeed strange that the political sermons of the pulpit, which on Sundays and even on week days, certain ministers drummed into the ears of excited congregations, should not have produced a more lasting effect. One reads today with horror the denunciations, the slanders, and the ferocious appeals that were mingled with the sacred and gentle words of Holy Writ in one great confusion of rhetoric and passion, uttered with no other purpose in the mind of the reviler than to further the objects of this party, which was to acomplish the downfall of "Popery" in America. How often did the lecture halls of the city resound with maledictions of Rev. Mr. Cheever, president of the New England Society. In fact, it was such abusive tirades that formed both the staple arguments and the political excitement in the association which made James Harper, Mayor of New York.[16]

The Nativist party and those not included in the membership knew that as long as the brave and militant Bishop Hughes continued to lead the Catholics, they had nothing to fear. A plot was therefore arranged to remove the prelate, who was the chief obstacle to their political success. However, before he was to feel the assassin's knife, he wished to place himself on record as making one last earnest appeal to those who where daily spurning his religion and covering him with insult. This letter was addressed to Mayor Harper and occupied many columns in the *Freeman's Journal.* We shall quote only the opening paragraph,

---

[13]*Ibid.*

[14]"Life of the Most Rev. John Hughes," by John R. G. Hassard, p. 247.

[15]"Life and Works of James Gordon Bennett." See also New York *Herald.* April 15, 1844.

[16]The *Freeman's Journal,* 1844.

as this contains the solemn warning notifying him that he was to be cut off from the number of the living.

"I am in receipt of a letter from a young Native American," writes the Bishop, "signed with his proper name, in which he advises me that he has provided himself with a 'poignard' by which I am to 'bite the dust'. If he had not put his name to this document, I should have destroyed it, as my rule is with all anonymous communications, without even glacing at its contents. I cannot answer such a correspondent; but placing his letter in your hands if you wish it, I shall pursue the tenor of my way, and be found wherever my duties as a Catholic Bishop and a citizen of the United States require me to be. I hope that I am at peace with God; I know that I am at peace, so far as in me lies, with all men; and thus I am ready to yield my life into the hands of its adorable Author when and as He may dispose."

The rest of the letter is a minute review of the causes that produced the evil spirit of the times and it lays particular emphasis on the influence exercised by the secular press, whose perverse ingenuity was in a large measure responsible for the recent Philadelphia riots.

The apprehension felt by the Catholics of New York was so great, that the prudent Bishop warned his flock to abstain from any sort of demonstration. On May 9, 1844, is seen the following advice from him in *Freeman's Journal*:[17]

"We notice by the papers that a public meeting of the 'Native American Party' is called to convene at the Park tomorrow afternoon. We perceive no possible motive of this injudicious and wicked proceeding, except it be to introduce into our city the torch of mortal discord, which is now enveloping Philadelphia in one ruinous conflagration. Were it worth while, we should invoke the public authorities, the guardians of property, those who have regard for the rights and lives of citizens, to interfere in a timely and efficient manner by the means with which the people have armed them for the maintenance of peace and order. Let all who can be influenced by our advice, lay it down as a rule for themselves and their neighbors, that their true course is to abstain from everything that could give occasion to the least disturbance. Let them not attend *under any pretext* any one of those meetings, which are gotten up with a view to invite the people to outrage. Let them remain as much as possible engaged in the usual attendance to their own

---

[17]*Freeman's Journal*, Vol. IV, May 9, 1844.

business, and when not thus occupied,—in the quiet of their homes. But if, as has already appeared in Philadelphia, it should be a part of Native Americanism to attack their houses and their Church, then it behooves them in case all other protection fail, to defend both with their lives. They should be particularly careful in whatever measure they may think proper to take for this purpose, to give no offense to anyone. Let them be cool and collected, abstaining 'till the last moment from the use of the means of self-defense with which they may be provided. But in *no* case let them suffer an act of outrage on their properties without repelling the aggression at all risks."

This advice of the Bishop served a double purpose—it was a solemn warning for the Catholics to beware of trouble; it was also an answer to any challenge coming from the Nativist Party. Its effect was that it set forever at rest the agitations of that association intent on destruction and murder.

Only two years were required to convince Eugene Casserly that Catholic journalism, as he found it in New York City, was far from being an earthly paradise.[18] Never did the social status of Catholics call for more anxious attention on the part of the journalist. The untrammelled expression of censure and correction had to be very judiciously exercised. To apportion blame, where it was due without fear of human respect, to eradicate dangerous opinions and bad passions, to displace distrust and diffuse better sentiments—these were but a few of the duties that presented themselves. Not only had he stemmed the tide of prejudice, but before retiring from the editorial chair, he had won the approval of even his boldest antagonists by the spirit of conciliation which characterized all his discussions. Mr. Casserly returned to the practice of the law and in 1850, joined the gold rush to California. In 1869 he was chosen United States Senator from that State, but resigned in 1873 before his term of office had expired.[19] He died in San Francisco, June 14, 1883.

Mr. Casserly's able management placed the *Freeman's Journal* on a fairly good basis. Thenceforth it was edited with varying success until 1848, when it was sold to McMaster. Then commenced the eventful career of one who holds a singular place in Catholic journalism. Hardly had the new editor taken up his pen, than it at once became evident that the resolute Bishop and the combative editor were to have many a lively discussion on the attitude that the *Freeman's Journal* should assume concerning the various grave religious questions then at issue. We can

---

[18]*Freeman's Journal,* Vol. IV, Oct. 5, 1844.
[19]"The Catholic Encyclopedia," Vol. III.

better appreciate the Bishop's relations with McMaster by examining a letter which the latter wrote to Brownson on September 9, 1848, shortly after he assumed his editorial duties:[20]

"All the address and finesse," he wrote, "that I know how to use, only just suffices to keep me from open hostility. It is easy to see that he deplores the necessity by which he was cornered into selling me the *Freeman's,* or having it sink alongside of a paper wholly independent of him; and you know him well enough, that the character and eminent success of the journal, since I have had it, does not render it more agreeable to him. But my course is taken with him. He is always managed by some one, never acts independently. I am going to undertake the job, and I think the Bishop will never sacrifice me as he has some others,—because I shall never trust him, never directly oppose him, and never suffer him to cease fearing me. By the aid of God and these interesting dispositions,—which I need not caution you that I do not proclaim on the housetops,—I look to weathering a good many storms, and being still editor when the Bishop shall have entered into his eternal reward. Generally of me it is thought, I am too hot and too heavy—and in truth I have no idea of keeping up so much excitement, as is raised about it just now. But in the first place, I want to increase its circulation and I find this just the way to do it; as nobody, who is any body, likes to miss seeing a paper that presents each week among other dishes one or two roasts."

Such sentiments, if, acted upon at the present time, would be characterized as detrimental. But McMaster lived at a period, when there was need of vigorous rhetoric. However, he would have displayed greater prudence, had he respected the opinions and the feelings of those who were his co-workers in the Catholic Church. It is said of him that "he spared no one high or low who differed with him, and his invective was as bitter as an unlimited vocabulary could make it."[21]

McMaster was a man of strong convictions, who like most of the converts of his time, was extremely sensitive of the Church's honor. One would have expected that age and experience would have softened the asperity and the impetuosity of his youthful days, but he retained these qualities till his death, so that it may be said that the history of the *Freeman's Journal* for the next forty years was also the life-story of its eccentric editor. People of this generation hardly realize how great an influence personal journalism exercised, for one gets but a few rare glimpses of its

---

[20]The *Catholic News,* April 11, 1908.
[21]The "Catholic Church in New York," by J. Talbot Smith, p. 395.

style and force in the twentieth century. But at the time of which we speak, that sort of newspaper-editing appealed to the average reader. At any rate, the editor's boldness and literary violence pleased the masses, if it did not always edify the more intellectual of his subscribers. As times and manners changed people expected higher ideals in journalism, so that in the last years of McMaster's life his prestige as a journalist waned.[22]

McMaster's early training was in part responsible for his peculiarities of temperament. He was born in 1820 at Duanesburg, Schenectady County, New York, and was reared under the influence of a Presbyterian father who traced his descent from the stern Scottish Covenanters, the Rev. Gilbert McMaster, a scholar who taught his son at home and then sent him to complete his studies at Union College.[23] Here the same rigid system was employed that McMaster had experienced in his own home. On that account he was afterwards known frequently to express his regret that he had never been a "boy". Although possessing more than sufficient talent, he did not complete his college course. He then became a tutor, and it was while teaching that he began to make inquiries about the Catholic religion. Very probably, he was led to examine its doctrines by the same spirit of inquiry, which brought hundreds of other persons to seek the truth during the progress of the Oxford Movement. He was frequently asked concerning the circumstances which first turned his mind in the direction of the Catholic faith, and his invariable answer was, "God only."[24] McMaster had the intention of becoming a Redemptorist priest, and for this set out for Belgium where a spiritual adviser persuaded him to remain in the world. He returned to New York and there began his long career as a journalist, on the very paper that two years later he was to control.[25]

McMaster had much to learn about the technicalities of journalism, but he was a ready student. He was filled with the classicism of the eighteenth century, and his labored and long drawn periods were calculated to put the reader to sleep. Consequently it became necessary to change his whole style, to fit it for newspaper work.[26] In the course of the year much improvement was noticed in his newspaper, and subscriptions were increasing. This fact so pleased Bishop Hughes that he gave the journal a strong letter of commendation.

After a year in his new role of editor, he vigorously attacked the Young Ireland Movement, the special object of the *Freeman's* onslaught being Thomas D'Arcy McGee. The feud between Mc-

---

[22]The *Freeman's Journal*, Vol. 50, Feb. 23, 1889.
[23]*Ibid.* See also the *Catholic News*, April 11, 1908.
[24]The *Freeman's Journal*, Vol. 50, Feb. 23, 1889.
[25]The *Catholic News*, April 11, 1908.
[26]The "Catholic Church in New York," by J. Talbot Smith, p. 390, et seq.

Gee and the *Freeman's Journal* was one of long standing. In fact even while editor of the *Pilot,* McGee had used the most abusive language when attacking this rival newspaper. When, after the suppression of the Young Ireland Movement by the Government, McGee escaped the general arrest of its leaders and returned to America, he located in New York City, where he edited a periodical called the *Nation.*[27]   Here he became a great source of annoyance to the *Freeman's Journal* and to the Archbishop, who heartily detested anyone claiming any connection with the Young Irelanders.   In the following year, 1849, he contributed a series of letters to the *Freeman's Journal,* in which he treated McGee and his paper, the *Nation,* with great severity.   Most of these letters were anonymous; the Archbishop signed himself "An Irish Catholic," but he took care to inform McGee personally that the Archbishop of New York was the writer. The editor of the *Nation,* in one of his articles, attempted to throw responsibility for the humiliating result of the Rebellion of 1848 on the Catholic clergy of Ireland.   But this was not the *Nation's* worst offense.   The prelate charged that "the paper was infidel in its tone," that it was "anti-Catholic directly in some instances, indirectly in all," and he urged "every diocese, every parish, every Catholic door to be closed against it."   Not only the *Nation* but the whole Young Ireland press in America was condemned in the strongest language.   We shall quote just one short passage, which appeared during the year 1849, in which he says:

"Let us get priests and religion out of the way; they make cowards of men; let priests be removed; let everything that tends to create a conscience be abolished forever.   These are their ideas, and you, my dear brethren, have found among you recently this new school of liberal teaching.   You have found among you editors and newspapers trafficking upon the ruins of a country which they have helped to degrade, and making their pages eloquent by a stupid imitation of Tom Paine and Voltaire.   These are the political confectioners who seal up the poison of their infidelity in sugar plums of flattery to popular prejudices, that they may sell them to the children of folly.   They call themselves Catholic too, even as Voltaire said he was a Catholic.   They say that they are Irishmen and they may be Irishmen, but not Irishmen of the legitimate stamp.   They are not of those Irishmen, who have preserved the nationality and honor of their country by preserving their Faith in the midst of every persecution."

McGee's persistent attacks upon the *Freeman's Journal* always

---

[27]Hassard, "Life of the Most Rev. John Hughes."   See also *Freeman's Journal,* Jan., 1849.

met with the censure which they deserved. In the beginning of the year 1854, he again attempted to begin an altercation with the editors of that newspaper. McMaster had lately taken as his associate J. McLeod Murphy, an engineer of some reputation. McGee began his attack by criticising the political tone of certain articles, which had recently been written in the *Freeman's Journal,* but especially those regarding the Mexican question, then at its height. One week the editor spoke of "Mexican Audacity," the next issue complained bitterly about "Mexican Perfidy." In fact, it seemed as if McMaster's journal had not a word to utter in favor of Mexico. McGee felt that there must be some reason for this attitude. He thought that he had solved the riddle, when he attributed the *Freeman's* jingoism to motives of self-interest. That interest he conceived to be a railway project known as the Tehuantepec Route, a project that was tempting to speculators. He intimated that these editors had been employed by a certain person in New York City to survey the route and to advocate its merits in the great metropolis. He had further ascertained that the same editors had been dispatched to Mexico in relation to the Gadsden treaty, as "bearers of dispatches and had returned to the city in that capacity." He was sure that he had obtained much inside information on the whole Mexican situation, since that paper had first reported the Mesilla Valley purchase.

In reply the editor of the *Freeman's Journal* stated that McGee was seeking revenge, because he had been the means three or four years before of stifling the *Nation,* which McGee was then conducting.[28] McMaster was ready with a full refutation of all the charges placed at his door. He stated that since Mr. Murphy had been with the paper, there had been no advocacy of the Tehuantepec route whatever in its columns. Some years before while Mr. Murphy was an officer of the Navy, the Tehauntepec Company engaged his services for their survey, on acount of his scientific ability and his previous knowledge of the Tehuantepec country. "The merits of the report of that survey," writes McMaster, "were greatly due to Mr. Murphy, and the proprietors of it avow that his services to the company were such as to render all the compensation made him or to be made him well and fully earned. Those, however, and the arrangement for his remuneration were settled previous to his connection with *Freeman's Journal.*"[29]

McMaster was the only editor of the paper that advocated the Tehuantepec route, but he was not employed by the company or by anyone else.

"Personal regard," he says, "for the American assignee of the Tehuantepec grant drew our private attention to the sub-

---

[28]*Freeman's Journal,* Feb. 19, 1854.
[29]*Ibid.*

ject. Our public advocacy of it was based on two considerations; first, that this route presented by far the quickest, shortest, and safest means of communication with the Pacific that was then seriously entertained by the public. At that time (1851) we did not believe in the practicability of a railroad to the Pacific across our own territory, although now, in our estimation, the certainty of this latter work being accomplished within a comparatively short time, has caused any and every transit across the Isthmus to sink into a secondary question. To establish the quickest and easiest possible communication between our Pacific and Atlantic coast, we justly consider as necessary to bind the former with its impetuous activity and self-dependence to the latter, and thus preserve the integrity of the Union. In this point of view, it was a question worthy the advocacy of every good citizen. The second consideration influencing us was that we thought and had reasonable grounds for thinking, that the grant referred to was a legal and just one, and that the rights of the American holder were valid.

"When Mr. Murphy declared his intention of associating himself with the paper, it became a matter of honor that the journal should have no bias whatever in favor of a grant in which Mr. Murphy might be supposed to have some pecuniary interest. There was a distinct and most explicit understanding between the editors, that neither of them could feel himself at liberty to use the name of the *Freeman's Journal* for any such advocacy."[30]

Here was a candid explanation of the suspicious circumstances noticed by Thomas D'Arcy McGee, and it was regarded by McMaster as a great victory. It speedily ended a controversy which threatened at one time to compromise the editor in the eyes of the public.

In 1851, Louis Kossuth, posing before the public as a Hungarian patriot, visited the United States. He stirred up a great deal of excitement among the more ignorant classes, few of whom had taken pains to examine the fact of the Hungarian Revolution or to inform themselves about the part played therein by this adventurer. He diverted a legitimate agitation for the rights of the Hungarian people into a general European movement against religion and society.[31] Immediately he was hailed as a champion

---

[30]*Ibid.*

[31]"Les Saints Lieux, Pelerinage á Jèrusalem, en passant par l'Autriche, la Hongrie, la Slavonie, les Provinces Danubiennes, Constantinople, l'Archipel, le Liban, la Syrie, Alexandrie, Malte, la Sicile, et Marseille," par Mgr. Mislin, Paris, 1851, pp. 21-24. See also *Brownson's Quarterly Review,* April, 1852.

of republican principles. Much cheap rhetoric was poured over Kossuth during his visit to New York, and orators without number almost deified him.

The *Freeman's Journal,* which had followed Kossuth's movements, saw through the whole deception, and was the first paper in New York City to expose him.[32] The editor showed that the condition of the southern negro was that of a dweller in Eden compared with the situation of the average Hungarian laborer. Furthermore he adduced incontestable evidence to show that the hands of Louis Kossuth were stained with blood, not in the fight for freedom but in committing murder for the purposes of robbery.

McMaster, it is probable, began this attack on Kossuth at the suggestion of Archbishop Hughes, for we know that the prelate communicated to the Austrian Minister certain expressions of opinion on Kossuth's anti-Catholic speeches in Europe. In this letter he speaks of the ex-Governor of Hungary in the following terms:[33]

"As regards Kossuth himself, my feelings towards him now are rather those of pity than of resentment. He is suffering in health; he is broken or breaking in spirit; he is disappointed in his mission to this country; he is by this time disgusted in his inmost soul, at the loud, hollow, deceptive acclamations which greeted his arrival. A great appearance of respect is still exhibited in his regard but even when it is sincere, under the shock of rebuke and disappointment, it brings him neither comfort nor confidence. One thing I am happy to know that the Catholics of this city, whether American, Irish, German, or French, have treated him with the utmost indifference; and in so doing, they have placed themselves in an honorable position, since it appears by the newspapers that the public men, who are supposed to have invited him, are utterly at a loss to know what to do with him now that he has arrived."

Horace Greeley in the New York *Tribune,* defending Kossuth, took issue with *Freeman's Journal,* but the facts in the case were so indisputably in favor of the Catholic paper, that the threatening storm became very soon only a tempest in a tea-pot.[34]

The finances of the *Freeman's Journal,* as years went by, greatly improved. When J. McLeod Murphy became associate editor, a design long entertained by McMaster was put to the test. The plan was to commence semi-weekly issues distinct from the regu-

---

[32]*Freeman's Journal* for the year 1851; *Ibid.* Vol. 50, Feb. 23, 1889.
[33]Hassard, "Life of the Most Rev. John Hughes, D.D.," p. 343.
[34]The *Freeman's Journal,* Vol. 50, Feb. 23, 1889.

lar paper. The three numbers were to form the substantial basis upon which to build eventually a Catholic daily.[35] This dream, however, was never realized for the *Freeman's Journal*. In fact the experience of a few weeks convinced the editors that the new venture had no possibility of paying its way. The Catholic daily presents the same problem now as it did then.

The most critical period of the *Journal's* whole existence commenced with the year 1856, when McMaster began a new course. Hitherto it had kept itself aloof from political parties, but at a time when the whole country was being agitated by an issue the result of which was threatening to disrupt the Union, religious papers of all shades of opinion were drawn into the struggle. The Catholic press also yielded to the temptation, not realizing that the steps it was taking, were soon to place some editors in a very embarrassing position. By advocating the election of James Buchanan for President, the *Freeman's Journal* made its first grave mistake.[36]

McMaster's sympathies for the South were very pronounced, and during the years of Buchanan's administration he gave full expression to his opinions, for he was an ultra States rights Democrat. During the Lincoln-Douglass debates, he flayed the former with his fiercest sarcasm. He saw clearly the trend of events and threw out solemn warnings, that the election of Lincoln would prove a national calamity. When Lincoln became President, however, McMaster's attitude changed. In spite of the principles he advocated, he wished to be loyal to the Union. He lamented the secession of the Southern States as keenly as any Northerner. In the issue of November 10, 1860, he writes:

"Lincoln must be sustained. Lincoln, elected according to the Constitution, must be inaugurated, and will be entitled to the loyal support of every good citizen in the execution of the laws within the limits of the Constitution. Whoever talks of resisting his inauguration is a traitor, and, if he attempt resistance, he ought to be hanged. The Constitution by which the general government and the government of South Carolina are alike bound, makes no provision for secession on any terms. South Carolina and each other State have no way of secession except by revolution—a revolution which the general government is under oath before God and man to put down. James Buchanan may make light of tampering with the oath to support the Constitution and enforce the laws made under it; he may prove still further the pliant tool of Southern disunionists—but the country will not hold him

---

[35]*Ibid.* files of year 1853.

[36]*Freeman's Journal* files for 1856 and succeeding years. See also issue of Feb. 23, 1889.

guiltless, and there has been no public functionary in this country whose death by the rope, for felony, if proven, would have met so little compassion as his would do. A perilous crisis has fallen upon us. We must meet it like men, not shrink from it. The South must bear the ungracious results of the wrong of her own factionists. As to resisting Lincoln, while he abides by the Constitution and the laws of the country—that is nonsense.

"Every citizen who keeps a good conscience owes allegiance to the United States Government. At the North, there will be no two opinions. The division, the contest, the war, if war alas! must be—will be at the South. It had better not be begun. The South certainly can deeply wound the North, but it will more deeply wound itself. Lincoln, within the Constitution and the laws, will and must be sustained."

When South Carolina formally seceded and the other States were about to follow in its path, the *Freeman's Journal* again protests vehemently. In the issue of January 21, 1861, we read:-

"Disunion for the sake of disunion rules the day there. A Charleston contemporary not long ago said that a man advocating such a thing must be sought in a lunatic asylum. Bedlam, however, has broken loose and lunacy is epidemic in Charleston. Under such circumstances how can we argue. Intellectually we cannot respect either the would-be leaders or the docile tools of South Carolinianism. In law, in morals, in policy, in good faith, South Carolinians have not a leg to stand on—not even a lame one. Their cause is not the cause of the South—it is the cause of a population so corroded by false principles that they cannot keep faith, and do not know the meaning of loyalty."

Again in the issue of April 27, 1861, we find the same uncompromising attitude.

"A lying spirit," says the editor, "has persuaded the Revolutionists of the South that they might fire on our flag, and even assail the capital of the country and yet find a divided North. They have passed the Rubicon. If we had forebearance, it was while forebearance was a virtue. They have this day to meet the stern resolve of a united North."

"War! War for what?" the editor asks on May 4. "On the side of the South we forebear to speak. From first to last —from the bolt in the Democratic convention in Charleston in April of last year down to the despicable act of Jefferson Davis and Major Beauregard in opening fire on the United States flag in Charleston harbor in April, we have had but one sentiment, and but one expression of condemnation and execration for the conspirators, who pretended to set up over the heads of the Southern people and without consulting them, a Revolutionary Confederacy. But for what is the North in arms? . . . . It is not to sustain a party but to vindicate an outraged country. It is not to uphold an administration but the Government."

No more loyal sentiments than these ever came from the lips of any American. McMaster at the time was as true a Unionist as drew breath in the United States. He had opinions, however as to how the war should be conducted. He freely exercised the privileges of criticizing the military preparations for the war, emphatically expressing the opinion that a very large army should be placed in the field from the start so as to put a speedy end to the insurrection. When the war commenced, he grew more and more pessimistic with each new victory of the Southern army. Again he denounced the withdrawal of liberty in the North, because of what he considered as the unconstitutional and arbitrary arrest of citizens without due process of law. This spirit of criticism created a bad impression on the authorities in Washington, whose censorship of the press was becoming daily more rigid. In the month of August, notice was given McMaster that *Freeman's Journal* was soon to be suppressed.[37] From that moment, its editor lost control of himself. Once aroused, he was not easily put down. After three more issues of his newspaper McMaster was arrested and imprisoned for eight months in Fort Lafayette. This term of confinement on what he considered no substantial charge, had only the effect of prejudicing McMaster still more against the administration, which in the year 1860 he had so loyally defended.

In April, 1862, the order excluding *Freeman's Journal* from the mails was rescinded.[38] When its editor once more obtained his freedom, his first thought was to make a declaration to those who had supported him in his hour of greatest tribulation. "We have uttered no sentiments hostile to our whole country," he said, "or to the Constitution that has made it a Union, or to any of the institutions that have made the country great and happy. We stand by the record we have made. We have not a retraction to make—not a single sentence or word." "Events have rapidly moved on," he adds, "during the more than seven months of our enforced silence. Positions have changed and have to do with new orders of phenomena. Dogmatism or blind attachment to any preconceived opinions or abstract theories will not do in the shifting scenes of so prodigious a revolution. We are not where we were nor shall we ever return thither."[39]

---

[37]*Freeman's Journal,* Vol. 50, Feb. 23, 1889.
[38]*Ibid.*
[39]The *Freeman's Journal,* May, 1862.

McMaster was too much filled with the thought of his recent imprisonment to banish all resentment towards Mr. Lincoln and his advisers. He came forth from prison more defiant than he had entered it, and almost every issue of his paper became more impassioned. These denunciations lack the dignity of his early efforts. The ravings of a sickened and excited brain caused him to write articles so bitter that Major General Banks stopped the delivery of *Freeman's Journal* at New Orleans, thus cutting off about six hundred subscribers;[40] but a protest was made by the editor and after a brief suppression, the paper was once more delivered as usual.[41]

Owing to the editor's imprisonment, the financial affairs of the newspaper were of course in the greatest confusion. The earnings of twenty years had almost disappeared. After the war, a systematic effort was made to obtain subscriptions. Friends spent leisure hours soliciting for the *Freeman's Journal*, and every week a dozen or more communications were found in the paper showing that the number of subscribers was increasing. By the year 1870, it had almost recovered from the ordeal of the Civil War epoch. From this time also, it turned its attention again more exclusively to religious topics, but the sad experiences of the sixties were costly lessons and those which the editor carried to the grave.

During the year 1874, the *Freeman's Journal* caused a stir among the leading journals of New York by being the first to publish the facts regarding a German intrigue for occupying one of the West Indies. For years, Germany had looked with envious eyes on Porto Rico. Spain at that time was in the height of the Carlist agitation, and was willing to yield certain territory in her colonies, provided she could get support against the Carlists. In some way, McMaster obtained inside information of the intended German plot, and opened the eyes of all America to the danger. Admiral Polo, Spanish Minister in Washington, was very much annoyed to learn that important information had been received from Madrid and published in the *Freeman's Journal* before it was officially announced to himself.[42] The statements made in the newspaper were identical with those received later by the Spanish Minister. This interesting communication was as follows:

"As the Government recognized the impossibility of suppressing the Carlist insurrection and the rebellion in Cuba without foreign help, and as the Government of His Majesty, the Emperor of Germany, has made us overtures at once

---

[40] The *Freeman's Journal*, March 14, 1863.
[41] *Ibid.* March 28, 1863.
[42] *Freeman's Journal*, 1874.

honorable and acceptable, it is desirable that this department should know what position the American Government would take in the event of the cession of our Isle to the Government of his Majesty, the Emperor."

Another note by the same courier explains that the German Government would see that a proposed loan to the Spanish Government offered in London would meet with success. Some cruisers were to be stationed along the Spanish coast to prevent the importations of articles, contraband of war. In return for all this "the Spanish Government agrees to cede to the Government of the German Empire by a provisional title, but one that may become perpetual, the island of Porto Rico in whole or in part." Admiral Polo, knowing that such an act would be an open violation of the Monroe Doctrine, refused to be a party to any such transaction, and he was therefore recalled. Hamilton Fish, then Secretary of State, and George Bancroft, the American Minister in Berlin, were ignorant of the whole proceeding. So the *Freeman's Journal* had the news even before it reached official circles in Germany. These tidings, published in a modest and unassuming Catholic weekly, produced a profound sensation on the public mind. "In the face of the Serrano-Bismarck negotiation," said the New York *Evening Post,* "all the other European news loses its interest for the people of this country." These were certainly busy days for McMaster. He was interviewed, questioned, and written up by every New York daily.

The attention of the notables among the New York journalists greatly pleased McMaster. To attract public notice was strictly in keeping with the eccentricities of his character. For similar motives, at an earlier date he affected to scorn Brownson, hoping thereby to keep attention riveted on himself, but all that his "barkings at the heels" of the great philosopher and journalist acomplished, was to bring scorn and ridicule upon himself. His *beau ideal* was the famous editor of the Paris *Univers.*[43] McMaster however, had neither the ability of his French colleague, nor was he placed in so lucky an environment. The bitter factional strife that existed in France during Veuillot's time was absent in America. The editor of the *Freeman's Journal,* in his attempts to imitate the art and the methods of this master, was compelled to create an atmosphere. This favorite means of reaching his end was frequently employed. He invariably singled out some prelate or other notable person and administered a severe scolding or a harsh criticism. Nothing produced greater satisfaction in McMaster's mind than when his words were heeded, and his op-

---

[43]The "Catholic Church in New York," by John Talbot Smith. See also the *Catholic News,* April 11, 1908; the *Freeman's Journal,* Vol. 50, Feb. 23, 1889.

ponent returned shot for shot. Most of the bishops, however, knew McMaster and his idiosyncrasies, and were amused rather than provoked at these paroxysms. The spirit of the *Freeman's Journal,* however, offended Bishop Baltes, who forbade its circulation in the Alton Diocese under pain of the denial of absolution to such as would read it. The *Journal* was classed by the Bishop with two other papers of the radical Irish type, as "offending against faith, morals, and ecclesiastical discipline."[44]

McMaster was sorely wounded first, because he was accused of heterodoxy, and secondly, because his journal was placed on the level of those that he had always despised. He was too much hurt to make any spirited reply, but nevertheless awaited a specific charge. "I, a Catholic layman," he wrote, "have for more than thirty years at some serious expense edited and published a Catholic journal in which, if one sentence has ever been published opposed to faith, morals, or the lawful discipline of any diocese in the United States, he will be my best friend who will make it known to me that I may correct it." He refrained from controversy with this prelate, although invited by him to do so.

The rebuke of the Bishop of Alton was still troubling McMaster, when someone rumored that Cardinal McCloskey, the Archbishop of his own diocese, had also placed his disapproval on the *Freeman's Journal.* The editor, however, promptly denied the truthfulness of the charge.[45]

"It is false to state," he said, "that the *Freeman's Journal* is or has been in any way officially disapproved by Cardinal McCloskey, our Archbishop. Were he not officially to admonish, but so much as to express his judgment to us in any conceivable manner of discussion, he knows that we would heed him. Once only on his first return from Rome, after being made Cardinal, he asked us to see him. With the kindness of a true father to a rough son, he praised us for some passing good things and in the gentlest and most exquisite manner, recognizing how far we were right, pointed out in what for the present we went farther than the Pope and the Holy Roman See! We took it as an admonition, though it was given so as not to hurt, were we weaker than we are, and yet though it touched a vital point in Catholic discipline, that 'instruction,' for it was that, which has ever since unnerved us in the discussion of the question, that we had looked at in a different light."

If McMaster ever bore any resemblance to Louis Veuillot, it is hardly discernible. Two characteristics, however, they possessed

[44]The *Freeman's Journal,* Vol. 50, Feb. 23, 1889.
[45]*Freeman's Journal,* Vol. 50, Feb. 23, 1889.

in common—a staunch devotion to truth and the militant quality
of fighting in defense of their principles. But one could naturally expect to find these traits in any Catholic editor. He had
none of the French journalist's distinguishing features, namely,
his art, his literary taste, his versatility.

The long and eventful career of James McMaster was now
drawing to a close. During the year 1880, he took as his associate Maurice Francis Egan. Mr. Egan came to New York from
Philadelphia in 1877 and edited for some time *McGee's Weekly.*
In 1879, he was associate editor of the *Catholic Review.*[46] Egan's
brilliant and attractive style gave a spicy flavor to the editorial
page of the *Freeman's Journal,* which it had never had before.
The young editor, however, was seriously hampered in the conduct of the paper by the whims and eccentricities of the aged
McMaster, whose irritability was intensified by sickness, a physical state in which he could eat almost nothing and with difficulty
ever slept.[47]

On the morning of December 29, 1886, James A. McMaster
died. The last years of his life were a constant preparation for
death. No morning that he was able to walk did he ever miss
Mass, and he was generally a weekly communicant. His end was
hastened by an accident that occurred on October 2. He fell
down a dark stairway leading from the editorial rooms of the
Freeman's Journal to the street. In this fall he seriously bruised
his shoulder and sustained also internal injuries.[48] Before the
accident, for three years or more he had not done much of the
writing for *Freeman's Journal,* but the stormiest weather never
found him away from his office, where he spent a few hours every
day, occupying his old chair in the editorial sanctum. "But," exclaimed a person who loved and admired him, "alas, the ink is
dry, the pen has fallen, and his crucifix, like that of Louis Veuillot, lies on his breast. The halo of a faithful life is around him.
He is within the portal of the Holy of Holies and the God whom
he never deserted is with him."[49]

After McMaster's death Maurice Francis Egan acquired from
the estate a half proprietorship of the paper,[50] which he successfully conducted alone until the middle of the year 1888, when it
was purchased by the Fords,[51] who in 1894 made the Rev. Louis
A. Lambert editor. He edited the newspaper up to the time of
his death, which occurred during the course of the year 1910.

---

[46]*Freeman's Journal,* Vol. 50. See also the *Catholic News,* April 11, 1908.
See also "Catholic Church in New York," by John Talbot Smith.
[47]*Ibid.*
[48]*Freeman's Journal,* Vol. 50, 23, 1889.
[49]*Freeman's Journal,* Vol. 50, Feb. 23, 1908.
[50]*Ibid.* Feb. 25, 1888.
[51]*Ibid.* Aug. 4, 1888.

Before he assumed charge of the *Freeman's Journal,* he was editor of the *Catholic Times,* of Buffalo, and a few years later conducted the *Catholic Times* of Philadelphia. His services to the cause of religion by the religious apostolate of the press, particularly for the sixteen years that he was editor of *Freeman's Journal,* gave him an exalted position among Catholic journalists. After the death of Father Lambert it was conducted by A. Brendan Ford, but during the World War its course meeting with the disapproval of the Government, its post office privileges were withdrawn and it suspended publication in July, 1918.

CHAPTER XXVII

Conclusion

The history of Catholic pioneer journalism has been nothing more nor less than a gigantic struggle, for the civil and religious liberty of the people. One cannot pick up a periodical in which that theme was not one of the leading purposes for which it was founded. It is as staunchly advocated by the national journals, which preceded the religious journals, as it was by the Catholic newspapers themselves. Notwithstanding the fact that the Fathers of our country had clearly enunciated the principles that should govern the people of the United States in questions of religion, the ink of the document containing these fundamental articles was hardly dry, when antipathy for Roman Catholics began to manifest itself.

The theme which we find consistently advocated by all opponents of Catholicism during this first period of Catholic journalism, and which applies to all movements that have ever been waged against the Church in America, may be reduced to this proposition: that it was the duty of all Americans to preserve the republic, its government, and its constitutional liberties against all enemies. Ignorance of the Catholic Church and her tenets, caused many to regard her as inimical to republican institutions. Any concerted and peaceful effort on the part of Catholics to safeguard their sacred rights and privileges was hailed as a conspiracy to subvert the Government.

The surest guarantee that could have been given to the people of the United States was the sincere desire of all Catholics to live at peace with their neighbors of other creeds. This was the appeal made by the Catholic press on all occasions. If the Catholic press had waged a war on the Protestant sects, such as was waged by the Protestant press upon the political and civil liberties and the religious rights of Catholics, there would have been a slight pretext for the unmitigated zeal with which they persecuted those of the ancient Faith. Not in a single instance did the Catholic press ever attempt to assail or to abridge the constitutional liberties of those who were directing and swaying the popular prejudice against them. Catholic periodicals based their claims for justice on the United States Constitution, and they maintained their ground on all occasions with a quiet but firm dignity. The standing motto of the *United States Catholic Miscellany,* the oldest and ablest defender of Catholic principles and doctrine was, from its very establishment, the exact wording of the first amendment to the Constitution, "Congress shall make no law respecting the establishment of religion or prohibit the free exercise thereof." In spite of these solemn warnings regarding constitutional rights and privileges, certain misguided zealots endeavored to abridge the liberties of Catholics. It was part and parcel of their system of operations to leave nothing undone, which would add to the discomfort of their opponents. Pulpits resounded with harangues against Catholics. Sunday schools inculcated uncompromising war against the "Pope and his degraded and slavish subjects." Publications, vile and obscene, which would be regarded as a contamination in the purlieu of a Sodom or a Gomorrah, found everywhere a ready market because they slandered the Catholic Church. We know that after the wicked falsehoods of one of the productions were exposed, and when the book was no longer salable, a certain clergyman in New York, the editor of a scurrilous and diabolical newspaper, quarreled with his iniquitious associates about a divison of the spoils.

Catholic journalism, then in its infancy, tried to avert the catastrophe that followed in the course of these persistent and gross fabrications, but failed. Then followed that wanton destruction of life and property which is almost without parallel in the religious history of this country. The Charlestown Convent was burned. In Philadelphia, St. Augustine's and St. Michael's churches met a similar fate. Murder was even committed. Yet infamous and belligerent newspapers and publications were wafted thick as leaves in autumn from the press. They warned the readers to beware of "Antichrist and Babylon and the Man of Sin." Who needs to be reminded of the organized assault made by the "Seventy-Three Calvinistic Ministers," who recommended the *Protestant,* a journal, the vulgarity of which Archbishop Hughes considered "better suited for the meridian of a fish market!" The very newsboys of the streets vociferously announced the hundreds of anti-Catholic articles published almost daily by the secular papers.

At that season, when the feelings of the religious public were excited to the highest pitch, there was formed, in the city of Philadelphia, the American Protestant Association. The Catholic press became astonished at the boldness of this combination of sects. Intelligent Protestants nervously inquired *cui bono,* for they knew that such bitterness and animosity must certainly produce a reaction. "Down with the Papacy and the abominations of the Romish Church." This was the slogan they adopted. It was the summons to renew the battle on the unoffending Catholics. Christian contended against Christian; the very altars of God were desecrated; the very bones of the dead were disinterred and scattered. They cast their sharpened swords without their scabbards and with these weapons of bloody strife they hoped to bring about the "extirpation of Popery."

Catholics needed able defenders against the terrible assaults of these religious fanatics. The spirit of the time produced therefore many militant journalists. Brownson, McGee, and McMaster were all men of strong convictions. They were also men of culture and learning. We can understand therefore why they took issue with their adversaries. Conscious of the truth of the Catholic religion they were anxious to repel with vigor the insults offered it on all sides. This defense developed what was known in that day as the personal element in Catholic journalism. No one, perhaps, possessed it more than McMaster. Among the clergy, Archbishop Hughes and Bishop England gave a stimulus and a prominence to Catholic newspapers.

With such representative men as editors and contributors, religion had nothing to fear. Catholic journalism, nevertheless, had its mediocrities, who sometimes did more harm than good. When one weighs, however, the fruits of all these pioneer efforts, the conclusion is reached that, had not a strong, vigorous, and sometimes militant Catholic press existed, the Church in America would not be occupying the splendid position which it holds in the twentieth century.

APPENDIX A

CHRONOLOGICAL LIST OF CATHOLIC PERIODICALS

The Michigan Essay	1809
The Shamrock or Hibernian Chronicle	1810
The Globe (a magazine)	1819
The United States Catholic Miscellany	1822
Erin (schismatic)	1822
The Catholic Herald and Weekly Register (schismatic)	1822
The Catholic Advocate and Irishman's Journal	1823
The Globe and Emerald	1824
El Habanero (a magazine)	1824
The Truth Teller	1825
The Irish Shield and Monthly Milesian (a magazine)	1828
The Catholic Press	1829
The Jesuit or Catholic Sentinel	1829
El Mensajero Semanal	1829
The Irishman and Charleston Weekly Register	1829
The Metropolitan (a magazine)	1830
The Protestant's Abridger and Expositor	1830
The Expostulator (juvenile)	1830
The Irishman and Southern Democrat	1830
The Irish Shield and Panorama	1830
The Catholic Telegraph	1831
The Irish Advocate	1831
The New York Weekly Register and Catholic Diary	1832
The Shepherd of the Valley	1832
The Catholic Intelligencer	1832
The Patriot and Shield	1832
The Irish Republican Shield and Literary Observer	1832
The Catholic Herald	1833
The Catholic Journal	1833
The Minerva (a magazine)	1834
The Catholic Advocate	1835
The Literary and Catholic Sentinel	1835
The Green Banner	1835
The Catholic Observer	1836
The Catholic Diary	1836
Boston Pilot	1836
Der Wahrheitsfreund	1837
The Pilot	1838
The Children's Catholic Magazine	1838
The Catholic Banner	1839
The New York Catholic Register	1839
The New York Freeman's Journal	1840
The Young Catholic's Magazine	1840

APPENDIX B

BIBLIOGRAPHY

American Catholic Historical Researches.
American Catholic Historical Society *Records.*
American Catholic Quarterly Review.
"Annals of the Propagation of the Faith."
"Annual Encyclopedia."
BARRETT, WALTER. "The Old Merchants of New York."
BAYLEY, THE REV. J. R. "A Brief Sketch of Early History of the Catholic Church on the Island of New York."
BENNETT, W. H. "Catholic Footprints in Old New York."
BOOTH, MARY L. "History of the City of New York."
"Boston Town Records."
BOURNE, WM. O. "History of the Public School Society of the City of New York."
BROADHEAD, JOHN R. "History of the State of New York."
BROWNSON, HENRY F. "Brownson's Middle Life from 1845 to 1855."
Brownson's Quarterly Review.
BURNS, REV. J. A., C.S.C. "The Catholic School System in the United States."
CAMPBELL, W. "History of Michigan."
"Catholic Directory."
"Catholic Encyclopedia."
Catholic World, The.
CLARKE, RICHARD H. "Lives of the Deceased Bishops of the Catholic Church in the United States."
CONDON, EDWARD O. "Irish Immigration to the United States." "Irish in America."
COOLEY, THOMAS M. "Michigan" (American State Series).
CRIMMINS, JOHN D. "Irish American Historical Miscellany."
CULLEN, B. "Story of the Irish in Boston."
DE COURCY, HENRY. "The Catholic Church in the United States."
DONAHOE, PATRICK. "The Burning of the Charlestown Convent." "Reminiscences of Early Catholic Journalism."
EASTMAN, F. S. "History of the State of New York."
"Encylopædia Britannica."
ENGLAND, RT. REV. JOHN. "Works" (Reynolds and Messmer editions).
FARMER, SILAS. "History of Detroit and Michigan."
FINOTTI, REV. J. M. "Bibliographia Catholica Americana."

Fitton, Rev. James. "Sketches of the Establishment of the Catholic Church in New England."

Greenleaf, J. "History of New York Churches."

Guernsey, R. S. "New York and Vicinity During the War of 1812-1815."

Guilday, Peter. "The Life and Times of John England, First Bishop of Charleston (1786-1842)."

Hassard, John R. G. "Life of the Most Rev. John Hughes, D.D."

Historical New York. "Half Moon Papers."

Houch, J. "History of the Catholic Church in Ohio."

Hudson, Frederick. "History of Journalism."

Janvier, Thomas A. "In Old New York."

Johnson, J. "Recollections of Brooklyn and New York."

"Journal of the American Irish Historical Society."

Kehoe, Lawrence. "Works of Archbishop Hughes."

Kirlin, J., Rev. "Catholicity in Philadelphia."

Lamb, Martha J. "History of New York."

Lossing, Benson J. "History of New York City."

McGee, Thomas D'Arcy. "History of Irish Settlers in North America."

McGuire, John F. "Irish in America."

McLaughlin, Andrew C. "History of Higher Education in Michigan."

Macneven, William James. "Pieces of Irish History, etc."

Madden, Richard Robert. "The United Irishmen, Their Lives and Times."
"History of Irish Periodical Literature."

Marty, Martin, O.S.B. "Dr. Johann Martin Henni, ein Lebensbild aus der Pionierzeit von Ohio und Wisconsin."

Meehan, Thomas F. "Catholic Periodical Literature in the United States" (Article in "Catholic Encyclopedia").
Articles in the *Catholic News* (1907-1908).
Articles in "Records and Studies" (U. S. Cath. Hist. Society).

"Metropolitan Catholic Almanac."

Michigan Pioneer and Historical Collection.

Middleton, Rev. Thomas C. "List of Catholic Periodicals in the United States" (Amer. Cath. Hist. Soc.).
"Supplementary List" (Amer. Cath. Hist. Soc.).

Missouri Historical Society Publications.

Mullany, M. "Catholic Editors I Have Known." (*St. John's Quarterly*).

Murray, John O'Kane. "Catholic Pioneers in America."
"Popular History of the Catholic Church in the United States."

New England Magazine.
O'BRIEN, REV. J. J. "Father Gabriel Richard." Article in "Records and Studies" (U. S. Cath. Hist. Soc.).
O'CALLAGHAN, E. B. "Documentary History of New York."
O'CONNELL, REV. J. J. "Catholicity in the Carolinas and Georgia."
O'DONNELL, REV. JAMES H. "History of the Diocese of Hartford."
O'GORMAN, RT. REV. THOMAS. "History of the Roman Catholic Church in the United States."
OLIVER, P. "The Puritan Commonwealth."
PALMER, A. E. "New York Public School."
PARKMAN, FRANCIS. "Half Century of Conflict."
RANDALL, S. S. "History of the State of New York."
ROBERTS, ELLIS H. "New York."
ROCHE, JAMES JEFFREY. "Life of John Boyle O'Reilly."
RODRIGUEZ, F. "Vida del Presbitero, Don Padre Felix Varela" (See also *American Catholic Quarterly Review*).
SCHARF, J. THOMAS. "Chronicles of Baltimore."
SHEA, JOHN GILMARY. "Catholic Churches in New York City."
"Hierarchy of the Catholic Church of the United States."
"History of the Catholic Church in America."
SHARP, W. "History of the City of St. Louis."
SHEPARD, J. "The Early History of St. Louis in Missouri."
SMITH, REV. JOHN TALBOT. "History of the Catholic Church in the Diocese of New York."
SMITH, WM. "History of New York."
SPALDING, RT. REV. JOHN LANCASTER. "Sketches of Early Missions in Kentucky."
"Life of Rt. Rev. Benedict Joseph Flaget."
SPALDING, MOST REV. MARTIN J. "Sketches of Catholicity in Kentucky."
STONE, WM. J. "History of New York City."
SULLIVAN, P. "Catholic Church in New England."
THOMAS, ISAIAH. "History of Printing in America."
ULLMAN, ALBERT L. "History of New York."
United States Catholic Historical Society. "Records and Studies."
United States Catholic Magazine.
VALENTINE, DAVID F. "History of the City of New York."
WASHINGTON, GEORGE. "Writings."
WILSON, JAMES GRANT. "Memorial History of the City of New York."
WILSON, RUFUS ROCKWELL. "New York, Old and New."

INDEX